## Praise for *Scattered Minds*

"One of the most comprehensive and accessible books
about ADD . . . challenges many accepted notions about
the condition."
—*Publishers Weekly* (starred review)

"Based on solid research and a strong humanistic sensibility . . .
written with humor and compassion, from an unsparingly
honest personal perspective."
—John J. Ratey, M.D., coauthor of *Driven to Distraction*

"Valuable for its stress on environmental issues and the author's
experience with the syndrome in his own family."
—*Library Journal*

"*Scattered Minds* asks questions that deserve to be considered about
this debilitating disorder—and the kind of society in which
it flourishes."
—*Maclean's* (Canada)

# SCATTERED MINDS

The Origins and

Healing of Attention

Deficit Disorder

Gabor Maté, M.D.

*Previously published as *Scattered*

AVERY
AN IMPRINT OF PENGUIN RANDOM HOUSE
NEW YORK

AVERY

an imprint of Penguin Random House LLC
penguinrandomhouse.com

Previously published in paperback as *Scattered* by Plume, an imprint of Penguin
Publishing Group, a division of Penguin Random House, LLC, New York, in 2000.
Originally published in a Dutton hardcover edition.

Most Avery books are available at special quantity discounts for bulk purchase for sales
promotions, premiums, fund-raising, and educational needs. Special books or book
excerpts also can be created to fit specific needs. For details, write SpecialMarkets
@penguinrandomhouse.com.

The Library of Congress has catalogued the Dutton hardcover edition as follows:

Maté, Gabor.
    Scattered: how attention deficit disorder originates and what you can do about it /
Gabor Maté.—lst American ed.
      p.   cm.
    Includes bibliographical references and index.
    ISBN 0-525-94412-5 (hc.)
        0-452-27963-1 (pbk.)
    1. Attention-deficit hyperactivity disorder—Psychological
aspects. 2. Attention-deficit hyperactivity disorder—Environmental
aspects. I. Title.
RJ506.H9M42326   1999
616.85'89—dc21                                  99-12999
                                                        CIP

Avery trade paperback ISBN: 9780593714379

Printed in the United States of America
5th Printing

PUBLISHER'S NOTE

*For my mother, Judith (Lővi) Maté, and for my late father, Andor Maté,
and for my own family, Rae, Daniel, Aaron and Hannah*

*Action has meaning only in relationship and
without understanding relationship, action on any level
will only breed conflict. The understanding of
relationship is infinitely more important
than the search for any plan of action.*

— J. KRISHNAMURTI

# Contents

# Acknowledgments

I owe thanks to all of the following.

Dr. John Ratey gave friendly encouragement, and his frank critique of my first draft was bracing and salutary. He also helped keep me abreast of current neuroscientific findings.

The intellectual debt I owe to Dr. Alan Schore and Dr. Daniel J. Siegel will be evident to readers of this book. I was fortunate to attend their lectures on infant-parent relationships and brain development in Seattle in 1996. Their forward-looking work gave substance to my own intuitive views and helped ground them in the literature of brain research and neuropsychology.

Diane Martin at Knopf Canada has made an indispensable contribution to the completion of this manuscript. She has spared the reader much unnecessary eyestrain. I came to look forward to reading her astute commentary and to positively enjoy cutting when she said cut, changing when she said change. I cannot imagine receiving more sensitive and sensible editorial advice.

Deborah Brody at Dutton in New York saw the possibilities in this work right from the beginning and has maintained a clear vision of the direction it needed to take. I had feared working with two editors would be a chore. It turned out to be a pleasure.

Denise Bukowski shaped a long and unwieldy book proposal into publisher-friendly form.

Copyeditor Alison Reid's expert and attentive work greatly enhanced the flow of the text without in any way detracting from its meaning.

My sister-in-law Noni Mate was the first to read the original several opening chapters. Her criticism was invaluable. Murray Kennedy also gave helpful feedback.

Dr. Michael Hayden gave his time and expertise to help clarify my understanding of genetics.

Betsy-Jo Spicer serendipitously started it all by inviting me to hear her story. Trish Crawford steered me in the right direction to find the neuroscientific research on brain development. Many adults with ADD and parents of ADD children have taught me by candidly sharing with me the stories of their lives.

I am grateful to four people whom I consider my teachers: the psychotherapist Andrew Feldmar, the developmental psychologist Dr. Gordon Neufeld, the psychiatrist Dr. Margaret Weiss and the family therapist Dr. David Freeman. The influence of all four is in these pages.

My friend Maria Oliverio, R.N., kept my office going through my successive absences as I wrote *Scattered Minds* and, more remarkably yet, manages to keep it organized even when I am there.

Rae, my life partner and soulmate, has shared the years of struggle, sorrow, laughter, learning and love that went into creating much of the raw material for this book. She has also worked as my most stringent editor: time and time again her insightful comments helped me get closer to the heart of what I was trying to say. Without her loving support, this book could not have become a reality.

Finally, I must express my gratitude toward my three children, Daniel, Aaron and Hannah, who have taught me more perhaps than they should have had to, and who have warmly supported the realization of my long-time desire to become an author.

# Author's Note

*Scattered Minds* is written in seven parts. The first four describe the nature of attention deficit disorder and offer an explanation of its origins, while the final three deal with the healing process. Part Five, on the ADD child, is intended not only for parents but also for adults with attention deficit disorder, as it gives information essential to their self-understanding. Similarly, parents who read the chapters concerning the ADD adult may gain further insights about their ADD children and, perhaps, also about themselves.

Attention deficit disorder is sometimes abbreviated to ADD, sometimes to ADHD. To further muddy the waters, the official designation is AD(H)D, meant to indicate the fact that one can have ADD with or without hyperactivity. By and large, ADD has become common usage. It is the least confusing form, and also the least awkward. It is the one employed exclusively in this book.

# Introduction

Attention deficit disorder is usually explained as the result of bad genes by those who "believe" in it, and as the product of bad parenting by those who don't. The aura of confusion and even acrimony that surrounds public debate about the condition discourages a reasoned discussion of how environment and heredity might mutually affect the neurophysiology of children growing up in stressed families, in a fragmented and highly pressured society and in a culture that seems more and more frenzied as we approach the turn of the millennium.

I have attention deficit disorder myself, and my three children have also been diagnosed with ADD. I do not think it is a matter of bad genes or bad parenting, but I do believe it is a matter of genes and parenting. Neuroscience has established that the human brain is not programmed by biological heredity alone, that its circuits are shaped by what happens after the infant enters the world, and even while it is in the uterus. The emotional states of the parents and how they live their lives have a major impact on the formation of their children's brains, though parents cannot often know or control such subtle unconscious influences. The good news is that major changes in the circuits of the brain can occur in the child and even in the adult if the conditions necessary for positive development are created.

Quick to arise whenever the environment is mentioned is the question of blame. "You mean it's the parents' fault?" people immediately ask. It is a simplistic notion that if something is wrong, someone has to be at fault. It would not help parents of children with ADD, besieged on all sides by the incomprehending judgments and criticality of friends, family, neighbors, teachers and even strangers in the street, to have yet one more finger pointed at them. This book does not do so.

A doctor in Ontario gave the father of a nine-year-old girl with attention deficit disorder a dramatically apt analogy. Imagine, he said, you're standing in the middle of a really crowded room. Everyone around you is talking. Suddenly someone asks you, "What did so-and-so just say?" That's what it's like inside the ADD brain and how it is for your child. A parallel analogy suits the situation the parents of ADD children find themelves in: you're stuck in the middle of heavy traffic at an intersection; the engine has stalled and you are trying your best to get moving. Everyone is yelling and honking angrily at you, but no one offers to help. Perhaps no one knows how to.

As parents who make every effort we can to raise our children in loving security, we do not need to feel more guilt than we already do. We need less guilt and more awareness of how the quality of the parent-child relationship can be used to promote our children's emotional and cognitive development. *Scattered Minds* is written to encourage such awareness.

The book is written also with two other sets of readers in mind. My hope is that adults with attention deficit disorder will find insights here that will help them gain a deeper understanding of themselves and of the path they could take toward their own healing. *Scattered Minds* is meant also to give health professionals with ADD clients and teachers working with ADD students a comprehensive view of a much misunderstood condition.

The analysis of ADD given in this book attempts to synthesize the findings of modern neuroscientific research, developmental psychology, family systems theory, genetics and medical science.[1] These are combined with an interpretation of social and cultural trends, as well with my own personal experience as an adult with ADD, as a parent and as a physician. To avoid giving the book an academic slant, references are given in the notes at the end, along with further comments intended for the professional reader and for lay readers seeking source information.

Case histories and quotations are from my files. With few exceptions, the names have been changed.

# PART ONE

The Nature of

Attention Deficit Disorder

# I

# So Much Soup

# and Garbage Can

Medicine tells us as much about the meaningful
performance of healing, suffering, and dying as chemical
analysis tells us about the aesthetic value of pottery.

— IVAN ILLICH, *Limits to Medicine*

U NTIL FOUR YEARS AGO, I understood attention deficit disorder about as well as the
average North American doctor, which is
to say hardly at all. I came to learn more through one of those
accidents of fate that are no accidents. As medical columnist for *The
Globe and Mail*, I decided to write an article about this strange
condition after a social worker acquaintance, recently diagnosed,
invited me to hear her story. She had thought I would be interested—or more likely she sensed it, with a gut-level affinity. The
planned column became a series of four.

To dip my toe in was to know that, unawares, I had been
immersed in it all my life, up to my neck. This realization may be
called the stage of ADD epiphany, the annunciation, characterized

by elation, insight, enthusiasm and hope. It seemed to me that I had found the passage to those dark recesses of my mind from which chaos issues without warning, hurling thoughts, plans, emotions and intentions in all directions. I felt I had discovered what it was that had always kept me from attaining psychological integrity: wholeness, the reconciliation and joining together of the disharmonious fragments of my mind.

Never at rest, the mind of the ADD adult flits about like some deranged bird that can light here or there for a while but is perched nowhere long enough to make a home. The British psychiatrist R. D. Laing wrote somewhere that there are three things human beings are afraid of: death, other people and their own minds. Terrified of my mind, I had always dreaded spending a moment alone with it. There always had to be a book in my pocket as an emergency kit in case I was ever trapped waiting anywhere, even for one minute, be it a bank lineup or supermarket checkout counter. I was forever throwing my mind scraps to feed on, as if to a ferocious and malevolent beast that would devour me the moment it was not chewing on something else. All my life I had known no other way to be.

The shock of self-recognition many adults experience on learning about ADD is both exhilarating and painful. It gives coherence, for the first time, to humiliations and failures, to plans unfulfilled and promises unkept, to gusts of manic enthusiasm that consume themselves in their own mad dance, leaving emotional debris in their wake, to the seemingly limitless disorganization of activities, of brain, car, desk, room.

ADD seemed to explain many of my behavior patterns, thought processes, childish emotional reactions, my workaholism and other addictive tendencies, the sudden eruptions of bad temper and complete irrationality, the conflicts in my marriage and my Jekyll and Hyde ways of relating to my children. And, too, my humor, which can break from any odd angle and leave people laughing or leave them cold, my joke bouncing back at me, as the Hungarians say, like "peas thrown at a wall." It also explained my propensity to bump into doorways, hit my head on shelves, drop objects and brush close to people before I notice they are there. No longer mysterious was my ineptness following directions or even remembering them, or my paralytic rage when confronted by a sheet of instructions telling me how to use even the simplest of appliances. Beyond everything, recognition revealed the reason for my lifelong sense of somehow never approaching my potential in terms of self-expression and self-definition—the ADD adult's awareness that he has talents or insights or some undefinable positive quality he could perhaps connect with if the wires weren't crossed. "I can do this with half my brain tied behind my back," I used to joke. No joke, that. It's precisely how I have done many things.

My path to diagnosis was similar to that of many other adults with ADD. I found out about the condition almost inadvertently, researched it and sought professional confirmation that my intuitions about myself were reliable. So few doctors or psychologists are familiar with attention deficit disorder that people are forced to become self-cultivated experts by the time they find someone who can make a competent assessment. I was fortunate. As a physician, I could negotiate the medical labyrinth and seek the best sources of help. Within weeks of having written my columns on ADD, I was assessed by an excellent child psychiatrist who also sees adults with the disorder. She corroborated my self-diagnosis and began treatment, at first by prescribing Ritalin. She also spoke with me about how some of the choices I was making in life reinforced my ADD tendencies.

My life, like that of many an adult with ADD, resembled a juggling act from the old Ed Sullivan show: a man spins plates, each balanced on a stick. He keeps adding more and more sticks and plates, running back and forth frantically between them as each stick, increasingly unsteady, threatens to topple over. He could keep this up only for so long before the sticks tottered and the plates began to shatter, or he himself collapsed. Something has to give, but the ADD personality has trouble letting go of anything. Unlike the juggler, he cannot stop the performance.

With an impatience and lack of judgment characteristic of ADD, I had already begun to self-medicate, even before the formal diagnosis. A sense of urgency typifies attention deficit disorder, a desperation to have immediately whatever it is that one may desire at the moment, be it an object, an activity or a relationship. And there was something else here too, well expressed by a woman who some months later came for help. "It would be nice to get a break from myself at least for a little while," she said, a sentiment I fully understood. One longs to escape the fatiguing, ever-spinning, ever-churning mind. I took Ritalin in a higher than recommended initial dose on the very day I first heard about attention deficit disorder. Within minutes, I felt euphoric and present, experienced myself as full of insight and love. My wife thought I was acting weird. "You look stoned" was her immediate comment.

I was not an undereducated teenager eager for kicks when I self-administered the Ritalin. Already in my fifties, I was a successful and respected family doctor whose columns of medical opinion were praised for their thoughtfulness. I practice medicine with a high value on avoiding pharmacology unless absolutely necessary, and needless to say, I have always advised patients against self-medicating. Such striking imbalance between intellectual awareness on the one hand and emotional and behavioral self-control on the other is characteristic of people with attention deficit disorder.

This plunge into impulsiveness notwithstanding, I believed there was light at the end of the tunnel. The problem was clear, the remedy elegantly simple: certain parts of my brain were dormant half the time; all that needed to be done was to rouse them from slumber. The "good" parts of my brain would then take control, the calm, sane, mature, vigilant parts. It did not work out that way. Nothing much seemed to change in my life. There were new insights, but what had been good stayed good and what had been bad stayed bad. The Ritalin soon made me depressed. Dexedrine, the stimulant I was next prescribed, made me more alert and helped me become a more efficient workaholic.

Since being diagnosed myself, I have seen hundreds of adults and children with attention deficit disorder. I now think that physicians and prescriptions for drugs have come to play a lopsidedly exaggerated role in the treatment of ADD. What begins as a problem of society and human development has become almost exclusively defined as a medical ailment. Even if in many cases medications do help, the healing ADD calls for is not a process of recovery from some illness. It is a process of becoming whole—which, it so happens, is the original sense of the word *healing*.

There is no disputing the malfunctioning neurophysiology in what we call attention deficit disorder. It does not follow, however, that we can explain all the problems of the ADD mind simply by referring to the biology of out-of-balance neurochemicals and short-circuited neurological pathways. A patient and compassionate inquiry is needed if we are to identify the deeper meanings manifested in the crossed neural signals, troubled behaviors and psychological tumult that together have been named ADD.

My three children also have attention deficit disorder—not diagnosed by me but according to evaluations at a hospital-based clinic. One has taken medication, with clear benefit, but none do so at the present time. In light of such a strong family history, it may seem surprising that I do not believe ADD is the almost purely genetic condition many people assume it to be. I do not see it as a fixed, inherited brain disorder but as a physiological consequence of life in a particular environment, in a particular culture. In many ways one can grow out of it, at any age. The first step is to discard the illness model, along with any notion that medications can offer more than a partial, stopgap response.

A certain mystique has recently evolved around ADD, but—despite what many people think—it is not a recent discovery. In one form or another, it has been recognized in North America since 1902; its present pharmacologic treatment with psychostimulants was pioneered more than six decades ago. The names given to it and its exact descriptions have gone through several mutations. Its current definition is given in the fourth edition of the

*Diagnostic and Statistical Manual,* scripture and encyclopedia of the American Psychiatric Association. The DSM IV defines attention deficit disorder by its external features, not by its emotional meaning in the lives of individual human beings. It commits the faux pas of calling these external observations *symptoms,* whereas that word in medical language denotes a patient's own felt experience. External observations, no matter how acute, are *signs.* A headache is a symptom. A chest sound registered by the doctor's stethoscope is a sign. A cough is both a symptom and a sign. The DSM speaks the language of signs because the worldview of conventional medicine is unfamiliar with the language of the heart. As the UCLA child psychiatrist Daniel J. Siegel has said, "The DSM is concerned with categories, not with pain."

ADD has much to do with pain, present in every one of the adults and children who have come to me for assessment. The deep emotional hurt they carry is telegraphed by the downcast, averted eyes, the rapid, discontinuous flow of speech, the tense body postures, the tapping feet and fidgety hands and by the nervous, self-deprecating humor. "Every aspect of my life hurts," a thirty-seven-year-old man told me during his second visit to my office. People express surprise when after a brief exchange I seem to be able to sense their pain and grasp their confused and conflicted history of emotions. "I'm speaking about myself," I tell them.

At times I have wished that the "experts" and media pundits who deny the existence of attention deficit disorder could meet only a few of the severely affected adults who have sought my help. These men and women, in their thirties, forties and fifties, have never been able to maintain any sort of a long-term job or profession. They cannot easily enter meaningful, committed relationships, let alone stay in one. Some have never been able to read a book from cover to cover, some cannot even sit through a movie. Their moods fly back and forth from lethargy and dejection to agitation. The creative talents they have been blessed with have not been pursued. They are intensely frustrated at what they perceive as their failures. Their self-esteem is lost in some deep well. Most often they are firm in the conviction that their problems are the result of a basic, incorrigible flaw in their personalities.

I would want any doubting Thomases to read and consider the autobiographical sketch submitted to me by John, a fifty-one-year-old unemployed single man. With his permission, I quote it exactly as written:

> Had Jobs work Do my Best I could never good enough. when people Talk to me they ask me if I Listening or I seem Bored. Shown emotion or I drift off or when I get to do Something can't finish it or start doing Something then eye start Something else. when I sometimes most of the time wait till Last minite To do things. Get a anxious feeling got to do it or else. feel pressured. Seem to mindwonder or daydream. for ever misplacing, loosing things. can't remember where I put Something away. "forgetful" confused, jumbled thinking. get mad about nothing people ask me whats wrong I say nothing. I can't seem to get what people want from me can't understand. when I was a kid. couldnt sit still figety. Report cards in school would always have something like doesn't pay Attention in class, doesn't sit still took me longer to Learn or understand. Always was in trouble was stuck sitting in front of class or in back of class or principal's office (strapped) been tied down in chair. always seeing counsellors. teachers always saying sit still be quiet. Sent to sit out in hall my dad was always telling me to sit still what lazy bum I am my room. was always yelling at me.

John's speech is far more articulate than his writing but no less poignant. "My dad," he said, "always rubbed my nose in it, that I should have been a doctor or a lawyer, or else I wouldn't amount to anything. After my parents divorced, the only time they would talk to each other was when my mother called my dad to say 'give him heck.'... I saw a video last week," he added. "Its title expressed how I feel: I Am Sick and Tired of Being Sick and Tired."

Patients are graphic about their feeling states, often almost lyrical. "Ah," a forty-seven-year-old man said with a discouraged wave of the hand and a smile that was resigned and mischievous at the same time, "my life is just so much soup and garbage can." What those words mean exactly, I could not say. Like poetry, they convey their meaning through the feelings and word associations they evoke. "Landed in the soup." "Fog as thick as soup." "Soup kitchen." "Treated like a piece of garbage." "I feel like garbage." Images of distress, loneliness and confusion, presented with a tinge of humor. The strangely dissonant imagery tells also of a troubled soul who found reality harsh—so harsh that the mind had to be fragmented in order to fragment the pain.

# 2

# Many Roads

# Not Traveled

To get through each day, natures that are at all high
strung, as was mine, are equipped, like motor cars,
with different gears. There are mountainous, arduous
days, up which one takes an infinite time to climb, and
downward-sloping days which one can descend at full
tilt, singing as one goes.

— MARCEL PROUST, *In Search of Lost Time*

ATTENTION DEFICIT DISORDER is defined by
three major features, any two of which suffice
for the diagnosis: poor attention skills, deficient impulse control and hyperactivity.

The hallmark of ADD is an automatic, unwilled "tuning-out,"
a frustrating nonpresence of mind. A person suddenly finds that
he has heard nothing of what he has been listening to, saw nothing
of what he was looking at, remembers nothing of what he was trying to concentrate on. He misses information and directions, mis-
places things and struggles to stay abreast of conversations. Tuning
out creates practical hardships, and it also interferes with the

enjoyment of life. "A continuous and whole experience of music is unknown to me," a high school teacher said. "My mind is off wandering after only a few chords. It is a major exercise for me even to hear one brief song through on my car radio." There is a sense of being cut off from reality, an almost disembodied separation from the physical present. "I feel like I am a human giraffe" is how one man described it, "as if my head is floating in a different world, way above my body."

This absence of mind is one cause of the distractibility and short attention spans that bedevil the adult or child with ADD, except around activities of high interest and motivation. There is an almost active not noticing, as if a person purposefully went out of her way to be oblivious of what is around her. I compliment my wife for a new decoration in our living room, only to be told that the very same item has been in that place for months or even years.

The distractibility fosters chaos. You decide to clean your room, which, typically, looks like a tornado has just passed through. You pick a book off the floor and move to replace it on the shelf. As you do so, you notice that two volumes of poetry by William Carlos Williams are not stacked side by side. Forgetting the debris on the floor, you lift one of the volumes to place it beside its companion. Turning a page, you begin to read a poem. The poem has a classical reference in it, which prompts you to consult your guide to Greek mythology; now you are lost because one reference leads to another. An hour later, your interest in classical mythology exhausted for the moment, you return to your intended task. You are hunting for the missing half of a pair of socks that has gone on furlough, perhaps permanently, when another item of clothing on the floor reminds you that you have laundry to wash before the evening. As you head downstairs, laundry hamper in arm, the telephone rings. Your plan to create order in your room is now doomed.

Completely lacking in the ADD mind is a template for order, a mental model of how order comes about. You may be able to visualize what a tidy and organized room would look like, but the mind-set to do the job is missing. To begin with, there is a profound reluctance to discard anything—who knows when you might need that copy of *The New Yorker* that has gathered dust for three years without ever being looked at? There is little space for anything. You never feel you can master the confused mess of books, papers, magazines, pieces of clothing, compact disks, letters to be answered and sundry other objects—you only shift portions of the chaos from one place to another. Should you nevertheless succeed now and then, you know full well that the order is temporary. Soon you will be throwing things about again, seeking some needed item you are sure you saw recently in some obscure nook or cranny. The law of entropy rules: order is fleeting, chaos is absolute.

A few people with ADD have extraordinary mechanical skills and are able to dismantle and assemble complex objects, pieces of machinery and the like almost intuitively. Coordination difficulties affect most others, particularly in the area of fine motor control. Things are dropped, feet are stepped on, balls fly in the wrong direction. Objects piled on top of each other during cleanup are fated to come crashing down. Telephone numbers are scribbled with the digits in the wrong order: even if it's possible to read what was written, you will still get the number wrong.

Like many others with ADD, I have little ability to conceptualize in three dimensions or to divine the spatial relationships of things, no matter how well they are explained. When in a novel I come to a physical description of, say, a room with a desk here, a bed there, a window, a nightstand, my mind's eye just glazes over. Asking for directions in the street, the person with ADD loses track by the time his informant is halfway through her first sentence. Fortunately, he has perfected the art of nodding. Ashamed to admit his lack of comprehension and knowing the futility of asking for clarifications that he would grasp with no greater success, he gives a masterful impersonation of one who understands. Then he heads off, entrusting himself to good fortune. "When there is a 50 percent possibility of choosing the wrong turn, I will do so about 75 percent of the time," one of my ADD patients said. The deficient visual-spatial sense works synergistically with the distractibility. Order just doesn't stand a chance.

The distractibility in ADD is not consistent. Many parents and teachers are misled: to some activities a child may be able to devote, if anything, compulsive, hyperconcentrated attention. But hyperfocusing that excludes awareness of the environment also denotes poor attention regulation. Also, hyperfocusing often involves what may be described as *passive attention*, as in watching television or playing video games. Passive attention permits the mind to cruise on automatic without requiring the brain to expend effortful energy. *Active attention*, the mind fully engaged and the brain performing work, is mustered only in special circumstances of high motivation. Active attention is a capacity the ADD brain lacks whenever organized work must be done, or when attention needs to be directed toward something of low interest.

A facility for focusing when one is interested in something does not rule out ADD, but to be able to focus, the person with ADD needs a much higher level of motivation than do other people. Ignorance of this fact has led many doctors to miss the diagnosis. "Indeed, the characteristic of our patient," wrote a psychiatrist of a college lecturer I had diagnosed with attention deficit disorder but whose GP wanted a second opinion, "is that he is able to focus his attention on something that he is really interested in, which for patients afflicted with ADD is very difficult." That is not what is very difficult. What can be immobilizingly difficult is to arouse the brain's motivational apparatus in the absence of personal interest.

ADD is situational: in the same individual its expression may vary greatly from one circumstance to another. There are certain classes, for example, in which the ADD child may perform remarkably well, while in others she is scattered, unproductive and perhaps disruptive. Teachers may conclude that the child is willfully deciding when or when not to buckle down and work diligently. Many children with ADD are subjected to overt disapproval and

public shaming in the classroom for behaviors they do not consciously choose. These children are not purposively inattentive or
disobedient. There are emotional and neurophysiological forces at
play that do the actual deciding for them. We shall examine them
in due course.

The second nearly ubiquitous characteristic of ADD is impulsiveness of word or deed, with poorly controlled emotional reactivity. The adult or child with ADD can barely restrain himself from
interrupting others, finds it a torture waiting his turn in all manner
of activities and will often act or speak impulsively as if fore-
thought did not exist. The consequences are predictably negative.
"I want to control myself," a thirty-three-year-old man said at his
first visit to my office, "but my mind won't let me." The impulsiveness may express itself as the purchase of unneeded items on a
whim, without regard for cost or consequence. "Impulse buying?"
another man exclaimed during our first interview. "If I had the
money I would impulse buy the whole world."

Hyperactivity is the third salient characteristic of ADD. Classi-
cally, it is expressed by trouble keeping physically still, but it may
also be present in forms not readily obvious to the observer. Some
fidgetiness will likely be apparent—toes or fingers tapping, thighs
pumping, nails being chewed, teeth biting the inside of the mouth.
The hyperactivity may also take the form of excessive talking. In a
minority of cases, especially in girls, hyperactivity may be absent
altogether. They may go through school inattentive and absent-
minded, but as they cause no trouble, they are "passed through"
from grade to grade. While the finding of hyperactivity is not
required for the diagnosis of ADD, it can be quite dramatic for
some patients. "The only thing that ever slowed me down was the
police siren when I was caught speeding," said a twenty-seven-
year-old woman.

The loquaciousness of many children with ADD is notorious.
One Grade 2 boy was called Talk Bird by his classmates, so incessant was his chatter. His parents, too, were often after him to be
quiet. It's as if such a child is saying, I'm cut off from people, so

anxious that if I don't work overtime to establish contact with them, I will be left alone. I only know to do this through my words. I know no other way. Some adults with ADD have told me that they speak so quickly partly because so many words and phrases tumble into their minds that they fear forgetting the most important ones unless they release them at a fast rate.

The individual with ADD experiences the mind as a perpetual-motion machine. An intense aversion to boredom, an abhorrence of it, takes hold as soon as there is no ready focus of activity, distraction or attention. An unremitting lack of stillness is felt internally—a constant background static in the brain, a ceaseless "white noise," as Dr. John Ratey, a Harvard psychiatrist, has put it. Merciless pressure in the mind impels without specific aim or direction. As long ago as 1934, an article in *The New England Journal of Medicine* identified a distressing quality to some people's lives, which the authors called "organic drivenness." I, for one, have rarely had a moment's relaxation without the immediate and troubling feeling that I ought to be doing something else instead. Like father, like son. At the age of eight or nine, my son said to me, "I always think I should be doing something, but I don't know what it is." The oldest person to whom I have prescribed a stimulant was an eighty-five-year-old woman who, on taking Ritalin, was able to sit still more than fifteen minutes for the very first time in her life.

The restlessness coexists with long periods of procrastination. The threat of failure or the promise of reward has to be immediate for the motivation apparatus to be turned on. Without the rousing adrenaline rush of racing against time, inertia prevails. Not once in high school or university did I begin an assignment or essay before the eve of the day it was due. In that era of manual typewriters, my rough copies had to serve as final copies. They resembled academic tossed salad: sheets pasted over with pieces of paper bearing hastily scribbled corrections. On the other hand, when there is something one wants, neither patience nor procrastination exist. One has to do it, get it, have it, experience it, immediately.

Frequent and frustrating memory lapses occur every day in the life of the person with ADD. A close friend of mine, Brian, has attention deficit disorder. He also has a dog. They take each other for daily walks. As Brian puts on his coat, hat and boots, the dog lies under the kitchen table, waiting. Brian leaves the house, and the dog doesn't move. The dog will not budge until Brian has come back into the house for the third time for key, wallet or whatever other items he has forgotten to take the first two times. The dog has learned from experience, which is more than can be said for his owner.

My most recent memory failure, as I write this, occurred four days ago. I showed up at Ben Gurion Airport in Tel Aviv, all packed and ready for the flight home to Vancouver. I was pleased with myself for getting somewhere on time for a change. At the airline counter, the ticket agent looked at my travel documents. Puzzlement spread across her face. "But your flight is booked for tomorrow," she finally said. Perhaps I was unconsciously trying to compensate for all the other occasions when I was perilously late getting to airports.

I am often asked how, with such traits, it was possible for me to get through the grind of medical school. The general answer is that there are many people who seem to be high achievers despite their ADD. ADD can blight various aspects of life. The apparent professional success of the workaholic can mask serious problems in other areas. It is also true with ADD, as with everything else, that there are degrees of it, with wide variations from one end of the range to the other.

Although I had planned to become a doctor all my life, I did not enter medical school until the age of twenty-eight, after several detours. In my early twenties, I had gradually scaled down my academic ambitions because I could not get myself to work at my studies consistently. One memorable day in second year, I walked into the examination room, bleary-eyed, having read five Shakespeare plays between midnight and seven o'clock in the morning. Unfortunately, I had the exam dates wrong—this particular examination was not in Shakespeare, but in European literature. So it went, term after term. In third year, I dropped out. In medical school I had a rough time of it for the first two years, when the emphasis was on basic sciences, taught in excruciating detail. Even then, I invariably began my exam preparations late the night before. I found it easier to become motivated and engaged as the courses became more practical and people-oriented in the higher years. And, challenging as it can be, medical school does present consecutive deadlines, exams to pass, hoops to jump through. It is less a long-term project than an extended series of short-term ones.

An adult with ADD looks back on his life to see countless plans never fully realized and intentions unfulfilled. "I am a person of permanent potential," one patient said. Surges of initial enthusiasm quickly ebb. People report unfinished retainer walls begun over a decade ago, partly constructed boats taking up garage space year after year, courses begun and quit, books half read, business ventures forsaken, stories or poetry unwritten—many, many roads not traveled.

Social skills are also an issue. Something about ADD hinders the capacity to recognize interpersonal boundaries. Although some ADD children shrink from being touched, in early childhood most of them literally climb all over adults and generally exhibit an almost insatiable desire for physical and emotional contact. They approach other children with a naive openness, which is often rebuffed. Impaired in their abilities to read social cues, they may be ostracized by their peers. For parents, it is heartbreaking to witness their child's exclusion from schoolyard games, birthday parties, sleepovers, Valentine card exchanges.

Although poor social skills generally accompany ADD, this is not universal. One type of ADD child is socially adept and wildly popular. In my experience, such success hides a lack of confidence in important areas of functioning and masks a very fragile self-esteem, but this may not emerge until these children grow into their late teens or early twenties.

Adults with ADD may be perceived as aloof and arrogant or tire-somely talkative and boorish. Many are recognizable by their compulsive joking, their pressured, rapid-fire speech, by their seemingly random and aimless hopping from one topic to the next and by their inability to express an idea without exhausting the English vocabulary. "I have never finished a thought in my life," one young man lamented. Men and women with ADD have about them an almost palpable intensity that other people respond to with unease and instinctive withdrawal. "It's as if I was from Mars and everyone else was from Earth," one forty-year-old woman said. Or, as another put it, "Everyone else seems to belong to some nice persons' club, and I am excluded." This sense of being always on the outside looking in, of somehow missing the point, is perva-sive. At social events, I tend to gravitate to the periphery, con-scious of a feeling that somehow I cannot enter into the spirit of things. I observe people talking to each other, people I may know quite well, acutely aware that I have nothing to say to anyone. Social conversation has always been a mystery to me. I have at times looked at people engaged in animated discussion and wished that I was invisible so that I could overhear them—not to eaves-drop but to find out once and for all exactly what there is to talk about. My patients with ADD tell me much the same thing about their experience. "I don't know how to make small talk, or I'm afraid of saying something stupid," a twenty-six-year-old woman said. And the truth is, when the ADD adult does join conversations, she often finds herself bored by the minute attention others devote to subjects that to her seem to skim only the surface.

To interview adults with attention deficit disorder is often to be ambushed by jokes. Unexpected turns of phrase and consciously absurd associations pepper life histories that in themselves are not much to laugh about. "Thank God it's only ADD," said one man after I confirmed his diagnosis. "I always used to think I was one crouton short of a Caesar salad." Children with ADD frequently act the part of the class clown.

The moods of the ADD child are capricious, happy smiles being transformed into frowns of displeasure or grimaces of despair in a matter of moments. Events anticipated with joy and begun with exuberant energy often end in bitter disappointment and a sulking, accusatory withdrawal. The emotional states of adults with attention deficit disorder also go through rapid and unpredictable up and down swings. Good days and bad days alternate without apparent reason.

The common theme on all days, good or bad, is a gnawing sense of having missed out on something important in life.

# 3

# We Could

---

# All Go Crazy

---

In everyday thought about especially complex
and emotionally charged situations oversimplified
generalizations are apt to be actively treasured.

   – DOROTHY DINNERSTEIN, *The Mermaid and the Minotaur*

A TTENTION DEFICIT DISORDER has been
called the "flavor of the nineties." Fueling
skepticism about its actual prevalence is the
fact that no feature of ADD is so unique that it cannot be found, to
one degree or another, in any number of people among the non-
ADD population. Lumping a group of personality characteristics
together in a psychiatric manual does not automatically establish a
pathology. Very reasonably, many people wonder why ordinary
traits are defined as symptoms of a medical disorder. Soon, the
critic warns, all human characteristics will be redefined as illness.
The February 1997 edition of *Harper's Magazine* contained a cru-
elly witty review by L. J. Davis of the DSM IV. According to current
psychiatric diagnostics, Davis wrote, "[E]very aspect of human life

(excepting of course the practice of psychiatry) can be read as pathology."

Health Canada statistics indicate that the amount of Ritalin consumed in Canada in 1997 represented more than a fivefold increase since 1990, including a 21 percent jump in the last year of that time period.[1] In the United States, too, the diagnosis of ADD has been spreading like wildfire. Are children being drugged to suit the convenience of adults? Some argue that the diagnosis is just another medical cop-out devised for the peace of mind of incompetent parents and lazy teachers—and of self-pitying adults too immature to face life's demands.

Even for those, such as myself, who recognize the existence of the neurophysiological and psychological impairments conjointly named attention deficit disorder, there are legitimate questions to be asked: about the way ADD is diagnosed, about how it should be understood and especially about its treatment. North American society tries to bury many problems under tons of medications, preferring to ignore the social and cultural causes of people's stressed mental states. The long-term social consequences of massive drug intake in the treatment of depression, ADD and a host of other conditions are yet to be known. I, too, am concerned about this, even though I prescribe medications to others and continue to take one myself.

It also seems to many people that a neurophysiological explanation of behavior is an attempt to excuse personal actions or the actions of others, blaming misdeeds and shortcomings on biology. Are we not to be held accountable for what we do, they ask. Is ADD a license for self-indulgent or hurtful behavior? In British Columbia recently, the defense lawyers in a rape/murder case argued that their client could not be held responsible because he suffers from obsessive compulsive disorder and attention deficit disorder. Wisely, the jury rejected that view. We must all accept responsibility for our actions, else the world becomes unlivable. Yet it would be a tremendous social advance if we made some effort to understand what experiences turn people into flawed or irresponsible or even antisocial beings. We would then approach the issue of crime, for one example, in a very different manner. Accountability does not necessarily call for the punitive inhumanity of the legal system as practiced in Canada and especially in the United States, which has more of its population in jail than any other Western country. There is little doubt that a significant percentage of prison inhabitants have ADD or some other preventible disorder of self-regulation.* Little doubt, too, that prison conditions could not have been more diabolically designed to exacerbate all these mental dysfunctions.

We are not helpless in the face of ADD, so on the personal level an attempt to shift the responsibility for negative behaviors onto brain circuits is unhelpful. It locks a person into victimhood. Regardless how sound neurophysiological explanations may be, no one's children, spouse, friends or co-workers should have to accept her right to disrespect or hurt them. Learning about the psychological and biological mechanisms of ADD gives a map to the self—but only a map, no more. Although people lacking it are left with little more than a discouraging sense of their failures, the map is not to be confused with the journey. It is still up to the individual to plot the course.

Some parents resist the idea of ADD for fear of seeing their children labeled and categorized. They do not like the idea of pinning a medical diagnosis on a child who, except in certain areas of functioning, seems quite well. Such fears are not baseless. Too often ADD seems no more than a judgment that characterizes a child as a problem student, incapable of normal activity. How people use language is quite revealing. People commonly say that this adult or that child "is ADD." That, indeed, is labeling, identifying the whole person with an area of weakness or impairment. No one *is* ADD, and no one should be defined or categorized in terms of it or any other particular problem.

---

* A 1998 Swedish study has shown ADD to be a very common finding in the prison population.

Recognizing a child's ADD should be simply a way of under-standing that helping him calls for some knowledgeable and creative approaches, not a judgment that there is anything funda-mentally or irretrievably wrong with him. This recognition should enable us to support the child in fullfilling his potential, not to fur-ther limit him.

That even open-minded people may have difficulty coming to terms with this diagnosis is only to be expected. Our usual mode of thinking about illness (or anything else, for that matter) is not comfortable with ambiguity. A patient either has pneumonia or does not; she either has some illness affecting the mind or does not. There is a popular discomfort with any condition of the mind per-ceived as "abnormal." But what if illness is not a separate category, if there is no line of distinction between the "healthy" and the "nonhealthy," if the "abnormality" is just a greater concentration in an individual of disturbed brain processes found in everyone? Then perhaps there are no fixed, immutable brain disorders, and we could all be vulnerable to mental breakdowns or malfunctions under the pressure of stressful circumstances. We could all go crazy. Maybe we already have.

ADD defies categories of normality or abnormality. If anyone who exhibits any trait of it were to be diagnosed with ADD, we might as well put Ritalin in the drinking water and sign up most of the industrialized world for group psychotherapy. As Drs. Hallow-ell and Ratey point out in *Driven to Distraction*, ADD is a diagnosis not of category but of dimension. At a certain point on the human continuum, the characteristics associated with ADD become intru-sive enough to impair a person's functioning to one degree or another.

Among professionals who work with ADD children or adults, it is easier to find agreement about what ADD looks like than about what it is. The term *disorder* is itself a misnomer. In medical terms it means an ailment or disease, which most assuredly ADD is not. Dis-order, however, has another meaning that predates its adaptation into medical terminology. "If you have many of the features of

ADD," I say to people, "and if they produce a lack of order in your life, then you have ADD. What is order? A sense of organization. A consciously planned sequence of activities. Knowing where things are and what you have done and what remains to be done. And what do we call a lack of order? Disorder."

I do not myself accept ADD as a disorder in the medicalized sense. ADD is not an illness, although some influential authorities have called it that. It is an *impairment*, like, for example, a visual impairment in the absence of any disease.

The question is, where do these impairments, the underlying physiological malfunctions and the associated behaviors and psychological problems, come from? At the present state of scientific knowledge, no definitive answers are yet possible, despite the astonishing growth of our understanding about the brain in the past decade.[2] Given what we know now—and given also what we don't know—the only test of any explanation for attention deficit disorder is whether it makes sense in the light of people's experience and the available research facts, and whether it can be used productively to help people.

Virtually all the authors of popular books on the subject assert that ADD is a heritable genetic disorder. With some notable exceptions, the genetic view also dominates much of the discussion within professional circles, a view I do not agree with.

I believe that ADD can be better understood if we examine people's lives, not only bits of DNA. Heredity does make an important contribution, but far less than usually assumed. At the same time, it would serve no purpose to set up the false opposition of environment to genetic inheritance. No such split exists in nature, or in the mind of any serious scientist. If in this book I emphasize environment, I do so to focus attention on an area that most books on the subject neglect and none explore in nearly enough detail. Such neglect frequently leads to crippling deficiencies in what people are offered by way of treatment.

There are many biological events involving body and brain that are not directly programmed by heredity, and so to say that ADD is

not primarily genetic is not in any sense to deny its biological features—either those that are inherited or those that are acquired as a
result of experience. The genetic blueprints for the architecture
and the workings of the human brain develop in a process of interaction with the environment. ADD does reflect biological malfunctions in certain brain centers, but many of its features—including
the underlying biology itself—are also inextricably connected to a
person's physical and emotional experiences in the world.

There is in ADD an inherited *predisposition*, but that's very far
from saying there is a genetic *predetermination*. A predetermination dictates that something *will* inevitably happen. A predisposition only makes it more likely that it *may* happen, depending on
circumstances. The actual outcome is influenced by many other
factors.

# 4

# A Conflictual

# Marriage: ADD

# and the Family (I)

A hallmark of a conflictual marriage is that husband and wife are angry and dissatisfied with one another. While the atmosphere of conflictual relationships is intensely negative much of the time, it is usually punctuated by periods of equally intense, sometimes very passionate closeness.... Conflict can have an addictive quality: It is both a familiar scene and a poignant reminder of how involved two people are with one another. People do not want conflict, but they have not found an alternative way of interacting.

— MICHAEL E. KERR, M.D., *Family Evaluation*

M Y WIFE, RAE, AND I have three children: two boys, aged twenty-three and twenty, and a ten-year-old daughter. They have all three been diagnosed with ADD, as have I.

Our family could almost be seen as poster perfect for the genetic argument: a financially secure, stable middle-class couple, married now nearly thirty years, who love each other and their children. There is no alcoholism or substance addiction, no family violence, no abuse. If these children have attention deficit disorder, surely it must be due to their genes. What about this environment could have caused ADD?

Environment does not *cause* ADD any more than genes *cause* ADD. What happens is that if certain genetic material meets a certain environment, ADD may result. Without that genetic material, no ADD. Without that environment, no ADD. The formative environment is the family of origin.

So far as marriages go, ours has been firmly at what may be called the "conflictual" end of the spectrum. We have worked things out, but it took decades and a lot of energy. In retrospect, we shudder at how hurtful and dark it felt at times, and particularly how our struggles burdened our children's lives.

Our marriage is now something we celebrate. Our ships, having been tossed and thrown about on heavy seas, have finally arrived safely in the same harbor. But the storms took their toll on our children. At the end of his delightfully candid 1972 essay, "My Own Marriage," the great American psychotherapist and teacher Carl Rogers wrote of the difficulties his adult children were having in their relationships. "So our growth together into a satisfying relationship for ourselves," he concluded, "has constituted no guarantee for our children." Children are a great incentive and impetus for parents to learn about themselves, about each other and about life itself. Unfortunately, much of the learning may occur at their expense.

There was never any question of a lack of love in our home. But love felt by the parent does not automatically translate into loving experienced by the child. The atmosphere in our home was often one of open or suppressed emotional conflict between the parents, mutually disappointed expectations and profound anxieties we were not even aware of.

My frustrations with life could, without warning, erupt against Rae or directly against the children in the form of rages or cold withdrawals. I could be supremely compassionate and helpful to relative strangers but present a double face of loving support and hostile rejection to those closest to me. Nowhere were my anxieties and unresolved tensions—which is to say, my unresolved grief—expressed as openly and as harmfully as in my own home.

During my children's early years, I was not comfortable with myself except as a superactive and sought-after doctor. Besides professional responsibilities, I frequently took on other highly demanding projects at the same time. I wore my beeper as a badge of distinction. Especially in the first few years, I would hope it would sound, so that other people might see how important I was. I might have felt satisfaction in every one of my activities, but I never felt satisfied with myself or my life. I had great difficulty turning down any new responsibility that came my way—except those at home. It was virtually impossible for me to say no to any request for help, no matter what the cost to my personal life. In honoring this overwrought sense of responsibility toward others, I neglected my responsibility toward the only people for whom I really was indispensable. This feeling of duty toward the whole world is not limited to ADD but is typical of it. No one with ADD is without it.

It is exhausting even to list the various activities I was pursuing at the time I first became aware of my ADD patterns less than four years ago. Besides my busy office practice, obstetrical work and the psychological counseling of patients, I also served as medical coordinator of the Palliative Care Unit at Vancouver Hospital, one of Canada's largest hospice wards. I was on call for the palliative service almost every night and every weekend for five years, except when on holiday. At any moment, I could be called away to attend a delivery or to look after the needs of a terminally ill person. On top of all this, I was writing a weekly medical column for *The Globe and Mail*. And just for something to do in my spare time, I was researching a book that—in fine ADD fashion—I dropped like a hot potato as soon as attention deficit disorder caught my interest.

One cannot live like that and not be affected. I was constantly on the go from one place to the next, always behind schedule. My newspaper columns were filed late at night, just before deadline. My office was invariably filled with patients who had been kept waiting much too long. I was semioblivious to the fact that my frenetic, catch-as-catch-can working style meant that others had to make adjustments and accommodations to their work that I had never formally negotiated with them. The palliative care nurses, with whom I had a mutually respectful and cordial relationship, said that working with me was like working in the center of a tornado. In her own efficient, quiet and calm way, my office nurse, Maria Oliverio—destined to win the Nobel Peace Prize someday—climbed the walls. People experienced me as tense, urgent, insistent.

The effect of this kamikaze juggling act on my family was devastating. On Rae's shoulders fell all the responsibility of organizing and maintaining not just a family home but the family itself. Without any discussion or conscious decision making, she was thrust into the position of the family's emotional lynchpin. She felt abandoned. She felt, too, that I saw her own calling as a painter as something of secondary importance.

There was also what I call the "weekend despair" of the driven personality. On Saturday mornings, there would be a crash. I was enveloped in a kind of enervated lethargy, hiding behind a book or a newspaper or staring morosely out the window. I was not only fatigued from the whirlwind week, but I did not know what to do with myself. Without the weekday adrenaline rush, I felt a lack of focus, purpose, energy. I was depleted and irritable, neither active nor able to rest.

Rae was hurt, anxious and angry. She withdrew emotionally. A vicious cycle was now complete, as my own fear and rage at abandonment were triggered. In such states of mind did we parent our children.

Young children cannot possibly understand the motives of adults. It means little to a young child that the parent feels love for him if that parent keeps disappearing at almost any time. The child experiences a sense of abandonment, a subliminal knowledge that there are things in the world much more important to the parent than he, the child, that he is not worthy of the parent's attention. He begins to feel, at first unconsciously, that there must be something wrong with him. He also begins to work too hard to get his needs met: demanding contact, acting out or trying to please the parent to gain approval and attention.

There were many good times, of course, when we would feel connected and our children felt the warmth of our love for each other. Our photo albums are full of happy memories. But the tough times came often enough to make it difficult for the children to construct in themselves a sense of security. The emotional climate was too unpredictable and confusing.

Not only was I physically absent much of the time, but there were also my difficulties staying focused in the present. Young children are completely in the right-brain feeling world of the here and now, precisely where I felt most uneasy. My ADD-based, tuned-out absentmindedness was such that I was quite capable of reading one of my sons or my daughter a story without following a word of it myself, engaging in thoughts or fantasies that took me far away. If the child asked me a question about what I had just read, I could not answer. Even without such evidence, children can sense this nonpresence of the parent. They suffer from it.

Some of our most stressful times came during two of Rae's pregnancies and in the first few years of our children's lives. When one of our children was twelve months old, Rae experienced a

full-blown clinical depression. During the worst of it, she was
hardly sleeping at all and could barely cope with the physical
demands of parenting. She was painfully conscious that she was
not providing the emotional contact the child needed and helpless
at the same time. She was not diagnosed or given the appropriate
care for many months. The failure occurred perhaps because she
was a doctor's wife—not an uncommon occurrence. I myself was
too close to her experience, too threatened by what was happening, too enmeshed in the process of it to see clearly.

There are things I wish I had not done during my children's
early years, but mostly I regret what I did not do: give my children
the gift of a mindful, secure and reliable parental presence. I wish I
had known how to allow myself to relax, to release myself from
the compulsions driving me and to fully enjoy the wonderful little
persons they were.

It may seem from what I have written here that I consider
myself the villain of the piece when it comes to our family. Not
so. I intend no judgment of myself, nor of anyone else. For one
thing, my contribution was responsible for only one half of the
strain between Rae and me. As I will discuss in a later chapter on
relationships, couples choose each other with an unerring instinct
for finding the very person who will exactly match their own level
of unconscious anxieties and mirror their own dysfunctions, and
who will trigger for them all their unresolved emotional pain. This
was certainly mutually true for us. Second, judgment or blaming
is not the point. Understanding is. In retrospect Rae and I can see
that between us there has been a coherent process at work all these
years. Everything that happened had to happen, given what we
knew, who we were, and what we each brought to the marriage.
It is also true that we gave our children the best that we could, and
continue to do so.

None of this personal history would be of interest if it were
simply an isolated tale of one family's emotional travails. It isn't. In
virtually every one of the families I have seen where one child or
another has ADD, I found stories that, while different in detail,

spoke similarly of tension and stress. While most parents are aware of the stresses in their lives during their child's early years, some report that the period of their ADD child's infant and toddler months were purely happy ones for them. On further discussion, they usually recognize that mixed in with happy times were also considerable stresses they had not at first identified. The fact is, we in this society are often quite removed from our own emotional reality. (More discussion of the families of adults and children with ADD is included in chapter 12.) I believe that it is in these stresses experienced by the parents in spite of their will to do the best for their children that the environmental roots of attention deficit are to be found. What research data exist also supports this view, even if not all researchers or scholars have drawn the same conclusion from the evidence before them. We will turn to that, after examining how the fascinating interplay of heredity and early childhood experience shapes the development of the human brain.

# 5

# Forgetting to

---

# Remember the

---

# Future

---

ADD is not a problem of knowing what to do; it is a
problem of doing what you know.

    — RUSSELL A. BARKLEY, PH.D., "Improved Delayed
    Responding"

T IS NOT THAT I WISH to be late. I do not
imagine for a moment that I *will* be late. I may
have to be somewhere, miles away, at 9:00 a.m.,
but as long as it is not yet nine, I fully believe I have time enough. I
am scheduled to attend ward rounds with nurses and other physicians at Vancouver Hospital. At 8:50 I leap into the shower, still
confident: there is space between the big hand of the watch and the
hour marker, so I am not late.

That the traveling always takes longer than I expect, that ice will have to be scraped off the car, that I will not find the keys, that I may get stuck in traffic do not arise in the mind as concrete possibilities. Two thought systems vie for control in the brain: the one logical and aware, the other the immature time sense of a young child. The latter is most often dominant.

It's only when nine o'clock strikes and I am searching for my car keys that irritability begins to set in. When I get outside and realize that frost has made the windshield completely opaque, I begin to curse. By the time I have to rush back up the stairs once, then twice, to find briefcase or lunch or stethoscope, I feel utterly frustrated.

I arrive on the ward fifteen minutes late—on a good day—removing my coat and hat and pulling my rubber galoshes off each foot in turn while hopping hurriedly down the hall on the other. Taking a deep breath outside the door, I steady myself. I enter the meeting room. Rounds are already in progress. "Okay, we can begin," I say. I notice that not everyone laughs.

Every adult with ADD can relate such anecdotes—funny to tell, not so funny to experience and never so jolly for others inconvenienced by the tardiness and disorganization. The ADD mind is afflicted by a sort of time illiteracy, or what Dr. Russell Barkley has called "time blindness." One is either hopelessly short of time, dashing about like a deaf bat, or else acts as if blessed with the gift of eternity. It's as if one's time sense never developed past a stage other people leave behind in early childhood.

To the very young child, any block of time seems infinite. Tell her that supper will be ready in three minutes: desperate wailing will signal her conviction that you have sentenced her to starvation. Tell her to hurry because time is running out, and she will not know what you are talking about. How can infinity run out? Only two units of time exist for the small child: the now and the not-now. The not-now is infinity.

The time sense of the ADD adult or child is warped in other ways. Ask people with ADD how long it will take to perform a particular task, and they will notoriously underestimate. A kind of magical thinking dominates, characteristic of young children: if I will it, it will happen. In magic anything is possible. Castles can be built or destroyed with the wave of a wand, worlds traversed in seven-league boots, you can get from Oz to Kansas by clicking your heels together. Magic vanquishes time.

No infant is born with a sense of time. The gradual acquisition of time sense is a task of development that begins in early childhood. At the outset, the infant has no categories such as time, space or causality, no awareness that one event leads to another. It is not until the age of seven or so, Jean Piaget found, that children begin to have a full understanding of time as a continuous flow. Until then, the child is in what Piaget, the great Swiss cognitive psychologist, called the "preoperational stage," when everything is observed and interpreted from only one point of view, the child's. "The preoperational child, in his egocentric manner, believes that he can stop time, speed it up, or slow it down."[1] The networks of nerve cells responsible for the various brain activities do not all develop the same way, at the same time, or, necessarily, to the same degree. With ADD we witness a delayed or permanently arrested maturation of the balanced time sense most people achieve by adulthood. In attention deficit disorder, the circuitry of time intelligence is underdeveloped.

Underdevelopment best explains another time-related malfunction of the ADD brain, the chronic incapacity to consider the future. The guiding assumption of the adult with attention deficit disorder, like that of the small child, seems to be that only the present exists and needs to be taken into account. He lives as if his actions had no implications for the future, no effects on future needs, relationships or responsibilities. The short-term goal is invariably chosen over the long-term, with the exception of activities or projects capable of arousing the sluggish motivation-reward nexus in the brain. The present impulse dominates. It has been aptly said that people with ADD forget to remember the future. In the moment of action or decision making, ADD adults are no more mindful of consequences than a young child.

Some aspects of the individual's mental and emotional functioning are normal for chronological age; others remain mired in an early childhood phase. "He can be so cooperative and mature one minute, and in the next he is behaving like a two-year-old," an exasperated mother will say of her preadolescent son. "Often I feel like a complete child," many adults with ADD have told me. Or, a wife will complain bitterly that living with her husband is like living with a young child. "Sometimes it feels like I am his mother. It's as if I have three children: two preschoolers and one age thirty-two."

The major impairments of ADD—the distractibility, the hyperactivity and the poor impulse control—reflect, each in its particular way, a lack of self-regulation. Self-regulation implies that someone can direct attention where she chooses, can control impulses and can be consciously mindful and in charge of what her body is doing. Like time literacy, self-regulation is also a distinct task of development in human life, achieved gradually from young childhood through adolescence and adulthood. We are born with no capacity whatsoever to self-regulate emotion or action. For self-regulation to be possible, specific brain centers have to develop and grow connections with other important nerve centers, and chemical pathways need to be established. Attention deficit disorder is a prime illustration of how the adult continues to struggle with the unsolved problems of childhood. She is held back precisely where the child did not develop, hampered in those areas where the infant or toddler got stuck during the course of development.

In general, we may speak of an underdevelopment of emotional intelligence. In his best-selling book *Emotional Intelligence*, Daniel Goleman, behavioral and brain sciences writer for *The New York Times*, defines this capacity as "being able to motivate oneself and persist in the face of frustrations; to control impulse and to delay gratification; to regulate one's moods and keep distress from swamping the ability to think…"[2] We have only to place a negative qualifier before the "being able" in that sentence, as in "not being able," and we arrive at a succinct description of the ADD personality.

Reactions can be gratifyingly mature at one time but distressingly immature at another. If some deeply unconscious anxiety is triggered, a person may respond with the lack of emotional self-regulation characteristic of an infant. A fully grown adult exhibiting the rage of an infant is terrifying and potentially dangerous.

We all have experiences as parents that we are ashamed of and wish we could erase. Such scenes always represent failures of self-regulation and impulse control. What happens during these times is that the brain centers where the deepest emotions of fear or rage are generated simply overwhelm the higher centers meant to govern them—as they normally would in a small child. "So-and-so is behaving like a baby" is quite an accurate description of the individual's neurophysiological state at such moments.

That the infant/toddler mode is so often dominant in attention deficit disorder reflects incomplete development of pathways in the cerebral cortex, and between the cortex and lower areas of the brain. *Cortex* means "bark," as in the bark of a tree, and refers to the thin rim of gray matter enveloping the white matter of the brain. Made up largely of the cell bodies of the nerve cells, or neurons, the cortex is where the most highly evolved activities of the human brain are processed. Spread out, it would be about the size and thickness of a table napkin. We can probably localize much of the organic basis of ADD in what is called the right prefrontal cortex, the area of the brain just behind the forehead. The evidence comes from the latest radiological studies, from sophisticated psychological tests, from animal experiments and from observing human beings who have sustained injury to this part of the brain.

In general, the functions of the right prefrontal cortex include impulse control, social-emotional intelligence and motivation. It also participates in the directing of attention. Human beings injured here, so-called prefrontal patients, exhibit distractibility, poor regulation of impulses and other classic signs of ADD. Monkeys deliberately lesioned in the right prefrontal cortex lose their ability to read social cues and to participate in socially essential activities such as mutual grooming. They are soon ostracized by other members of the group. When separated from mother, infant monkeys similarly lesioned become hyperactive, as do rats lesioned in this area of the brain.

Neuroimaging studies such as scans and magnetic resonance imaging (MRI) that reveal the architecture and functioning of brain structures also implicate the right prefrontal cortex. MRI pictures have shown smaller than normal structures in the right prefrontal areas of ADD patients.

Another way to study the brain is the use of electroencephalograms, or EEGs, which measure electrical wave activity. EEG studies performed in Edmonton, at the University of Alberta, have cast some light on how ADD may be reflected in brain functioning.[3] The EEGs of a group of preadolescent boys with ADD were compared with those of a matched group of non-ADD peers. The two groups had similarly normal EEGs at rest, but the ADD group showed excessive "slow wave" activity during directed tasks such as reading or drawing. As would be expected normally, the non-ADD group had increased fast-wave electrical responses to the same task. In other words, in the ADD group electrical activity in the cerebral cortex, or gray matter, slowed down just when it would have been required to speed up.

It may seem paradoxical to consider that hyperactivity of mind or body can be caused by an underactivity of the cortex. It would also seem odd to think of hyperactivity being stopped by a stimulant medication. The paradox is best understood by means of an analogy. Imagine a busy urban street corner where major thoroughfares converge, each conveying a high volume of traffic. In our model, the drivers have no capacity to regulate themselves. They rely on the order kept by a policeman who ensures that when traffic flows east-west, the vehicles traveling on the north-south axis are stopped until it is their turn to move, and that cars are allowed to make turns in an organized fashion. Traffic flow, in short, is alternately inhibited in one direction while being permitted in another. There is *order*. Now imagine that the policeman falls asleep on the job. There will ensue tremendous activity as cars from all directions attempt to move through the intersection, their drivers increasingly frustrated, their horns joined in a deafening cacophony. Despite all the commotion, there is little progress. Fewer and fewer cars are able to move purposefully. There is *disorder*.

The prefrontal cortex may be seen as that policeman. One of its major tasks is inhibition. It evaluates the myriad impressions, thoughts, sensations and impulses reaching it from the environment, from the body and from the lower brain centers. It must select what is essential and helpful and inhibit input and impulses that are not useful to the organism in a given situation. Our initial response to a stimulus, whether anxiety-producing or pleasurable, is unconscious. It comes not from the cortex but from lower brain centers where emotions originate. The cortex has a split second to decide whether to give permission to the impulse or to cancel it.[4] One way to understand ADD neurologically is as a *lack of inhibition*, a chronic underactivity of the prefrontal cortex. The cerebral cortex in the frontal lobe is not able to perform its job of prioritizing, selection and inhibition. The brain, flooded with multiple bits of sensory data, thoughts, feelings and impulses, cannot focus, and the mind or body cannot be still. In short, the policeman is asleep. If we want the traffic to move, we need to rouse him. Similarly, the cortex is functioning at a semidormant level, as indicated by the EEG finding of slowed activity. Hence the efficacy of stimulant medications: they arouse the inhibitory function. They wake up the cop, alert the underdeveloped and underactive circuitry of the prefrontal cortex.

Recognizing that ADD is a problem of development rather than one of pathology takes us in a direction completely different from that dictated by a narrowly medical approach. When we ask why the medical disorder ADD develops, we are adopting the *illness model* of ADD. Implied in the illness model is the presence of a pathological entity in the brain, analogous to, say, inflammation of joints in rheumatoid arthritis or bacterial invasion of the lungs in pneumonia. Such a way of formulating the question of how ADD originates almost demands a medicalized answer. We look for the narrowly biological, exclusively physiological explanation.

If we choose not to see ADD as medical disorder or illness, the question of causation is turned around and examined from the opposite angle. Recognizing that time sense, self-regulation and self-motivation are nature driven and necessary developmental tasks, we ask the following: What conditions are needed for human physiological and psychological maturation? What conditions would inhibit or interfere with that growth process? *Instead of asking why a disorder or illness develops, we ask why a fully self-motivated and self-regulated human personality does not.*

Nature, we may say, has an agenda for the comparatively long development phase of humans, eighteen years or even longer: the maturation of an autonomous, self-motivated individual in harmony with the community and environment that he is a part of. In ADD, the natural agenda is frustrated. Why? Posing the question this way immediately resolves the vexing and confusing issue of how it could be that "symptoms of a disorder" are distributed so widely among the population, even in those without the supposed disorder. Not many human beings are born into ideal situations. Throughout the industrialized world and particularly in North America, families are under enormous strain from a frenzied lifestyle and the breakdown of traditional supports. Since perfect parenting is almost impossible, there will be partial flaws of development, to a greater or lesser degree, in just about everyone. "So few children grow up in truly optimal circumstances," Stanley Greenspan, a leading American child psychiatrist, has written, "that we have no idea of what the parameters of development really are."[5]

In some people, there will be a greater concentration of developmental problems. This may be because their specific circumstances were worse, or because they were more sensitive, deeply affected by conditions that others with more robust temperaments could better withstand. They are the ones likely to be diagnosed with ADD or with some other "disorder."

On the westernmost shores of Canada, on Vancouver Island, one sees scruffy and twisted little conifers, stunted relatives of the magnificent fir trees that dominate the landscape just a short distance inland. We would be wrong to see these hardy little survivors as having some sort of plant disease; they have developed to the maximum that the relatively harsh conditions of climate and soil allow. If we wish to understand why they differ so dramatically from their inland relatives, we need to know under what conditions majestically tall, stout and ramrod-straight fir trees are able to thrive. It is the same with human beings. We do not have to look for diseases to explain why some people are not able to experience the full flowering of their potential. We have only to inquire what conditions sustain unfettered human development and what conditions hinder it.

The answer to underdevelopment is development, and for development the appropriate conditions must exist. No matter how efficiently they are able to arouse the higher brain centers, medications offer only a partial solution to the problems posed by ADD. We may not be able to prescribe development directly, but we can promote an environment that makes development possible. Fortunately, as we will see when we come to the chapters on the healing process in ADD, neurological and psychological maturation can take place at any time during the life cycle, even in late adulthood.

# PART TWO

How the Brain Develops

and How the Circuits and

Chemistry of ADD Arise

# 6

# Different Worlds:

# Heredity and the

# Environments of

# Childhood

The family I grew up in was not the family my brothers grew up in. They grew up in a family that was on the road constantly, never in the same place longer than a couple of months at best. They grew up in a family where they watched the father beat the mother regularly, battering her face until it was a mortified, blue knot. They grew up in a family where they were slapped and pummelled and belittled for paltry affronts... I grew up in a world so different from that of my brothers, I may as well have grown up under a different surname.

— MIKAL GILMORE, *Shot in the Heart*

A GENETIC FUNDAMENTALISM permeates public awareness these days. It may be summed up as the belief that almost every illness and every human trait is dictated by heredity. Simplified media accounts, culled from semidigested research findings, have declared that inflexible laws of DNA rule the biological world.

It was reported in 1996 that according to some psychologists, genes determine about 50 percent of a person's inclination to experience happiness. Social ability and obesity are two more among the many human qualities now claimed to be genetic. "Each week ... brings the discovery of a gene that is associated with some disease or trait," noted a tongue-in-cheek contributor to *The New York Times*. "With thousands yet to be discovered, you can just imagine what is out there, or in there...The Line Dancing Gene. The Loves British Cuisine Gene...The Tendency to Go on TV Talk Shows and Embarrass Yourself Gene..."

True or not, narrow genetic explanations for ADD and every other condition of the mind do have their attractions. They are easy to grasp, socially conservative and psychologically soothing. They raise no uncomfortable questions about how a society and culture might erode the health of its members, or about how life in a family may have affected a person's physiology or emotional makeup. As I have personally experienced, feelings of guilt are almost inevitable for the parents of a troubled child. They are all too frequently reinforced by the uninformed judgments of friends, neighbors, teachers or even total strangers on the bus or in the supermarket. Parental guilt, even if misplaced, is a wound for which the genetic hypothesis offers a balm.

There is a significant hereditary contribution to ADD—sensitivity, subject of the next chapter—but I do not believe any genetic factor is *decisive* in the emergence of ADD traits in any child.[1] Genes are codes for the synthesis of the proteins that give a particular cell its characteristic structure and function. They are, as it were, alive and dynamic architectural and mechanical plans. Whether the plan becomes realized depends on far more than the gene itself. It is determined, for the most part, by the environment. To put it differently, genes carry *potentials* inherent in the cells of a given organism. Which of multiple potentials become expressed biologically is a question of life circumstances.

Were we to adopt the medical model—only temporarily, for the sake of argument—a genetic explanation by itself would still be unsuitable. Medical conditions for which genetic inheritance are fully or even mostly responsible, such as muscular dystrophy, are rare. "Few diseases are purely genetic," says Michael Hayden, a geneticist at the University of British Columbia and a world-renowned researcher into Huntington's disease. "The most we can say is that some diseases are strongly genetic." Huntington's is a fatal degeneration of the nervous system based on a single gene that, if inherited, will almost invariably cause the disease. But not always. Dr. Hayden mentions cases of persons with the gene who live into ripe old age without any signs of the disease itself. "Even in Huntington's, there must be some protective factor in the environment," Dr. Hayden says.

Genes can be activated or turned off by factors in the environment. In the Cree population of northwestern Ontario, for example, diabetes is found at a rate five times the Canadian national average, despite the traditionally low incidence of diabetes among native peoples. The genetic makeup of the Cree people cannot have changed in a few generations. The destruction of the Crees' traditional physically active ways of life, the substitution of high-calorie diets for their previous low-fat, low-carbohydrate eating patterns and greatly increased stress levels are responsible for the alarming rise in diabetes rates. Although heredity is involved in diabetes, it cannot possibly account for the pandemic among Canada's native peoples, or among the rest of the North American population, for that matter. We will see that in similar ways changes in society are causing more and more children to be affected by attention deficit disorder.

It is easy to jump to hasty conclusions about genetic information. Some studies have identified certain genes, for example, that are said to be more common among people with attention deficit disorder or with other related conditions, such as depression, alcoholism or addiction. But even if the existence of these genes is proven, there is no reason to suppose that they can, on their own, induce the development of ADD or any other disorder. First, not everyone with these genes will have the disorders. Second, not everyone with the disorders will be shown to carry the genes.

Studies do show that if parents or siblings have ADD, a child in that family will have a greatly increased statistical risk for having ADD as well. ADD is also found more commonly in people whose first-degree relatives are alcoholics or suffer from depression, anxiety, addiction, obsessive-compulsive disorder or Tourette's syndrome. It may appear from such facts that this motley collection of related syndromes is largely hereditary—but to assume that would be like believing that if there are three generations of butchers or bakers or candlestick makers in a family, then meat cutting, baking and candle manufacturing must also be genetic. The family atmosphere in which the child spends the early formative years has a major impact on brain development. It is obvious that brain/mind problems such as ADD are far more likely to develop in families where the parents are struggling with dysfunction or psychological problems of their own. It would be astonishing if children growing up in such unsettled environments did not develop some of the same problems. No genes need be involved at all for these conditions to run in families.[2]

There has been an enduring misconception in psychological studies that comparing identical twins adopted by different families can separate out genetic effects from environmental ones. Because identical twins adopted by different parents are brought up under different circumstances, any similarities in personality traits are assumed to be due to the shared heredity; any differences in character are thought to be caused by differences of environment. This misbelief has heavily influenced the conventional understanding of attention deficit disorder. It has been shown, for example, that if one of the twin pair has ADD, there is a 50 to 60 percent likelihood that the other will have it as well. The technical term for this likelihood is *concordance*. Such a high degree of concordance is taken to prove a hereditary causation—but only if one ignores the most obvious question: *since identical twins have exactly the same genes, why is the concordance not closer to 100 percent?* Also ignored is a powerful environmental factor: *the adoption itself.*

A consistently available nurturing caregiver is a fundamental need of the human infant. Adoption means separation from the birth mother to whose body, voice, heartbeat and biorhythms a newborn is attuned by the time of birth. We cannot simply discount the devastating effect such separation may have on the impressionable nervous system of the infant. Not a few adoptions—including a significant number of the adoptions examined in published studies—take place several months or longer after birth. Many adoptee infants must endure several changes of caregiver without any single, consistently reliable mothering figure to provide them with a constant, safe relationship. Given that emotional security is an absolute human need in infancy, it is astonishing that adoption is so often forgotten as a possibly crucial influence.

It is also a fact, as a number of adoptive mothers have told me, that even when a newborn adopted at birth is welcomed into a family with the greatest joy and goodwill, some time may have to pass before the truly symbiotic, two-way, physiologically and emotionally attuned relationship is established between mother and infant. Everything being equal, this process is smoother when the mother has herself carried the child within her body for nine months.

There is another environment that adopted twins have shared: nine months in the same uterus. Stress on the mother during pregnancy can unbalance the levels of hormones in her body, particularly of the stress hormone cortisol (cortisone). Both during and after intrauterine life, cortisol directly affects the developing nervous system. The vast majority of pregnancies ending in adoption occur in mothers under severe stress. They are often unwanted pregnancies, many in teenage girls facing enormous personal, family and social pressures. Infants—twins or single—who are adopted out are likely to have been exposed to high levels of stress hormones throughout the nine months of gestation, a negative influence on their developing brains even before birth.[3]

For such reasons, we can expect all adopted children to be at unusually high risk for psychological problems in general, ADD in particular, without any recourse to genetic explanations. Such is the case. Any health professional working with ADD cases is struck by the large proportion of clients, children or adults, who were adopted in early childhood. A 1982 study found that "the rate of adoption among ADD patients in the clinical population was *8 to 16 times the prevalence of adopted children in the population at large.*"[4] If you have ADD, you have a far higher than average chance of having been adopted.

None of this is to say that all babies are born alike, or that there are no important inborn differences in neurological systems from one infant to the next. Mothers report being aware of some characteristic features in the personalities of their babies right from birth, and even before. Some infants, for example, may be more difficult to arouse, others to quiet down. Some may be extremely sensitive, others relatively insensitive, to environmental stimuli such as noise or touch. Stanley Greenspan calls these "patterns of reactivity." In his 1997 volume, *The Growth of the Mind*, Dr. Greenspan observes that the same combination of biological traits—the very same pattern of reactivity—can come to embody many positive human qualities, or may serve as the basis of highly disturbed characteristics. "Whether these features become talents or problems depends, in short, on how the child's nature is nurtured," he writes.[5] The critical difference is the environments in which children are reared.

A view of ADD that recognizes the importance of the environment is inherently optimistic. If environmental causes are largely responsible for a problem, perhaps environmental approaches can be employed to help resolve it. When we come to the chapters dealing with the treatment of attention deficit disorder, we will see that long-term positive changes are indeed possible, based on changing the environments of children, and even of adults.

A dramatic illustration of how environment shapes personality is the story of the Gilmore family.

On January 17, 1978, in Utah, the convicted double murderer Gary Gilmore was executed by firing squad, his unyielding refusal to appeal his death sentence having gained him a measure of international notoriety. The shattering story of his childhood, blighted by family violence, alcoholism and spite was chronicled later by his brother Mikal Gilmore in the memoir *Shot in the Heart*. Mikal, the youngest of four boys, was born when Gary was eleven years old. If children reared in the same family shared the same environment, the differences between siblings would have to be due to genetic inheritance. In the case of the Gilmores, it is easy to see why Mikal, born at a time when the family was enjoying a period of relative stability, would feel he had been brought up in a different world, why the misery of his childhood, as he put it, had been so radically different from the misery of his brothers' childhood. Even without such vast chasms in experience, the environment of siblings is never the same.

Environment has far greater impact on the structures and circuits of the human brain than was realized even a decade ago. It is what shapes the inherited genetic material. I believe it to be the decisive factor in determining whether the impairments of ADD will or will not appear in a child.

Many variables will influence the particular environment a child experiences. Birth order, for one, automatically places siblings in dissimilar situations. The older sibling has to suffer the pain of seeing parental love and attention directed toward an intruder. The younger sibling may need to learn survival in an environment that harbors a stronger, potentially hostile rival, and never comes to know either the special status or the burden of being an only child. The full weight of unconscious parental expectations is far more likely to fall on the firstborn. Historical studies of birth order have established it as an important influence on the shaping of the personality, comparable with sex.[6]

The parents' economic situation may be better around the birth of one child than when other children are born. Or, as in the case of my family of origin, historical or social circumstances may have enormous consequences on the parents' emotional states and therefore on the personalities of their children. I was born in 1944 to Jewish parents in Budapest, Hungary, having made the miscalculation of entering the world two months before the Nazi occupation of my birthplace, over a year before the end of World War II. The first of my two brothers was born two and a half years later, during a time of peace, optimism and immense emotional relief. It goes without saying that the psychological equilibrium of my parents would have changed dramatically between my birth and that of my brother, as would the degree of anxiety they transmitted to their sons.

The younger of my brothers was born in Canada, less than two years after our family settled here as penniless refugees. We had fled Hungary after the 1956 revolution, when my parents, then close to middle age, decided to leave the insecurities and upheavals of Eastern Europe behind forever. Fortunately perhaps, they could not have foreseen the difficulties of adjusting to a new life on a new continent. Their third son arrived in the midst of economic hardship and uncertainty about the future. My mother recalls that she wept throughout the nine months of her pregnancy, and she still has feelings of guilt about the deep postpartum depression she suffered during the first year of her youngest son's life.

Three brothers and, I would say, three different sets of parents. I do not believe it is coincidental that my youngest brother and I have both been treated for depression and attention deficit disorder. Our middle brother has not.

Even without world wars, revolutions and emigration, siblings growing up in the same home almost never share the same environment. More accurately, brothers and sisters share some environments—usually the less important ones—but they rarely share the one single environment that has the most powerful impact on personality formation. They may live in the same house, eat the same kinds of food, partake in many of the same activities. These are environments of secondary importance. Of all environments, the one that most profoundly shapes the human personality is the invisible one: the emotional atmosphere in which the child lives during the critical early years of brain development. The invisible environment has little to do with parenting philosophies or parenting style. It is a matter of intangibles, foremost among them being the parents' relationship with each other and their emotional balance as individuals. These, too, can vary significantly from the birth of one child to the arrival of another. Psychological tension in the parents' lives during the child's infancy is, I am convinced, a major and universal influence on the subsequent emergence of ADD. We will return to it in later chapters.

A hidden factor of great importance is a parent's unconscious attitude toward a child: what, or whom, on the deepest level, the child represents for the parents; the degree to which the parents see themselves in the child; the needs parents may have that they subliminally hope the child will meet.

For the infant there exists no abstract, "out-there" reality. The emotional milieu with which we surround the child is the world as he experiences it. In the words of the child psychiatrist and researcher Margaret Mahler, for the newborn, the parent is "the principal representative of the world."[7] To the infant and toddler, the world reveals itself in the image of the parent: in eye contact, intensity of glance, body language, tone of voice and, above all, in the day-to-day joy or emotional fatigue exhibited in the presence of the child. Whatever a parent's intention, these are the means by which the child receives his or her most formative communications. Although they will be of paramount importance for development of the child's personality, these subtle and often unconscious influences will be missed on psychological question-naires or observations of parents in clinical settings. There is no way to measure a softening or an edge of anxiety in the voice, the warmth of a smile or the depth of furrows on a brow. We have no instruments to gauge the tension in a father's body as he holds his infant or to record whether a mother's gaze is clouded by worry or clear with calm anticipation.

It may be said that no two children have exactly the same parents, in that the *parenting* they each receive may vary in highly significant ways. Whatever the hopes, wishes or intentions of the parent, the child does not experience the parent directly: *the child experiences the parenting.* I have known two siblings to disagree vehemently about their father's personality during their childhood. Neither has to be wrong if we understand that they did not receive the same *fathering,* which is what formed their experience of the father. I have even seen subtly but significantly different mothering given to a pair of identical twins.

In the case of the Gilmores, two of the four brothers—Gary and Galen—turned out "bad" and came to violent ends, and the other two—Frank and Mikal—with great difficulty managed to gain a sense of themselves as self-respecting human beings. When they looked back on their childhoods, Frank and Mikal clearly recognized that their unfortunate siblings had been given their parents' darker sides, while they themselves received what little lightness there was in their father and mother.

The effects of the environment on brain development and personality formation vary from child to child. As we see, these influences are different to begin with. They are also acting on different individuals. How the infant reacts to the environment has a major impact on the nature of his experience of the world. It would be virtually impossible for two children to inhabit the same environment, even if their worlds could be exactly matched to the minutest detail.

# 7

# Emotional Allergies:

# ADD and Sensitivity

If a mother has eight children, there are eight mothers.
This is not simply because of the fact that the mother was
different in her attributes to each of the eight. If she
could have been the same with each...each child would
have had his or her own mother seen through individual
eyes.

— D. W. WINNICOTT, F.R.C.P., *Home Is Where We
Start From*

UPPERTIME. THE EIGHT-year-old daughter is taking her time leaving her toy or book
or reveries. "Hurry up. We want to eat," the
father says, tense with hunger and work overload.

The daughter covers her ears. "Don't yell at me," she complains.

"I am not yelling," the man answers, this time hearing himself
raise his voice.

The child's face turns into a picture of pain and despair.
"Mommy, Daddy's being mean to me," she cries.

If the decibel count in that kitchen had been measured when the father first instructed his daughter to hurry, it would not have registered at levels most people would define as yelling. The daughter's reaction, however, is genuine. She picks up, senses, experiences the tension in the father's voice, the edge of controlled impatience and frustration. That is what is translated in her brain as "yelling." She is feeling exactly the same fear and outrage as another child would if shouted at in an angry manner. It is a matter of sensitivity, of the degree of reactivity to the environment. This child is emotionally hypersensitive.

The derivation of *sensitivity* is from the Latin word *sensir*, "to feel." Degrees of sensitivity reflect degrees of feeling. Of the various *Oxford Dictionary* definitions of *sensitive*, it will be useful to keep three in mind. Each is exquisitely apt as a description of the ADD child: *1. Very open to or acutely affected by external stimuli or mental impressions. 2. Easily offended, or emotionally hurt. 3. (As of an instrument) responsive to or recording small changes.* The word has another connotation, that of being empathetic, respectful of other people's feelings. The two meanings may coexist in the same individual, but not in every case. Some of the most sensitive people in terms of how they react may be the least mindful of the feelings of others.

Some human beings are hyperreactive. A relatively negligible stimulus, or what to other people would seem negligible, sets off in them an intense reaction. When this happens in response to physical stimuli, we say the person is allergic. Someone allergic to, say, bee venom may choke, wheeze and gasp for air when stung. The small airways in the lungs may go into spasm, tissues in the throat may swell, the heartbeat may become irregular. His life may be in peril. The nonallergic person, had she been stung by the same bee, would experience no more than a momentary pain, a welt, an irritating itch. Was it the bee sting that sent the first victim into physiological crisis? Not directly. It was his own physiological responses that brought him close to death. More accurately, it was the combination of stimulus and reaction. The precise medical term for an allergy, for this hyperreactivity, is *hypersensitivity*.

People with ADD are hypersensitive. That is not a fault or a weakness of theirs, it is how they were born. It is their inborn temperament. That, primarily, is what is hereditary about ADD. Genetic inheritance by itself cannot account for the presence of ADD features in people, but heredity can make it far more likely that these features will emerge in a given individual, depending on circumstances. It is sensitivity, not a disorder, that is transmitted through heredity. In most cases, ADD is caused by the impact of the environment on particularly sensitive infants.

Sensitivity is the reason why allergies are more common among ADD children than in the rest of the population. It is well known, and borne out again and again in clinical practice, that children with ADD are more likely than their non-ADD counterparts to have a history of frequent colds, upper respiratory infections, ear infections, asthma, eczema and allergies, a fact interpreted by some as evidence that ADD is due to allergies. Although the flare-up of allergies can certainly aggravate ADD symptoms, the one does not cause the other. They both are expressions of the same underlying inborn trait: sensitivity. Since emotionally hypersensitive reactions are no less physiological than the body's allergic responses to physical substances, we may say truthfully that people with ADD have emotional allergies.

Almost any parent with an ADD child, or any adult living with an ADD spouse, will have noticed in the ADD person a touchiness, a "thin skin." People with ADD are forever told that they are "too sensitive" or that they should stop being "so touchy." One might as well advise a child with hay fever to stop being "so allergic."

With its usual wisdom, everyday language has found an accurate description of hypersensitivity when it speaks of someone having a thin skin. If one had an area on one's thigh with part of the epidermis destroyed by, say, scalding hot water, one literally would have a thin skin: the nerve endings would be closer to the surface. A slight gust of air might cause a highly unpleasant sensation, even pain, whereas surfaces with full-thickness skin would feel little or nothing. The emotionally sensitive person lives, as it were, with the nerve endings that send emotional stimuli to the brain centers very close to the surface. Like the exposed nerve endings in scalded skin, they are very easily irritated. Hence, my daughter's complaint that I was yelling. Of course, I was the short-tempered father in the anecdote. The suppertime set-to used to be familiar in our home.

Parents, teachers and doctors may doubt a child's reports of his sensations. Some hypersensitive children, feeling physical pain or discomfort, will express what to others may seem an excessive and exaggerated distress. They are accused of malingering or playacting or of looking for attention. In fact, there is no dissimulation in their behavior around pain or discomfort, only, in a phrase of Friedrich Nietzsche's, "a refined susceptibility to pain." Sensitivity is affected by emotional states. People's pain tolerance is lower when they feel anxious or depressed, partly because of changes in stress hormone levels and in the levels of endorphins, the body's innate painkillers.

Sensitive children come to be called "difficult" because adults have trouble understanding their temperament and because parenting methods that work with other children are frustratingly inadequate with this group. Like the related phrase "terrible twos," "difficult child" shows grown-up bias. In the child's experience, it is the adult who is ornery. Were children the arbiters of language, we would hear of the "difficult parent" and the "terrible thirties."

Physiological differences in the human nervous system help explain differences in levels of emotional reactivity from one child to the other. In some children, the nervous system is always in a state of hair-trigger alert. Researchers at the University of Washington, Seattle, measured the electrical activity of an important nerve, the vagus nerve, in five-month-old babies.[1] (The vagus connects the central nervous system with the heart, the lungs and the stomach.) Infants with a higher baseline "tone" in the vagus nerve were also "more emotionally reactive to both positive and mildly stressful stimuli." These same infants at fourteen months were more reactive to maternal separation.

Like hypersensitive instruments, sensitive children register and record even minute changes in their emotional environment. It is not a matter of choice for them; their nervous systems react. It is as if they had invisible antennae projecting in every direction, picking up and conducting into their bodies and their minds the psychic emanations around them. They may have no conscious knowledge of this, any more than an instrument is consciously aware of what measurements it is registering. Unlike instruments, however, the sensory equipment of human beings is not easily shut off. My wife and I learned to recognize our daughter's moods and behaviors as real-time, instantaneous computer printouts of the psychological atmosphere in our home. If we wanted to know how we were doing as individuals or as a couple, we needed only check the facial expressions and emotional responses of our daughter. What was recorded there did not always reassure us.

Abdominal cramps in sensitive children are often clues to unresolved tensions in the family environment. They are common and all too frequently misinterpreted. These are the children who go pale with "inexplicable" tummy aches and are dragged from doctor to doctor, from clinic to emergency ward, from specialist to specialist, subjected to examinations, tests, X-rays and over and over again are pronounced "perfectly healthy." The parents are assured there is no reason for the pain. There is reason. Their child's body is a barometer for the stresses on the whole family system, his symptoms the markings on a minutely calibrated instrument.

As pointed out in chapter 6, there are a small number of debilitating conditions with a strong genetic basis, such as muscular dystrophy or Huntington's disease. These are rare, affecting about one person in ten thousand or even fewer. They do not pose a significant threat to the survival of the species. If, however, we add up the numbers of people plagued by depression or ADD or the other common psychological problems people in this society struggle with, including alcoholism and anxiety, we will have identified no less than a third of the North American population. Genetic explanations for these conditions assume that after millions of years of evolution, nature would permit a very large number of disordered genes, handicapping a third of humankind, to pass through the screen of natural selection—a highly unlikely proposition.

We face no such difficulty if we see that what is being transmitted genetically is not ADD or its equally ill-mannered and discombobulating relatives, but *sensitivity*. The existence of sensitive people is an advantage for humankind because it is this group that best expresses humanity's creative urges and needs. Through their instinctual responses the world is best interpreted. Under normal circumstances, they are artists or artisans, seekers, inventors, shamans, poets, prophets. There would be valid and powerful evolutionary reasons for the survival of genetic material coding for sensitivity. It is not diseases that are being inherited but a trait of intrinsic survival value to human beings. Sensitivity is transmuted into suffering and disorders only when the world is unable to heed the exquisitely tuned physiological and psychic responses of the sensitive individual.

ADD is not a natural state. It is, to adapt a famous phrase of Sigmund Freud's, one of civilization's discontents.

# 8

# A Surrealistic

# Choreography

One of the most striking peculiarities of the human brain
is the great development of the frontal lobes—they are
much less developed in other primates and hardly evident
at all in other mammals. They are the part of the brain
that grows and develops most after birth.

— OLIVER SACKS, M.D., *An Anthropologist on Mars*

THE HUMAN BRAIN is the most complex entity in the universe. It has between fifty and
one hundred billion nerve cells, or neurons,
each branched to form thousands of possible connections with
other nerve cells. It has been estimated that laid end to end, the
nerve cables of a single human brain would extend into a line
several hundred thousand miles long. The total number of connections, or *synapses*, is in the trillions.[1] The parallel and simultaneous
activity of innumerable brain circuits, and networks of circuits,
produces millions of firing patterns each and every second of
our lives. The brain has well been described as "a supersystem of

systems." Even though fully half of the roughly hundred thousand genes in the human organism are dedicated to the central nervous system, the genetic code simply cannot carry enough information to predetermine the infinite number of potential brain circuits. For this reason alone, biological heredity could not by itself account for the densely intertwined psychology and neurophysiology of attention deficit disorder.

Experience in the world determines the fine wiring of the brain. As the neurologist and neuroscientist Antonio Damasio puts it, "Much of each brain's circuitry, at any given moment in adult life, is individual and unique, truly reflective of that particular organism's history and circumstances."[2] This is no less true of children and infants. Not even in the brains of genetically identical twins will the same patterns be found in the shape of nerve cells or the numbers and configuration of their synapses with other neurons.

The microcircuitry of the brain is formatted by influences during the first few years of life, a period when the human brain undergoes astonishingly rapid growth. Five-sixths of the branching of nerve cells in the brain occurs after birth. At times in the first year of life, new synapses are being established at a rate of three billion a second. In large part, each infant's individual experiences in the early years determine which brain structures will develop and how well, and which nerve centers will be connected with which other nerve centers, and establish the networks controlling behavior.[3] The intricately programmed interactions between heredity and environment that make for the development of the human brain are determined by a "fantastic, almost surrealistically complex choreography," in the apt phrase of Dr. J. S. Grotstein of the department of psychiatry at UCLA. Attention deficit disorder results from the miswiring of brain circuits, in susceptible infants, during this crucial period of growth.

Of all mammals, the human animal has the least mature brain at birth. Early in their infancy, other animals perform tasks far beyond the capabilities of humans for many months. A horse can walk on the first day of life; infant apes cling to mother's fur within a few weeks of birth. Human beings are able to coordinate the visual skills, muscle control, balance and orientation in space required for comparable activities only near the end of the first year.

In the period following birth, the human brain, unlike that of our closest evolutionary relative, the chimpanzee, continues to grow at the same rate as in the womb. Whereas the chimpanzee brain will no more than double from birth to reach its adult size, the brain mass of humans will have *tripled* by age four. By adulthood, the size of our brain will have *quadrupled*, meaning that fully three-quarters of our brain growth takes place outside the womb following birth, with most of this increase occurring in the early years.

One way to see this is as a compromise negotiated by nature. We were permitted to walk, freeing our forelimbs to evolve into arms and hands capable of many delicate and complicated activities—a development that gave impetus to a large expansion in brain size, particularly of the frontal lobes. These lobes coordinate the movements of the hands. They also perform the problem solving and the social and language skills that have given humankind abilities to thrive in a wide variety of habitats. Were we born with our wiring rigidly fixed by heredity, the frontal lobes would be far more limited in their capacity to learn and to adapt to the many different possible environments that human beings inhabit.

To accommodate our upright stance, the human pelvis had to narrow, so growth inside the womb longer than nine months would have resulted in infants too large to be born safely. Already at the end of the nine months of human gestation, the head is the largest part of the body, the one most likely to get stuck in our journey through the birth canal. The bargain forced on our evolutionary ancestors was that the tremendously large human brain has to develop outside the relatively safe environment of the womb, highly vulnerable to potentially adverse circumstances.

According to the latest insights of modern neuroscience, brain development in the human infant involves a process of competition that has been described as "neural Darwinism."[4] Nerve cells, circuits, networks and systems of networks vie with one another for survival. The neurons and connections most useful to the organism's survival in its given environment are maintained. Others wither and die. Nerve pathways lacking the full conditions for growth will not develop, or will develop dysfunctionally and incompletely. The stores of neurochemicals that are underutilized diminish, and the brain's capacity to manufacture them declines. By the elimination of unused cells and synapses, and by the formation of new ones favored by the environment, specialized circuits gradually develop that conduct the varied and multiple activities of the human brain.

Neural Darwinism means that our genetic potential for brain development can find its full expression only if circumstances are favorable. To understand this, we need only imagine an infant kept in a dark room, held, physically cared for and fed, but never spoken to. After a year of such deprivation, the brain of this infant would not be comparable to those of other infants, no matter what her inherited potential. Despite perfectly good eyes at birth and healthy nerves to conduct visual images to the brain, the thirty or so neurological units that together make up visual sense would not develop. Even the neurological components of vision present at birth would atrophy and become useless if this child never saw light for about five years. Irreversible blindness would be the result. If we surrounded the child with silence for the first ten years, he would never be able to learn human speech. Attention deficit disorder is also an example of how the neural circuitry and biochemistry of the brain may be held back from developing optimally when appropriate input from the environment is interfered with. What, then, are the optimal conditions for full brain development?

The three conditions without which healthy growth does not take place can be taken for granted in the matrix of the womb: nutrition, a physically secure environment and the unbroken relationship with a safe, ever-present maternal organism. The word *matrix* is derived from the Latin for "womb," itself derived from the word for "mother." The womb is mother, and in many respects the mother remains the womb, even following birth. In the womb environment, no action or reaction on the developing infant's part is required for the provision of any of his needs. Life in the womb is surely the prototype of life in the Garden of Eden where nothing can possibly be lacking, nothing has to be worked for. If there is no consciousness—we have not yet eaten of the Tree of Knowledge—there is also no deprivation or anxiety.

Except in conditions of extreme poverty unusual in the industrialized world, although not unknown, the nutritional needs and shelter requirements of infants are more or less satisfied. The third prime requirement, a secure, safe and not overly stressed emotional atmosphere, is the one most likely to be disrupted in Western societies.

The human infant lacks the capacity to follow or cling to the parent soon after being born, and is neurologically and biochemically underdeveloped in many other ways. The first nine months or so of extrauterine life seem to have been intended by nature as the second part of gestation. The anthropologist Ashley Montagu has called this phase *exterogestation*, gestation outside the maternal body.[5] During this period, the security of the womb must be provided by the parenting environment. To allow for the maturation of the brain and nervous system that in other species occurs in the uterus, the attachment that was until birth directly physical now needs to be continued on both physical and emotional levels. Physically and psychologically, the parenting environment must contain and hold the infant as securely as she was held in the womb.

For the second nine months of gestation, nature does provide a near-substitute for the direct umbilical connection: breast-feeding. Apart from its irreplaceable nutritional value and the immune protection it gives the infant, breast-feeding serves as a transitional stage from unbroken physical attachment to complete separation from the mother's body. Now outside the matrix of the womb, the infant is nevertheless held close to the warmth of the maternal body from which nourishment continues to flow. Breast-feeding also deepens the mother's feeling of connectedness to the baby, enhancing the emotionally symbiotic bonding relationship. No doubt the decline of breast-feeding, particularly accelerated in North America, has contributed to the emotional insecurities so prevalent in industrialized countries.

Even more than breast-feeding, healthy brain development requires emotional security and warmth in the infant's environment. This security is more than the love and best possible intentions of the parents. It depends also on a less controllable variable: their freedom from stresses that can undermine their psychological equilibrium. A calm and consistent emotional milieu throughout infancy is an essential requirement for the wiring of the neurophysiological circuits of self-regulation. When interfered with, as it often is in our society, brain development is adversely affected. ADD is one of the possible consequences.

# 9

# Attunement and

# Attachment

From early infancy, it appears that our ability to regulate
emotional states depends upon the experience of feeling
that a significant person in our life is simultaneously
experiencing a similar state of mind.

— DANIEL J. SIEGEL, M.D.

THE AREAS OF THE CORTEX responsible for
attention and self-regulation develop in response to the emotional interaction with the
person whom we may call the mothering figure. Usually this is the
birth mother, but it may be another person, male or female, depending on circumstances. Although, for the sake of convenience,
I will at times refer to this person only as the mother, the word
should always be understood to refer to whoever the primary nurturing figure may be—father, mother, or grandparent, foster parent
or adoptive parent of either gender. Because the formation of the
child's brain circuits is influenced by the mother's emotional states,
I believe that ADD originates in stresses that affect the mothering

parent's emotional interactions with the infant. They cause the disrupted electrical and chemical circuitry of ADD. Attachment and attunement, two crucial aspects of the infant-parent relationship, are the determining factors. They are the subject of this chapter.

The right hemisphere of the mother's brain, the side where our unconscious emotions reside, programs the infant's right hemisphere. In the early months, the most important communications between mother and infant are unconscious ones. Incapable of deciphering the meaning of words, the infant receives messages that are purely emotional. They are conveyed by the mother's gaze, her tone of voice and her body language, all of which reflect her unconscious internal emotional environment. Anything that threatens the mother's emotional security may disrupt the developing electrical wiring and chemical supplies of the infant brain's emotion-regulating and attention-allocating systems.*

Within minutes following birth, the mother's odors stimulate the branching of millions of nerve cells in the newborn's brain. A six-day-old infant can already distinguish the scent of his mother from that of other women. Later on, visual inputs associated with emotions gradually take over as the major influences.

By two to seven weeks, the infant will orient toward the mother's face in preference to a stranger's—and also in preference to the father's, unless the father is the mothering adult. At seventeen weeks, the infant's gaze follows the mother's eyes more closely than her mouth movements, thus fixating on what has been called "the visible portion of the mother's central nervous system." The infant's right brain reads the mother's right brain during intense eye-to-eye mutual gaze interactions. As an article in *Scientific American* expressed it, "Embryologically and anatomically the eye is an extension of the brain; it is almost as if a portion of the brain were in plain sight."[1] The eyes communicate eloquently the mother's unconscious emotional states:

---

*The circuitry and brain chemistry involved are described in the next chapter.

[O]ne person uses another's pupil size as a source of information about that person's feelings or attitudes; this process usually occurs at unconscious levels. Dilated pupils occur in states of pleasure and are an indicator of "interest"... Experiments have shown that women's eyes dilate in response to a picture of a baby. Most importantly...viewing enlarged dilated pupils elicits larger pupils in the observer. In a developmental study, infants smiled more when a female experimenter's eyes were dilated rather than constricted...

Everyone has had the experience of suddenly feeling intense physiological and psychological shifts internally at trading glances with another person; such shifts can be exquisitely pleasurable or unpleasant. How one person gazes at another can alter the other's electrical brain patterns, as registered by EEGs, and may also cause physiological changes in the body. The newborn is highly susceptible to such influences, with a direct effect on the maturation of brain structures.

The effects of maternal moods on the electrical circuitry of the infant's brain were demonstrated by a study at the University of Washington, Seattle.[2] Positive emotions are associated with increased electrical activity in the left hemisphere. It is known that depression in adults is associated with *decreased* electrical activity in the circuitry of the left hemisphere. With this in mind, the Seattle study compared the EEGs of two groups of infants: one group whose mothers had symptoms of postpartum depression, the other whose mothers did not. "During playful interactions with the mothers designed to elicit positive emotion," the researchers reported, "infants of non-depressed mothers showed greater left than right frontal brain activation." The infants of depressed mothers "failed to show differential hemispheric activation," meaning that the left-side brain activity one would anticipate from positive, joyful infant-mother exchanges did not occur—despite the mothers' best efforts. Significantly, these effects were noted only in the frontal areas of the brain, where the centers for the self-regulation of emotion are located. In addition to EEG changes, infants of depressed mothers exhibit decreased activity levels, gaze aversion, less positive emotion and greater irritability.

Maternal depression is associated with diminished infant attention spans. Summarizing a number of British studies, Dale F. Hay, a researcher at the University of Cambridge, suggests "that the experience of the mother's depression in the first months of life may disrupt naturally occurring social processes that entrain and regulate the infant's developing capacities for attention."[3]

Just how important a close moment-to-moment connection between mother and infant can be was illustrated by a cleverly designed study, known as the "double TV experiment," in which infants and mothers interacted via a closed-circuit television system. In separate rooms, infant and mother observed each other and, on "live feed," communicated by means of the universal infant-mother language: gestures, sounds, smiles, facial expressions. The infants were happy during this phase of the experiment. "When the infants were unknowingly replayed the 'happy responses' from the mother recorded from the prior minute," writes the UCLA child psychiatrist Daniel J. Siegel, "they still became as profoundly distressed as infants do in the classic 'flat face' experiments in which mothers-in-person gave no facial emotional response to their infant's bid for attunement."[4]

Why were the infants distressed despite the sight of their mothers' happy and friendly faces? Because happy and friendly are not enough. What they needed were signals that the mother is aligned with, responsive to and participating in their mental states from moment to moment. All that was lacking in the instant video replay, during which infants saw their mother's face unresponsive to the messages they, the infants, were sending out. This sharing of emotional spaces is called *attunement.*[5] Emotional stress on the mother interferes with infant brain development because it tends to interfere with the attunement contact.

Attunement is necessary for the normal development of the brain pathways and neurochemical apparatus of attention and emotional self-regulation. It is a finely calibrated process requiring that the parent remain herself in a relatively nonstressed, non-anxious, nondepressed state of mind. Its clearest expression is the rapturous mutual gaze infant and mother direct at each other, locked in a private and special emotional realm, from which, at that moment, the rest of the world is as completely excluded as from the womb.

Attunement does not mean mechanically imitating the infant. It cannot be simulated, even with the best of goodwill. As we all know, there are differences between a real smile and a staged smile. The muscles of smiling are exactly the same in each case, but the signals that set the smile muscles to work do not come from the same centers in the brain. As a consequence, those muscles respond differently to the signals, depending on their origin. This is why only very good actors can mimic a genuine, heartfelt smile. The attunement process is far too subtle to be maintained by a simple act of will on the part of the parent. Infants, particularly sensitive infants, intuit the difference between a parent's real psychological states and her attempts to soothe and protect the infant by means of feigned emotional expressions. A loving parent who is feeling depressed or anxious may try to hide that fact from the infant, but the effort is futile. In fact, it is much easier to fool an adult with forced emotion than a baby. The emotional sensory radar of the infant has not yet been scrambled. It reads feelings clearly. They cannot be hidden from the infant behind a screen of words, or camouflaged by well-meant but forced gestures. It is unfortunate but true that we grow far more stupid than that by the time we reach adulthood.

In attunement, it is the infant who leads and the mother who follows. "Where their roles differ is in the timing of their responses," writes John Bowlby, one of the century's great psychiatric researchers.[6] The infant initiates the interaction or withdraws from it according to his own rhythms, Bowlby found, while the "mother regulates her behaviour so that it meshes with his... Thus she lets him call the tune and by a skillful interweaving of her own responses with his creates a dialogue." The tense or depressed mothering adult will not be able to accompany the infant into relaxed, happy spaces. He may also not fully pick up signs of the infant's emotional distress, or may not be able to respond to them as effectively as he would wish. The ADD child's difficulty reading social cues likely originates from her relationship cues not being read by the nurturing adult, who was distracted by stress.

In the attunement interaction, not only does the mother follow the child, but she also permits the child to temporarily interrupt contact. When the interaction reaches a certain stage of intensity for the infant, he will look away to avoid an uncomfortably high level of arousal. Another interaction will then begin. A mother who is anxious may react with alarm when the infant breaks off contact, may try to stimulate him, to draw him back into the interaction. Then the infant's nervous system is not allowed to "cool down," and the attunement relationship is hampered.

Infants whose caregivers were too stressed, for whatever reason, to give them the necessary attunement contact will grow up with a chronic tendency to feel alone with their emotions, to have a sense—rightly or wrongly—that no one can share how they feel, that no one can "understand."

Attunement is the quintessential component of a larger process, called *attachment*.[7] Attachment is simply our need to be close to somebody. It represents the absolute need of the utterly and helplessly vulnerable human infant for secure closeness with at least one nourishing, protective and constantly available parenting figure. Essential for survival, the drive for attachment is part of the very nature of warm-blooded animals in infancy, especially of mammals.

In human beings, attachment is a driving force of behavior for longer than in any other animal. For most of us it is present throughout our lives, although we may transfer our attachment need from one person—our parent—to another—say, a spouse or even a child. We may also attempt to satisfy the lack of the human contact we crave by various other means, such as addictions, for example, or perhaps fanatical religiosity or the virtual reality of the Internet. Much of popular culture, from novels to movies to rock or country music, expresses nothing but the joys or the sorrows flowing from satisfactions or disappointments in our attachment relationships. Most parents extend to their children some mixture of loving and hurtful behavior, of wise parenting and unskillful, clumsy parenting. The proportions vary from family to family, from parent to parent. Those ADD children whose needs for warm parental contact are most frustrated grow up to be adults with the most severe cases of ADD.

Already at only a few months of age, an infant will register by facial expression his dejection at the mother's unconscious emotional withdrawal, despite the mother's continued physical presence. "(The infant) takes delight in Mommy's attention," writes Stanley Greenspan, "and knows when that source of delight is missing. If Mom becomes preoccupied or distracted while playing with the baby, sadness or dismay settles in on the little face."[8]

# 10

# The Footprints

# of Infancy

The mind emanates from the interface between
neurophysiological processes and interpersonal relationships. Experience selectively shapes genetic neuronal
potential and thus directly influences the structure and
function of the brain.

— DANIEL J. SIEGEL, M.D.

BEHIND THE FOREHEAD in the vicinity of
the right eye is where one of the most
important regulatory centers in the brain is
located: the orbitofrontal cortex.[1] It is part of the prefrontal cortex,
that area of the gray matter most involved in social intelligence,
impulse control and attention. It is also important in short-term
working memory. The orbitofrontal cortex—so named because of
its proximity to the eye socket, known as the orbit—is more
developed on the right side and appears to dominate its counterpart in the left hemisphere.

A complex condition like ADD cannot be traced to just one part of the brain. Many circuits and systems must be involved. According to a lot of recent evidence, however, disturbances of the orbitofrontal cortex are, indeed, implicated in disorders of impulse inhibition and emotional self-regulation, including ADD. It is probably here that the neurophysiological effects of stressed attunement and attachment are most pronounced.'

Nature's goal for human growth is for the eventual maturation of a self-motivated, self-regulated and self-reliant adult. The infant lacks these attributes. We may say that the natural agenda is really the transformation of regulation from dependence on another individual to independence, from external regulation to internal regulation. This shift from external to internal regulation requires the development of the prefrontal cortex, the cortex in the very anterior portion of the brain, including and especially the orbito-frontal cortex.

The right orbitofrontal cortex, which for the sake of brevity we will call the OFC, has connections with virtually every other part of the cortex. It also has rich connections with the lower brain structures, where the body's internal physiological states are controlled and monitored, and where the most primitive and powerful emotions such as fear and rage are generated. It is at the center of the brain's reward and motivation apparatus and contains more of the reward chemicals associated with pleasure and joy—dopamine and endorphins—than almost any other area of the cortex.

Via its connections with the vision centers of the cortex, the OFC plays a role in visual-spatial orientation, the locating of objects in space. When visual-spatial orientation is impaired, a person tends to bump his head a lot or run into people unseeingly and have difficulty following physical directions—all features of ADD I am intimately familiar with.

The OFC has a major role in the control of attention. From all the information about the external environment and internal body states entering our brain, the OFC helps to pick out what to focus on. While the explicit meaning of words spoken is analyzed in the left hemisphere, the right OFC interprets the emotional content of communications—the other person's body language, eye move-ments and tone of voice. It carries out a constant and instan-taneous computation of the emotional significance of situations. It is deeply concerned with the assessment of relationships between the self and others. According to a number of studies, it is "domi-nant for the processing, expression, and regulation of emotional information."[2]

The OFC also functions in impulse control, helping to inhibit the lower centres in the brain where urgent emotional drives orig-inate. When it is working smoothly, it can delay emotional reac-tions long enough to allow mature, more sophisticated responses to emerge. When its connections are disrupted, it lacks this capac-ity. At such times primitive, unprocessed emotions will flood our minds, overwhelm our thinking processes and control our behavior.

Finally, the OFC records and stores the emotional effects of experiences, first and foremost the infant's interactions with his or her primary caregivers during the early months and years. Its imprinting of the earliest interactions with the primary caregivers is the unconscious model from which all later emotional reactions and interactions will be formed. Groups of neurons in the OFC encode the emotional footprints of these important experiences—footprints in which, willy-nilly, we tend to follow later in life, again and again and again.

The great Canadian researcher Donald Hebb showed that groups of neurons that have fired together once are more likely to fire simultaneously in the future. This Hebbian principle has been expressed as "neurons that fire together wire together." The early emotional imprinting is encoded in the form of potential neuronal patterns: groups of nerve cells primed to fire together. We ex-perience them later in life when we find to our surprise that some relatively minor stimulus, being cut off in traffic, for example, trig-gers in us an irrational rage, leaving us scratching our head and wondering, What was that about? It was about the early imprint-ing of the OFC with the rage and frustration of the infant and tod-dler, and about the Hebbian principle. Each time we scream at someone in traffic, we are telling a story from the earliest part of our life.

A vast body of research supports this understanding of the functions of the right prefrontal cortex. Most dramatic to observe are the deficiencies and impairments suffered by people who have been injured in this area of the brain.[3] Their behavior and emotional reactions are like a textbook description of ADD. Among other ADD-like features, these so-called prefrontal patients often digress and have to be frequently reminded to finish a line of thought; are easily distracted; when listening, will often shift attention to whatever snippet of speech catches their interest; during tasks will often seem to lose track of what the instructions were; will be given to childish emotional outbursts; will have difficulty inhibiting their physical impulses; will find it nearly impossible to learn from experience.

Sustaining physical damage, such as an injury to the brain, is not the only way that the chemical and electrical functions of the prefrontal cortex may become disrupted. In ADD there is no brain damage, but there is impaired brain development. As I wrote in an earlier chapter, *it is not that a disorder develops, but that certain important brain circuits do not develop. Interference with the conditions required for the healthy development of the prefrontal cortex, I believe, accounts for virtually all cases of ADD.*

Emotional interactions stimulate or inhibit the growth of nerve cells and circuits by complicated processes that involve the release of natural chemicals. To give a somewhat simplified example, when "happy" events are experienced by the infant, endorphins—"reward chemicals," the brain's natural opioids—are released. Endorphins encourage the growth of nerve cells and of connections between them. Conversely, in animal studies, chronically high levels of stress hormones such as cortisol have been shown to cause important brain centers to shrink.

Emotions affect not only the release of brain chemicals in the short term but also the long-term balance of neurotransmitters, the molecular messengers telegraphing electrical impulses from one nerve cell to another. Just as the infant's early interactions with the nurturing caregivers help to shape the structure of brain centers and circuits, so, too, do they play a role in determining the chemistry of the brain. Throughout the human life span there remains a constant two-way interaction between psychological states and the neurochemistry of the frontal lobes, a fact that many doctors do not pay enough attention to. One result is the overreliance on medications in the treatment of mental disorders. Modern psychiatry is doing too much listening to Prozac and not enough listening to human beings; people's life histories should be given at least as much importance as the chemistry of their brains.

The dominant tendency is to explain mental conditions by deficiencies of the brain's chemical messengers, the neurotransmitters. As Daniel J. Siegel has sharply remarked, "We hear it said everywhere these days that the experience of human beings comes from their chemicals." Depression, according to the simple biochemical model, is due to a lack of serotonin—and, it is said, so is excessive aggression. The answer is Prozac, which increases serotonin levels in the brain. Attention deficit is thought to be due in part to an undersupply of dopamine, one of the brain's most important neurotransmitters, crucial to attention and to experiencing reward states. The answer is Ritalin. Just as Prozac elevates serotonin levels, Ritalin or other psychostimulants are thought to increase the availability of dopamine in the brain's prefrontal areas. This is believed to increase motivation and attention by improving the functioning of areas in the prefrontal cortex. Although they carry some truth, such biochemical explanations of complex mental states are dangerous oversimplifications—as the neurologist Antonio Damasio cautions:

> When it comes to explaining behavior and mind, it is not enough to mention neurochemistry... The problem is that it is not the absence or low amount of serotonin *per se* that "causes" certain manifestations. Serotonin is part of an exceedingly complicated mechanism which operates at the level

of molecules, synapses, local circuits, and systems, and in which sociocultural factors, past and present, also intervene powerfully.[4]

The deficiencies and imbalances of brain chemicals are as much effect as cause. They are greatly influenced by emotional experiences. Some experiences deplete the supply of neurotransmitters; other experiences enhance them. In turn, the availability—or lack of availability—of brain chemicals can promote certain behaviors and emotional responses and inhibit others. Once more we see that the relationship between behavior and biology is not a one-way street. As an example, in troops of monkeys the dominant, most successfully aggressive males have been found to have less serotonin than the others. This would seem to prove that low serotonin levels cause aggression. However, the serotonin levels drop only *after* these males achieve dominant status. So while the relative lack of serotonin may help to *maintain* the dominant male's aggressive capacities, it could not have *caused* them. Emotional stress can similarly affect serotonin levels, contributing to symptoms of depression. When we prescribe Prozac, we are not so much treating the biology of inheritance as the biology of living and having experiences in the world.

Environmental influences also affect dopamine. From animal studies, we know that social stimulation is necessary for the growth of the nerve endings that release dopamine and for the growth of receptors that dopamine needs to bind to in order to do its work. In four-month-old monkeys, major alterations of dopamine and other neurotransmitter systems were found after only six days of separation from their mothers. "In these experiments," writes Steven Dubovsky, Professor of Psychiatry and Medicine at the University of Colorado, "loss of an important attachment appears to lead to less of an important neurotransmitter in the brain. Once these circuits stop functioning normally, it becomes more and more difficult to activate the mind."[5]

A neuroscientific study published in 1998 showed that adult

rats whose mothers had given them more licking, grooming and other physical-emotional contact during infancy had more efficient brain circuitry for reducing anxiety, as well as more receptors on nerve cells for the brain's own natural tranquilizing chemicals.[6] In other words, early interactions with the mother shaped the adult rat's neurophysiological capacity to respond to stress. In another study, newborn animals reared in isolation had reduced dopamine activity in their prefrontal cortex—but not in other areas of the brain. That is, emotional stress particularly affects the chemistry of the prefrontal cortex, the center for selective attention, motivation and self-regulation. Given the relative complexity of human emotional interactions, the influence of the infant-parent relationship on human neurochemistry is bound to be even stronger.

In the human infant, the growth of dopamine-rich nerve terminals and the development of dopamine receptors is stimulated by chemicals released in the brain during the experience of joy, the ecstatic joy that comes from the perfectly attuned mother-child mutual gaze interaction. Happy interactions between mother and infant generate motivation and arousal by activating cells in the midbrain that release endorphins, thereby inducing in the infant a joyful, exhilarated state. They also trigger the release of dopamine. Both endorphins and dopamine promote the development of new connections in the prefrontal cortex. Dopamine released from the midbrain also triggers the growth of nerve cells and blood vessels in the right prefrontal cortex and promotes the growth of dopamine receptors. A relative scarcity of such receptors and blood supply is thought to be one of the major physiological dimensions of ADD.

The letters ADD may equally well stand for Attunement Deficit Disorder.

# PART THREE

The Roots of ADD

in Family and Society

# 11

# An Utter Stranger:

# ADD and the Family

# (II)

I see the world being slowly transformed into a
wilderness, I hear the approaching thunder that, one day,
will destroy us too, I feel the suffering of millions.
  — ANNE FRANK, *The Diary of a Young Girl*

IN A PHOTOGRAPH OF ME at age four months,
a dark, intense face with a look that belongs to one
much older stares directly toward the camera. The
infant is tense, even fearful. The eyes appear to look through the
observer to some reality far away. The mother supports the child
under the arms, somewhat stiffly perhaps, her face bent toward her
son with an expression of soft, loving absorption. To know why this

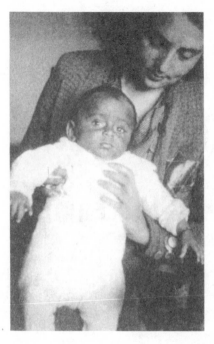

four-month-old should be so world-weary and wary, one needs to glance to the right of his shoulder, where a yellow silk star on the mother's jacket reflects the flashbulb. It is the badge of shame Jews had to wear in countries under Nazi rule.

As I've mentioned, I was born in Budapest in January 1944, the first child of Jewish parents. Two and a half months later, Hungary came under German occupation. In the wake of the German army followed SS Lt. Col. Adolf Eichmann and his Sondereinsatzkommando, charged with the annihilation of Hungarian Jewry, the only large population of Jews left in the German sphere of influence. In three months, half a million human beings, two-thirds of the Jewish population of Hungary, were deported and killed in the death camps. Nowhere else had the Nazi death machine murdered so many people in so short a time. As Eichmann was to tell his Israeli captors nearly two decades later, "The operation went like a dream."

My mother kept a diary of those times. In it the reports of a newborn's typical problems and milestones are interspersed with matter-of-fact descriptions of the devastation the terrible realities were wreaking on our life. The diary, its entries addressed to me, has been in my possession for decades. Strangely—or perhaps not so strangely—I did not read it until I was over fifty years old. In neurophysiological terms, my prefrontal cortex would never let me. A powerful ennui and drowsiness would come over me whenever I opened the diary, and that was seldom. It must have evoked painful emotions I was not prepared to reexperience on the conscious level.

My mother is now eighty. Three years ago, she suffered an injury. As I faced the possibility of her death, my thoughts returned to the diary. I asked her to read it all to me, partly because I wanted to record it in her own voice for myself and for future generations, but also because her handwriting is nearly illegible (despite the fact that she never went to medical school). This is my translation of the first entry, written ten days after my birth:

Still in my maternity bed, only today can I finally begin the task of recording the peculiar circumstances of the life of my little Gabi. As much as possible, I hope to write down for him everything, from his very first moments, so that if, with God's help, he grows up, he will be able to see in front of him the first years of his life exactly as they were....

January 6 was the great day. At 3:00 in the morning I was wakened by the first pains. Anyu, your grandmother, phoned Dr. Sandor at eight o'clock. He told us to come in to the hospital. We arrived there at 9:30, accompanied by Anyu and your aunt Viola....

It was at four in the afternoon that I came to from the anesthetic and they showed me my little son. I am deliberately not writing about the details of labor. I can no longer recall the pains, only the joy he brought me by his birth. My first thought, which I expressed out loud, was that my dear Andor will be so happy to know that he has a son. In the interests of historical accuracy I must note that we are now in the year 1944, a time when forced labor is still the fashion. This means that my Andor is in Szentkiraly-Szabadjan in Transylvania, breaking up rocks instead of marveling at his newborn son....

He had, and has, beautiful long black hair, black eyelashes, a small mouth. There have been interesting changes in his nose, as at birth he had a large nose like his father whereas by now he has a cute little nose. He first suckled at the breast at noon, on January 7; right away he showed himself to be quite a talented beginner.... Today, by the way, he demonstrated a neat little trick. With a well-aimed and powerful stream he nearly peed into his own mouth, but for nurse Rozsi clamping her hand over his face....

My father was also to write a few notes in the diary, during a leave of absence he was allowed to spend with his wife and newborn child, a few weeks after my birth. We would not see him again for fourteen months. For much of that time, my parents knew nothing of each other's fate. Part of his entry for January 30 reads:

A few years ago there arose a universal massacre of human beings, more horrible than any before, which they call a world war. Here in Central Europe it claims its victims just as in China or Japan....

Naturally, we ourselves are most concerned with our own situation as Jews. These days, as so often in the past, we have again become "undesirable elements," so called. As such, we are not worthy to be called up for military service, but since we must still fulfill our responsibilities to our homeland, we do so as forced laborers....

Enough of this preamble. The chief thing is, after a long separation we shall be together for thirty days....

Two days after the German occupation, my mother called the pediatrician. "Would you come to see Gabi?" she requested. "He has been crying almost without stop since yesterday morning."

"I'll come, of course," the doctor replied, "but I should tell you: all my Jewish babies are crying."

Now, what did Jewish infants know of Nazis, World War II, racism, genocide? What they knew—or rather, absorbed—was their parents' anxiety. They drank it in with their mothers' milk, heard it in their fathers' voices, felt it in the tense arms and bodies that held them close. They inhaled fear, ingested sorrow. Yet were they not loved? No less than children anywhere. If in the photograph the love may be seen in my mother's face, her fear and worry are reflected in mine.

Among Eichmann's victims were my maternal grandparents, Dr. Josef Lővi and Hannah Lővi, from what is now the town of Kosice in southern Slovakia. On June 4, they were transported by train to Auschwitz, where my grandfather's fellow physician Dr. Josef Mengele selected them for immediate death in the gas chambers. This photograph is the last one they ever saw of their first grandson.

After her parents were taken away, my mother wanted to kill herself. She would lie on her bed for hours on end in a state of complete despondency. "You saved my life," she told me when she was dictating her diary. "Only the sight of you next to me, in your crib, gave me reason to go on." There were no entries in my mother's diary for weeks around this time, except for some recipes in my pediatrician's handwriting: feeding formulas for the guidance of a gentile couple who were to adopt me secretly in case my mother was also deported. My mother refused to part from me until the final possible moment. "I will give up my son when they're here to throw me into the cattle train," she said, "not one second before."

In June, the Hungarian government put an end to the deportations, due to international protests and even threats. The Jews of Budapest were spared the death camps, but not the continued terror. On June 21, all Jews were ordered to move into overcrowded "starred houses"—houses marked with a yellow star—in the center of town. The day we were forced to leave our home, my mother's breast milk dried up.

Deportations resumed later in the fall. In December, we sought refuge in a so-called protected house under the nominal and very tenuous protection of the Swiss embassy. There were two thousand people in that two-story office building. The conditions were unimaginable. Toilets were overflowing, and people had to use latrines dug in the courtyard. There was no possibility to wash diapers. Everyone was infested with lice. There was hardly anything my mother could feed me. On the spur of the moment, she gave me to a complete stranger, a gentile woman visiting her Jewish husband, who agreed to push me in my buggy to the home of a relative. This cousin of my mother had managed to stay outside the ghetto with his family by finding employment in a German army bakery. With them at least I had a chance of survival.

"When I think of it now," my mother says, "I could not have been in a normal state of mind. Otherwise I could not have been as strangely calm as I was, as if nothing unusual was happening."

We were reunited three weeks later, when the Red Army took Budapest, but my mother remained in complete darkness about the fate of my father, and also about the fate of her sister, who had been transported to Auschwitz along with my grandparents. In April, after the last German soldier had left Hungary, my father came back. In time so did my aunt. She weighed less than ninety pounds and was wearing the only clothing she could find: a discarded German army uniform.

My mother tells me that when I saw her again after our three weeks of separation, I responded as if she were an utter stranger to me. I would not so much as look at her for days.

In photographs of me taken later in childhood can be seen both the intensity and the distance from the present first evident in the picture of my mother and me taken in May 1944. They depict a young boy with a contemplative and perhaps perturbed expression. Unlike my brother, I avoid the gaze of the camera—perhaps as a toddler may cover his eyes to avoid being seen. Or perhaps I am scanning the far horizons of the future, or of the past. It's all the same. What do our fears or fantasies of the future reflect, if not our past?

I have told the story of my infancy for two reasons. First, I know of no clearer illustration of how our relationship with our primary caregiver and her emotional states shape our brains, our minds, our personalities. My mother and I had little opportunity for normal mother-infant experiences. These were hardly possible, given the terrible circumstances, her numbed state of mind and having to concentrate her energies on basic survival. Second, there can be no more vivid example of how the attunement I wrote about in the previous two chapters can be severely interfered with despite the deepest feelings of love a mother may have.

I don't say that only the war prevented my mother and father from being perfect parents. As an adult I have felt resentment toward my parents and have had to do psychological work around my relationship with them concerning issues not directly connected with my first year and a half of life. I have no way of knowing whether I might not have developed attention deficit disorder regardless, without those trying events of 1944. What I do know is that I can make sense of my ADD traits when I consider them in the light of this formative period in my life.

What we are investigating here is how the psychological states of the parents form the brain and mind of the infant. As may be seen from the example of my own nuclear family, my wife and three children, you don't need a world war and genocide for a mother to be stressed or for a father to be an absent figure. You don't need horrors to trigger deep conscious and unconscious anxieties in the parents. You don't need privation for infants to live their formative period during a time when the parents are distracted—knowingly or unknowingly—from the parenting task. These negative factors can be present in any family, even when the material circumstances are ideal, and even when the parents love their children and have nothing but the best intentions.

# 12

# Stories within

# Stories:

# ADD and the

# Family (III)

Yet they who belong to the distant past are in us, serving as impetus, as a burden to our fate, as blood that can be heard rushing, as a gesture rising out of the depths of time.

— RAINER MARIA RILKE, *Letters to a Young Poet*

THE MAJORITY OF THE parents referred to me with concerns about their child's ADD could be described in the same terms as Rae and me: conscientious people who love their children and are trying to do their best. Over and over again I see some mix of stresses and problems that parallel our own: hectic lifestyles, unresolved personal problems, tensions conscious or unconscious. Without realizing it, many of these parents clearly exhibit signs of ADD themselves. With ADD or not, many mothers and especially fathers are not infrequently described as having a short fuse and an unpredictable temper. No matter whom they had consulted, not one of the couples I have seen in my practice had ever before been encouraged to look closely at how their emotions, lives and marriages might affect their children. Their idea of stress is financial disaster or serious illness or death in the family, or perhaps a nuclear bomb going off outside their home. It seems to them just normal human existence to live at a hectic pace and in tense relationships, nerves stretched taut as piano wire. Sensitive children, as all children with ADD are, will be particularly affected.

Asked the appropriate questions, concerned parents, almost without exception, confirm the history of stress in the family. When I am able to interview the parents of adults who come for assessment, they almost invariably recall discord or major pressures on the family that their children, the adults I am seeing, have little knowledge of.

On occasion, when I probe the history of their child's earliest months and years a parent may say, "Oh, but the divorce didn't come until my son/daughter was eight years old"—an interpretation that misses something important. It is not divorce *per se* that is emotionally most wearying for the child: it is the long-term tensions and emotional heaviness that precede every divorce. No happily married couple wake up one morning and decide to leave each other. The stresses that finally separate a wife and husband wreak subterranean damage for years before they erupt into the open. Almost every divorce is the culmination of months and years of disappointment, acrimony, dejection and pain. Where there is unremitting emotional or physical abuse, the divorce itself is even a positive step, both for the abused partner and for the children.

In the minority of cases where the parents are adamant that what I am saying about stress in their lives simply does not apply,

I am still usually left with the feeling that there is more beneath the surface than the couple are psychologically ready to realize.

People can be deeply affected by unconscious anxieties and stresses they have no conscious knowledge of whatsoever. (This is often my impression, for example, whenever I meet anyone who tells me that they are a "happy person" or who says that "I believe in thinking positively.") A woman recently came to talk to me about her thirteen-year-old daughter, who had already been diagnosed with attention deficit disorder. This mother insisted that the problem began when the child was four years old. Around this time her husband became severely depressed and the couple went through difficulties that resulted in the breakup of the marriage. "The first years after my daughter's birth were the happiest years of our lives," she said. I told her I accepted her report of feeling happy, but that I still believed—although, of course, I could not prove—that there had been significant *unconscious* stresses which would have made their sensitive child emotionally insecure and interfered with the attunement process. I suggested that if her husband became profoundly depressed, he would have carried within him all his life the seeds of that depression, namely the unconscious and unresolved effects of some difficult childhood experience. "That's true," she agreed, "he did have a troubled childhood." In many ways, I told her, she would have had to be taking care of him emotionally all throughout their relationship, even before the birth of their daughter. "I did," she agreed, "I found that out in therapy after our divorce." That would have taken an emotional toll on her, I offered, even if she wasn't aware of it—and the fact that she was not aware of her mothering role toward him meant that she, too, must have carried within her the traces of painful childhood experiences. Somehow, early in her life, she must have learned to repress her own needs in order to serve the needs of others. "That's also true," she replied, "but you can't tell me I wasn't happy when I was." We ended the session, agreeing to disagree. Now, as of this writing, three weeks after that appointment, she has not yet returned for follow-up. I do not suppose that she will. It was not her memory of happy feelings that I questioned, only her belief that her daughter's infancy had been free of major emotional stresses. I had not demanded that she accept my opinion, but not unnaturally, she may feel uncomfortable about continuing with a physician who, in her view, is making false assumptions.

Sometimes a couple will deny the tensions between them and focus on what they believe to be wrong with their child as a means of avoiding conflict with each other. One father who clearly had an alcohol problem refused even to consider that this may have affected (and may continue to affect) his teenage son. His wife did not challenge him, for fear, no doubt, of angering him. They both denied any marriage problems to me, but one could have cut the tension between them with a knife.

It is not unusual for only the mother to show up for the first interview, even though both parents were asked to come in. "I've already seen two doctors," a woman quoted her husband as saying, "I don't need to see another one." Her voice broke with emotion as she related this. As happened between Rae and me, many of the mothers have been burdened with full responsibility for the family's emotional well-being. They may be pushing themselves beyond the limit of their energies, as they have done for years. Such unequal division of emotional labour is, I believe, one of the main reasons why more women than men become depressed. One also sees many single mothers, separated or divorced. Others have remarried and are having problems with a child from the first marriage.

Stress, maternal depression, marital discord, separation and divorce are more common in the families of children with ADD. "Besides problems with parenting stress, self-esteem and depression," writes Russell A. Barkley, "parents of ADD children are more likely to report a significantly greater number of stress events not associated with parenting."[1] He adds:

One such source of distress is in the marital relationship of these parents. Parents of ADD children are more likely to have marital disturbances than those of normal children... We have found that over an 8-year follow-up period, families of ADD children are three times more likely to experience separation and/or divorce of the biological parents than are families of normal children.... Mothers of ADD children rated themselves as more depressed and their marriages as more distressed than the mothers of normal children.

It could be argued, of course, that the child's ADD behavior is what depresses the mothers and causes fault lines to widen in marriages. Looking after an ADD child can be very stressful, but how parents respond to that task depends very much on what stress factors and coping skills they carry within themselves. The stresses and the discord are almost always present before the child exhibits ADD behavior, quite often before the child is born.

The most heartrending cases are adults in their midlife or beyond who simply have not been able to make much sense of their world or their lives, despite obvious warm qualities, intelligence and creative potential. When you listen to their stories, you find that many of them have suffered abuse of one form or another and may not even be aware of it. Events may be recalled, but the emotions that would naturally arise from those events are suppressed. If the emotions are remembered, their effects on the present state of mind are not understood.

Stefan is a thirty-year-old who at his first visit said, "I'm here because I'm not getting anywhere except older and grayer." He spoke with a sardonic wit, which I felt was a way of distancing himself from some deeply distressing feelings. "There's a bunch of things I want to do," he stated, "but I can't think of them right now. I don't even start anything any more because I'll never get finished with anything anyway." Despite his evidently high intelligence, he had not even completed high school. He had done well in subjects that he could immediately and instinctively grasp, but he proved completely incapable of studying. He was now working in a warehouse.

Asked about his childhood, Stefan said it had been "fine and dandy, I guess." He did say, on being further questioned, that "my mother laid down a lot of the law, and occasionally got out the spoon." Asked what that meant, he replied in the same offhand, sardonic fashion that "the wooden spoon was applied liberally to our backsides as a disciplinary measure." He recalled his father being distant and absent. Of his parents' relationship, Stefan said that his mother married his father because she felt sorry for him, but she never felt that he cared about her. "One of the disappointments of my mother's life," he said, "is that she had three sons just like my father."

What if Stefan had not learned to use his irony of tone and language as protection? He would have said that there was little love in his family, that his father was unavailable for contact and that his mother beat him—not fine and dandy but very painful, in fact. He also would have understood that his problems did not arise from some mysterious defect of his own. As it was, he blamed everything on what he called "biology." "My thermometer is set low, at blue, and that's why I'm prone to depression, dissatisfaction and hopelessness."

"My head is all scrambled," said David, a thirty-seven-year-old unemployed man. "I'm a motormouth." He was very critical of himself. He had been tested for intelligence, which confirmed his own estimate of himself as quite smart. He believed his intelligence should have been able to prevent him from making careless mistakes, from being so forgetful and disorganized: "I feel," he said, "as if my impulsiveness and hyperactivity run the show; I can't trust myself for decisions." David has a low frustration tolerance. Often, he reported, he made the wrong decision "simply to get through a situation." He told of having bought an inappropriate set of tires for his car just because he was too impatient to look for the right set.

David's parents divorced when he was four years old. Following that, he rarely saw his father, while his mother went through many unsatisfactory relationships. Both parents drank. David said they were jovial under the influence of alcohol, only sometimes "moderately angry, nothing really too severe." When asked what happened when his parents were "moderately angry," David recalled being hit hard with an orange-colored belt by his mother, when he was six or seven years old. He did not recall why his mother did this, but he did remember feeling bewildered and humiliated. He also recalled having once to grab a stick from his father's hand and experiencing "total fear." These are the experiences he described as "nothing too severe."

Almost all the adults minimize the effects of the trauma they had experienced. They have pushed out of conscious awareness the anger and despair of a small child assaulted by the very people he must rely on for support and protection, or they see such experiences as normal life events. One woman answered in the negative when I asked her if there had ever been any violence in her home of origin. It turned out that she used to be whipped by her father, ostensibly as a form of punishment. I asked her what she had meant by her original answer. "I can see it, now that you mention it," she replied. "But when I thought of the word *violence*, I thought you meant something much worse."

When people first mention violence they experienced in the family home, it is not unusual for them to do so with a smile. They use dismissive phrases they would never employ if they were describing the same events happening to someone else, particularly to any small child they know. They feel they brought their punishments on themselves. "Just kid stuff," said a thirty-six-year-old woman whose father used to hit her with a stick. "I was not an easy kid," said one man, "I warranted discipline." "I didn't get what I didn't deserve," said another. I ask them whether they would smile or call it "just kid stuff" if they themselves were to witness a child being subjected to such "discipline." The answer is always a somber no.

Among the recurrent themes blighting the childhoods of adults I have seen with severe cases of ADD are family strife and divorce; adoption, depression—especially in the mother; violence—

especially from the father; alcoholism; and sexual abuse. A 1994 study found that in a group of sexually abused girls 28 percent met the criteria for attention deficit disorder, compared with 4 percent of the nonabused group.[2] What is the connection? Although the trauma of sexual abuse can reinforce ADD traits such as tuning out, the association between ADD and sexual abuse goes deeper. It predates the abuse. Families in which sexual abuse is likely to occur are families that are psychologically stressful to grow up in from the moment of birth. So it's not that sexual abuse later in childhood causes ADD, but that the psychological atmosphere that later will make abuse possible is already present in infancy. Something amiss in relationships in a family will have negative effects on brain development in early childhood.

It has been suggested that, in general, hyperactive kids are the ones most likely to get abused. Even if that were so, the abusive inclination of the parent is not caused by the child's ADD. On the contrary—as with sexual abuse—ADD is more likely to arise in a family where physical mistreatment is a possibility, whether expressed or only latent. The psychological atmosphere in such families will have been disturbed prior to the child's birth, because the parents themselves carry the psychic scars of abuse. Only people abused in their youth will go on to abuse their own children—and they will do so almost inevitably unless they have recognized the facts of their own childhood histories and have taken up the task of healing.

Many people said that their families had moved a lot in their childhoods, which may very well reflect some ADD tendencies in their parents. Some say they attended schools in different towns almost every year. There was no stability of domicile, school or friendships. "I could describe to you the inside of the principal's office at six different high schools," said a woman who told of being punished frequently for not paying attention, being late and other ADD-related behaviors. A perhaps non-violent but forbiddingly stern, angry father is often mentioned. "We felt like we were walking on eggshells around him" is a common phrase.

"When I read the material on ADD, there is very little that doesn't describe me," says Anthony, a twenty-nine-year-old salesman. He seems depressed and reports a lack of enthusiasm or sense of deep engagement with aspects of his life, including his relationship with his common-law partner. Like many adults with ADD, Anthony has very few recollections of childhood events before the age of eight or nine, although a number of relatives have told him that he had been psychologically abused in the family home. His father, it seems, was mercilessly critical of him and played "mind games" at his expense. My consultation report to Anthony's family doctor goes on:

> Anthony says he doesn't have clear memories of too many of these incidents. His clearest memory is of when he was around seventeen years old, following his father's remarriage. A yelling match with his father in which he was called "lazy" and "bum" left him in tears. A few minutes later, his father returned to him and told him that "the only reason I am doing this is because you are a great guy and you could be doing so much more." Anthony says, "The whole incident made me feel like shit."

"There are two possibilities why your memories of childhood are so hazy," I suggest to people. "Either nothing happened worth remembering, or too much happened that may be hurtful for you to recall." As we shall see in a later chapter, human beings can tune out entire periods of their lives that were characterized by emotional pain.

"Before I was even old enough to go to school, I had to look after my mother whenever she was in a drunken stupor," one young woman recalled. Since a child cannot possibly be up to the task of taking care of a self-destructive adult, one given such responsibility inevitably develops a profound sense of inadequacy. Fourteen to 25 percent of ADD children have experienced parental alcoholism. Customarily, even if their drinking does not reach levels that may be called alcohol abuse, the parents of children with

ADD still consume more alcohol than the parents of their non-ADD peers. The significance is that these parents are probably using alcohol as a relaxant, as self-medication for stressed, depressed or agitated mind states.

ADD children are far more likely than other children to have parents who have suffered major depression, about 30 percent compared with 6 percent.[3] That figure would be even higher, I believe, were it to include the many people whose depression never reaches a diagnosed clinical state but who live their lives in the grip of low moods and irritability that seem normal to them. (John Ratey and Catherine Johnson have called such subclinical states "shadow syndromes" in their book of the same name.) I have often seen patients who do not know just how down their moods had been until medications or some other mode of therapy lifts the weight of depression from their shoulders. When I first took an antidepressant in my midforties, I was amazed at the difference. Curiously, I felt much more like myself. It was as if a fog had evaporated and I saw that for years previously I'd had only periodic glimpses of a life not burdened by negative feelings.

Family strife and parental depression contribute to the child's ADD problems not just because of their negative influence on attunement during brain development. Stressed or depressed mothers are found to be more short-tempered, more controlling and more angry with their children. Depression, particularly in the mother, also evokes an aggressive response from many a young child, quite probably due to the child's rage at what she unconsciously interprets as the emotional withdrawal of the mother. One mother of an ADD child told me that when she had been depressed, her daughter, then a toddler, became inexplicably aggressive toward playmates or even children she did not know.

If we are to make sense of all the stressed lives—the depressions, the increased prevalence of alcoholism, the violence some of these adults with attention deficit disorder experienced in their childhoods, the recognized or unrecognized ADD of the parents themselves who bring in their children for assessment—we have to go back farther into the family histories. Marilyn, a twenty-seven-year-old teacher, has ADD, and both her brothers have been treated for depression. She says, "I always have an underlying feeling of something being wrong." This feeling is accompanied by a physical sense of heaviness, which she feels paralyzes her at times. She finally discovered that she could understand her own childhood only if she recognized the early circumstances that shaped her mother's life. "My mother lived through a terrible childhood," Marilyn said. "She didn't show it to us, but underlying things I picked it up."

There is a telling bit of research evidence that deserves more attention than it has received: parents of ADD children report fewer contacts with their extended families, "and when such contacts occur, report them to be less helpful."[4] Parents of ADD children, in other words, seem to be relatively alienated from their own families of origin. They do not see their brothers, sisters, mothers and fathers as often as others tend to. When they do see their families, the interaction tends not to be satisfactory. ADD children are less likely to have the comfort and support that only loving grandparents can give. Something had already gone wrong at least one generation before these children were born, in the family of origin of their parents.

Lance Morrow, journalist and writer, succinctly expressed the multigenerational nature of suffering in his book *Heart*, a wrenching and beautiful account of his encounters with mortality, thrust upon him by near-fatal heart disease: "The generations are boxes within boxes: Inside my mother's violence you find another box, which contains my grandfather's violence, and inside that box (I suspect but do not know) you would find another box with some such black secret energy—stories within stories, receding in time."

My children, I know, suffered because of the distortions in my personality imposed by my first years. That is not an excuse, only a fact. They can avoid passing my infant suffering, and their own, on to their children, but they will have to work at understanding themselves and the influences that helped to shape them.

The family as an institution has been put under enormous strain by vastly powerful forces in our society and culture. If we want to find the sources of ADD, that is where we need to look—a task we will take up in the next chapter. But the family is the most immediate environment to act on us. We are all part of a multi-generational family system that does not begin or end with our parents. When we consider our childhoods, we are in many ways considering the effect that our grandparents' attitudes, unconscious processes and behaviors had on our parents during the latter's formative years. To understand ourselves, we need to understand the concentric "stories within stories," in Lance Morrow's phrase, which place us at the central point—and the resting point, until we have children ourselves.

Marilyn was right. The seeds of her own troubled childhood were sown long before she was born, in her mother's troubled childhood, and even long before her mother was born. We bequeath to our children not only what we honor in ourselves and in our parents; each generation also passes much of its own negative experiences on to the next, quite without wishing to do so. We need not be helpless in deciding how the story of our families will continue in the future, but first we have to recognize the themes and events that have shaped our present.

Blame becomes a meaningless concept if one understands how family history stretches back through the generations. "Recognition of this quickly dispels any disposition to see the parent as villain," wrote John Bowlby, the British psychiatrist who showed the decisive importance of attachment in infancy and childhood.[5] Who should we end up pointing the accusing finger at? At Adam and Eve, or perhaps at some poor anthropoid ape ancestor digging at the earth, a crudely sharpened stick held between palm and prehensile thumb.

# 13

# This Most Frenetic

# of Cultures:

# The Social Roots

# of ADD

To understand in a satisfactory manner the brain that fab-
ricates human mind and human behavior, it is necessary
to take into account its social and cultural context.

— ANTONIO DAMASIO, M.D., PH.D., *Descartes' Error*

ATTENTION DEFICIT DISORDER is found in
higher proportions of the population in North
America than overseas, even if we accept that it
may be overdiagnosed on this side of the Atlantic. In *Driven to Distraction*, Drs. Hallowell and Ratey speculate that North America
may have a different gene pool to account for the difference:

The people who founded our country, and continued to popu-
late it over time, were just the types of people who might have
had ADD. They did not like to sit still. They had to be willing to
take an enormous risk in boarding a ship and crossing the
ocean, leaving their homes behind; they were action-oriented,
independent, wanting to get away from the old ways... The
higher prevalence of ADD in our current society may be due to
its higher prevalence among those who settled America.[1]

This theory is psychologically attractive and may account for
some of the prevalence of ADD in the New World, but it does not
entirely square with history. The overwhelming majority of immi-
grants were not adventurers but solid artisans, merchants, farmers
and workers escaping economic hardship, political oppression,
religious persecution or catastrophes such as the Irish potato
famine. Nor could this theory apply to African blacks brought
here as slaves, or to Native North Americans subdued by guile and
force. It would also fail to account for the rising incidence of ADD
in Britain. A related theory says that today's ADD population are
the descendants of yesterday's hunters: fast on their feet and quick-
witted, restless and individualistic, in contrast to the non-ADD
population whose ancestors were farming people: stolid, patient,
hardworking traditionalists. Beautiful metaphor, questionable
genetics. It is not obvious—or at least not to me—how an incapacity to keep still, a tendency to be clumsy, careless and absent-
minded, and having a poor sense of direction would combine to
make someone a great hunter.

The greater prevalence of ADD in North America is rooted in
something more prosaic and more disturbing than genes from
adventuresome forebears: the gradual destruction of the family by
economic and social pressures in the past several decades. This
process is more advanced in North America than elsewhere in the
industrialized world.

We have seen that the individual's brain circuits are decisively
influenced by the emotional states of the parents, in the context of

the multigenerational family history. Families also live in a social and economic context determined by forces beyond their control. If what happens in families affects society, to a far greater extent society shapes the nature of families, its smallest functioning units. The human brain is a product of society and culture just as it is a product of nature. John Bowlby wrote that "the behavioural equipment of a species may be beautifully suited to life within one environment and lead only to sterility and death in another." Each species has what Bowlby calls its "environment of adaptedness," the circumstances to which its anatomy, physiology and psychological capacities are best suited.[2] In any other environment, the organism or species cannot be expected to do so well, and may even exhibit behavior "that is at best unusual and at worst positively unfavourable to survival." How poorly today's North American way of life serves the needs of the human body may be gauged by the high levels of, say, heart disease, diabetes and obesity on this continent. The situation of the human brain is analogous. The miswired ADD circuits of the prefrontal cortex are as much the effect of unhealthful circumstances as are the cholesterol-plugged arteries of atherosclerotic coronary disease.

The psychoanalyst Erik H. Erikson devoted a chapter in his Pulitzer Prize–winning book, *Childhood and Society*, to his reflections on the American identity. "This dynamic country," he wrote, "subjects its inhabitants to more extreme contrasts and abrupt changes during a generation than is normally the case with other great nations." Such trends have only accelerated since Erikson made that observation in 1950. The effects of rapid social and economic shifts on the parenting environment are too well known to need detailing here. The erosion of community, the breakdown of the extended family, the pressures on marriage relationships, the harried lives of nuclear families still intact and the growing sense of insecurity even in the midst of relative wealth have all combined to create an emotional milieu in which calm, attuned parenting is becoming alarmingly difficult. The result in successive generations of children is seen in alienation, drug use and violence—what

Robert Bly has astutely described as "the rage of the unparented." Bly notes in *The Sibling Society* that "in 1935 the average working man had forty hours a week free, including Saturday. By 1990, it was down to seventeen hours. The twenty-three lost hours of free time a week since 1935 are the very hours in which the father could be a nurturing father, and find some center in himself, and the very hours in which the mother could feel she actually has a husband." These patterns characterize not only the early years of parenting, but entire childhoods. "Family meals, talks, reading together no longer take place," writes Bly. "What the young need— stability, presence, attention, advice, good psychic food, unpolluted stories—is exactly what the sibling society won't give them."

Although society has created economic pressure on women to participate in the workforce when children are very young, it has made little provision for the satisfaction of children's needs for emotional nourishment and stimulation. In neither Canada nor the U.S. has public support for the care of young children of working parents come close to adequate. Because caring for young children is undervalued in our society, day care is politically undersupported and underfunded. The most recent insights of developmental psychology and direct research both indicate that even with all the goodwill in the world, it is difficult for a non-relative to meet an individual young child's attunement needs, especially if several other infants or toddlers are vying for that caregiver's attention. Although many day cares are well run and staffed by dedicated, albeit poorly paid workers, standards are far from uniform. For example, the state of New York demands that no more than seven toddlers can be under the care of any one worker. The regulation prescribing this hopelessly unwieldy ration is reportedly one of the *most stringent* in the United States.

There is no getting away from the fact that one-to-one, attuned parenting is the ideal situation for child development in the early years, but this is not a call for women to resume their traditional roles in the home, denied an opportunity for work and career. The natural agenda would seem to put the birth mother in the role of primary caregiver during the "second nine months of gestation"—by and large the breast-feeding period—but it does not follow that women have to be restricted to that role or men excluded from it. A physiological inability to breast-feed does not disqualify one from changing diapers or emotionally nurturing an infant. And there are no biologically based differences when it comes to parenting once breast-feeding is no longer the main source of the infant's nutrition. If women have a more finely honed instinct for mothering, it is not an instinct necessarily rooted in the biology of their sex. As many men have proven, mothering—the sensitive nurturing of the child—can be learned when one needs to learn it, or when one decides to do so.

Feminism is not wrong in calling for equality of the sexes and for an evenhanded sharing of nurturing responsibilities. I have noted in the previous chapter that the unequal division of emotional work is a major cause of depression in women, and therefore an important negative influence on the developing brain of the young child. As Dorothy Dinnerstein points out in *The Mermaid and the Minotaur*, this "female monopoly of early child care" is also a source of distortions in the psychology of both males and females, and in their relationships with each other. The answer to the need of the young child for close parental contact is not the ghettoization of women in the home. It is the recognition by society at large that there is no more important task in the world than the nurturing of the young during the earliest years. From the strict financial point of view alone, the benefits to society would be enormous if this were accepted—so much costly social dysfunction would be prevented, so many productive and creative forces allowed to unfold. There would be much less ADD, and much less of other disorders of development as well, if fathers as well as mothers were encouraged to consider the child's interests paramount in the formative years, and were not denied the required social and economic support.

Quite the opposite is true now. Far from being helped, working women are actively penalized if they wish to extend the time they are at home caring for their children. For men, it is not even considered reasonable to think of "interrupting" their careers in order to share in that process. Society does little to establish expert and compassionate day care for those children during whose early years the parent(s), for one reason or another, cannot avoid the necessity of working outside the home. Poor women, especially in the U.S., are economically terrorized by the welfare system into entrusting their infants to appallingly inadequate care situations, and then must spend hours daily traveling to low-paying jobs that barely allow their families a subsistence income.

The effects of disrupted family life on mental functioning are magnified by cultural influences. "American society," Drs. Hallowell and Ratey observe, "tends to create ADD-like symptoms in all of us. We live in an ADD-ogenic culture." They identify what they call "pseudo ADD," people living lives in conformity with the frenzied society and culture around them but not impaired in their functioning by the neurophysiological attributes of ADD. It can look like ADD from the outside, but it is not ADD from within.

> What are some of the hallmarks of American culture that are also typical of ADD? The fast pace. The sound bite. The bottom line. Short takes, quick cuts. The TV remote-control clicker. High stimulation. Restlessness... Speed. Present-centered, no future, no past. Disorganization... Going for the gusto. Making it on the run. The fast track. Whatever works. Hollywood. The stock exchange. Fads...[3]

Cultural manifestations such as television cannot in themselves create ADD, if by that we mean the neurophysiological miswiring of self-regulation and attention. ADD arises in the infant and toddler because of stresses in the family environment. These stresses are imposed by society, but before the child is directly exposed to popular culture. However, as Hallowell and Ratey point out, culture can feed ADD and reinforce it. Current social trends make it more daunting for people with attention deficit disorder to overcome their ADD-related problems. They make some ADD-driven behaviors seem even desirable and rewarding.

Three decades ago, the television program *Sesame Street* was developed to teach the basics of reading and counting to inner-city children in the eastern United States. These children, mostly of racial minorities living under conditions of deprivation and in families stressed even beyond the general norm, would be precisely the ones we would predict to have ADD. The program offered a warm, friendly environment and rapidly alternating vignettes, sketches and educational sound bites of very short duration. The purpose was not to overtax the brief attention spans of the intended audience and to hold their interest, which otherwise would quickly wane. In short, whether or not the producers identified it in these precise terms, *Sesame Street* was a response to the socially engendered ADD of poor children.

Since then, we have evolved into a culture that celebrates a short attention span. If one were to watch a news or interview program dating from around the time *Sesame Street* first appeared, one would still hear people speaking in full sentences, beginning and completing a thought. The camera would hold them in its gaze. Today, news items are shorter and give less information. The average sound bite is under ten seconds long. The camera jumps around like a nervous rabbit. If our teenagers do not have ADD, they surely would have it—were it possible to develop it at their age—from watching the dazzling, hyperkinetic music videos in which camera angles are maintained no longer than the blink of an eye. Television programmers may no longer have the benign educational goals of *Sesame Street*, but they seem to take for granted that the entire population's ability to pay attention has become impaired.

In his final dispatch, Martin Walker, for nine years Washington correspondent of the British newspaper *The Guardian*, referred to U.S. society as "this most frenetic of cultures." A well-chosen phrase. One does not need prophetic powers to foretell that the first decades of the next millennium will see more ADD than even our present time.

# PART FOUR

The Meaning of ADD Traits

# 14

# Severed Thoughts

# and Flibbertigibbets:

# Distractibility and

# Tuning Out

The King is mad. How stiff is my vile sense
That I stand up and have ingenious feeling
Of my huge sorrows. Better I were distract.
So should my thoughts be severed from my griefs...
— WILLIAM SHAKESPEARE, *King Lear*, Act 4., Sc.7

ABSENTMINDEDNESS IS on the continuum of normal human traits, as are all other manifestations of ADD. It is one of the psychological byproducts of living in a complex society. Few can maintain an absolute mindfulness, an unhindered awareness of the present.

Life would hardly be possible without an ability to shut out a large proportion of the stimuli received by our brains at every moment—sights, sounds, physical sensations, reports about the internal functions of the body. With attention deficit disorder, the question is not how we develop a capacity to shut out certain aspects of reality, but how this normal capacity becomes distorted into a mind dysfunction severe enough to interfere with daily experience of the world.

In the language of psychology, mental absence, tuning out, is an example of a mind state known as *dissociation*.[1] It is employed in clinical psychiatry to refer to specific syndromes such as multiple personality disorder, but I use the term in its general sense. Dissociation, including the tuning-out of ADD, originates in a defensive need—it is a form of psychological defense. Gloucester's motive to be "distract," in the fourth act of *King Lear*, is very close to the source of the "distractness" of ADD. It is a way of coping with emotional hurt. The original purpose of dissociation is to separate conscious awareness from some emotional pain we are experiencing, to *dis-associate* one from the other. We may think of dissociation as a psychological anesthetic.

Under what circumstances does a human being need a psychological anesthetic to free him from awareness of pain? The answer is not as obvious as it may seem, because pain itself serves a crucial function in survival. We would not survive without pain. Physical pain warns us of physical danger, such as the heat of a fire or the cutting edge of a blade. Emotional pain warns us that a situation threatens our psychic well-being.

Dissociation is a nature-given emergency survival technique. It is not meant for everyday use but is to be employed in the rare circumstance when to feel pain threatens survival more than not to feel pain. Since tuning out can be perilous even as it protects, only under certain dire conditions will nature allow us to use it as defense. The first condition is *severe distress*. One does not have to tune out the hurt of a stubbed toe. The second condition is *helplessness*. If help is available, it is safer to feel the pain and scream for assistance than to tune it out. In her book *Betrayal Trauma* Jennifer J. Freyd, professor of psychology at the University of Oregon, gives an illuminating analogy:

> Suppose Deanna breaks a leg on a skiing accident while travelling with a companion. The pain is so severe that Deanna is unlikely to want to move at all, and she is certainly unlikely to stand up and walk. Instead, she waits while her companion goes to get a rescue team. On the other hand, if Beverly has a similar accident while travelling alone, there is a good chance that she will spontaneously block perception of the leg pain and get up and try to hobble to safety. In the first case, the pain is protecting Deanna from further damage that may be caused by walking on a broken leg. In the second case, the blockage of pain is allowing Beverly to escape the life-threatening situation of being trapped alone in the snow. Presumably Beverly abhors pain as much as does Deanna, but only Beverly's circumstance is likely to create the spontaneous blockage of pain.[2]

For a person with ADD, tuning out is an automatic brain activity that originated during the period of rapid brain development in infancy when there was emotional hurt combined with helplessness. At one time or another, every infant or young child feels frustration and psychological pain. Episodic experiences of a distressing nature do not induce dissociation, but chronic distress does—the distress of the sensitive infant with unsatisfied attunement needs, for example. The infant has to dissociate chronic emotional pain from consciousness for two reasons. First, it is too overwhelming for his fragile nervous system. He simply cannot exist in what we might call a state of chronic negative arousal, with adrenaline and other stress hormones pumping through his veins all the time. It is physiologically too toxic. He has to block it out. Second, if the parent's anxiety is the source of the infant's distress, the infant unconsciously senses that fully expressing his own emotional turmoil will only heighten that anxiety. His distress would then be aggravated—a vicious cycle he can escape by tuning out.

The survival value of all psychological defenses is relatively short-lived. Sooner or later dissociation becomes a hindrance, interferes with life and slows psychological growth. The tuned-out individual has difficulty learning from experience and is hampered in making contact with others. The inner retreat from psychological reality means that he may never learn to cope with emotional setbacks in a creative and positive way. We may compare any psychological defense to a heavy fur coat a man in a cold northern climate puts on to keep from freezing. Wearing the fur coat saves his life. Let's imagine that he is suddenly transported to the equator, coat still on. He would soon find that the clothing that helped him survive in the north makes him most uncomfortable or even ill in his new circumstances. Of course, our traveler is free to remove his coat. The problem with unconscious psychological defenses is that they cannot be shed at will. They were induced without our conscious will in the first place, indeed before we had any will at all.

Once in place, a defense mechanism such as tuning out takes on a life of its own. Little or nothing of a distressing nature need be there in the immediate environment for it to happen. It becomes, as it were, the "default" setting in the cerebral apparatus of awareness: unless some other special switch is turned on, tuned out will be the state that the brain automatically returns to. Because tuning out is based on deeply entrenched neurological responses, their later activation requires very little stimulus. Once a circuit is established, signals will travel along it much more easily than along alternative routes, in a manner analogous to the ease of walking along a beaten path rather than through grass or bush on either side of it, or water flowing in a channel instead of across flat ground. If we want the stream to run in a different direction, we will have to create new courses for it.

Given their automatic tuning out, ADD children forever find themselves being told to "pay attention"—a demand that completely misunderstands both the nature of the child and the nature of attention. The obvious monetary connotation of "pay" is that attention is something the child *owes* the adult, that the child's attention belongs to the adult by right. The phrase takes for granted that being attentive is always a consciously chosen act, subject to one's will. Both of these assumptions are faulty.

Nobody is born with "attention." Like language or locomotion, being attentive is a skill we acquire. As with all other skills, the conditions necessary for the development of attention have to be present. It is not an isolated attribute of the child's but the product of a relationship between the child and her environment. "A skill is a characteristic neither of a person nor of a context, but of a *person-in-context*," write the brain researchers Kurt Fischer and Samuel Rose.[3] To understand what we call inattention, we have to consider the child, the context and the relationship between the two. There can be no automatic expectation of owing or paying attention. Attention is complex, the result of complex brain activity with multiple components. The deficit of attention in ADD is not just a matter of some sluggish brain mechanism to be set in action by admonishments or rewards, or simply to be lubricated by this or that pharmaceutical product.

The brain's level of arousal is a major factor in determining our capacity to give attention, as the neuroscientist Joseph LeDoux explains:

Arousal is important in all mental functions. It contributes significantly to attention, perception, memory, emotion, and problem solving. Without arousal, we fail to notice what's going on—we don't attend to the details. But too much arousal is not good either. If you are over aroused you become tense and anxious and unproductive. You need to have just the right level of activation to perform optimally.

Because of insufficient self-regulation, children with ADD are often underaroused or overaroused. In the first state, they cannot get going on a task; in the second, they cannot focus on it. "Arousal locks you into the emotional state you are in," LeDoux points out. "This can be very useful (you don't want to get distracted when you are in danger), but can also be an annoyance (once the fear system is turned on, it's hard to turn it off—this is the nature of anxiety)."[4] Arousal levels reflect such obvious factors as rest or fatigue, but are also deeply affected by the emotional context.

Many people with ADD have noticed that a strange drowsiness may come over them in the midst of some emotionally charged situations, as, for example, during a conflict with a spouse. All of a sudden, they start yawning and their eyelids grow heavy. Their partners naturally believe that the drowsiness is a sign of boredom and a lack of caring. Or the emotionally stressed ADD child may suddenly—and genuinely—complain of being "tired," only to regain energy a few minutes later if the source of anxiety, which may be some homework she feels beyond her capacities to do, is removed. The parent may conclude that the child is malingering. What is really happening is that the right prefrontal cortex is over-inhibiting a network of neurons in the brain stem, known as the *reticular formation*—an important part of the circuitry of arousal—because the emotions are too threatening. The reticular formation sends axons (nerve cables) to the cortex, where chemicals are released that make the cortical cells more alert, more responsive to incoming information. The cortex, in turn, projects axons to the reticular formation and can inhibit its arousal function, as in the case of our drowsy individual or the tired child. For the person in emotional distress, drifting off to sleep would permit at least a temporary escape—an unconscious defense closely connected with tuning out. I have experienced this not only during emotional conflict, but, the reader may recall, also when I tried in past years to read the diary my mother kept during my infancy.

Another reaction to fear or anxiety can be overarousal, due to the activity of the brain center where those emotions are generated, the *amygdala*. Once the amygdala is activated, it magnifies arousal and floods the cells in the cortex with messages of danger. The cortex now becomes hyperfocused on the perceived source of the anxiety, initiating a cycle: anxiety–arousal–more anxiety–more arousal, in the midst of which all other information is blocked out. A person in this state cannot concentrate on much else, as anyone who has ever been anxious can verify. An example in the classroom may be a young pupil with ADD in whom the gruff commands of a perhaps well-meaning but authoritarian teacher trigger anxiety. The child will become overaroused and will not "pay attention," which raises the teacher's ire. His disapproval, in turn, will further lock the child into his anxious state. "Marty would do much better if he would only learn to concentrate," the teacher will write in his report card. Yet in another class with a teacher whose personality style he finds encouraging instead of intimidating, Marty does well. He may have ADD, but his attention skills are not set according to some inflexible gauge. He is a "person in context." The problem for him in this context is not attention as such, but his difficulty regulating his internal emotional environment. It is all too easily discombobulated by the roughness his sensitive nervous system picks up in the teacher's tone of voice.

Arousal is only one aspect of attention. Other factors such as interest, motivation and the child's emotional priorities contribute. So does the body's internal environment, as a highly sensitive child may be distracted by physical sensations. Unbalanced chemical states, such as blood sugar levels at either the high or low ends of the normal range, are notoriously powerful negative influences on the ADD child's ability to concentrate or to remain emotionally balanced. All these separate streams flow together into the composite mind activity we call attention.

Although we think of attention as a function of the intellect, its deepest roots are in the subsoil of emotion. From the evolutionary point of view, this could not have been otherwise. Imagine a nutritionally challenged saber-tooth tiger charging us: to motivate us in that situation, we don't need intellect but raw fear. Better to scoot first and ask questions later. Emotion divorced from thought is hazardous, but human life is equally impossible when thought rules without emotion. The emotionless Vulcan space traveler in *Star Trek*, Mr. Spock, may be the television ideal of rationality, but as a human being he couldn't think his way out of a paper bag.

What is true for humankind as a species is also true for the individual human. In infancy, emotional development precedes intellectual growth because the brain centers that process emotion and motivation mature before those that serve thinking and logic: emotion before intellect, right brain before left brain. Attention first develops as an activity of the emotion-processing parts of the brain. Emotions remain the basis of attention, even after the intellect comes to dominate our conscious thought.

The newborn can no more focus his attention than he can focus his vision. In fact, there is a close link between the visual and attentional systems: a powerful incentive for the development of both is the infant's emotional relationship with the mothering adult. As we have seen, the brain center in the prefrontal cortex that tracks the emotionally important object—that adult—also helps to select what in the environment receives the infant's attention. The direct, calm interest of the caregiver first kindles the infant's own interest in the world and helps to organize his attention. The ecstatic joy exchanged between them during mutual gaze interactions motivates the infant to explore the environment.

The first stage in the building of the architecture of the mind is what Stanley Greenspan calls "making sense of sensations":

> Equipped with an immature nervous system, a baby arrives into a clamorous world of stimuli that come both from within and without her growing body. In the early months of life, a normally developing child begins the task of making order out

of sensations that stream unbidden and unchanneled through her maturing senses. First she must attain control over her body's motions and internal sensations and over her own attention. She must learn to remain calm while simultaneously attending to and sometimes taking action on objects or events outside herself... The infant who has attained calm attention has taken a first gigantic step on the road to fulfilment of her human potential.[5]

The skill of attention that begins during the initial stages of brain growth and mental development goes through several important phases, but the central buttress of them all is the secure attachment/attunement relationship with the primary caregiver. Without that, the infant will not focus. Without it, the toddler will be hesitant or unregulated about how he explores the environment. Happy interactions between caregiver and infant generate motivation and arousal by triggering the release of the reward brain chemicals, endorphins and dopamine. In a positive interaction with mother lasting only ten seconds, an underaroused toddler is energized, his unfocused attention transformed into focused attention.[6]

Attention and emotional security remain intertwined throughout childhood. What looks like a deficit of attention may be a preoccupation with something important to the child but hidden to the observing adult: the child's emotional anxieties. The classroom behavior of ADD children, to give a common example, is frequently said to be disruptive. They seem to have more interest in interacting with their peers than in the material the teacher would have them study—which may simply mean that they are obsessed with trying to get their relationship needs met. If they tend not to do this very successfully, they do it all the more desperately. Their brain's attentional system cannot switch into "schoolwork mode" when it is consumed by anxieties about the child's emotional connection with the world.

For people deeply hurt, the internal world may offer more

meaning than the real one. A woman in her thirties whose ADD was never noticed because she was not hyperactive, only a day-dreamer, told me that she spent entire school days staring out the window, lost in fanciful adventures with imaginary friends. From the outside, one might have described her as "distracted." The Latin root of *distract* is "draw away"—drawing her away from the inside was her hiddenmost emotional longing. Her brain unconsciously assigned greater value to a self-created internal universe than to anything or anyone in the classroom.

The nagging hunger for emotional contact explains the oft-observed "paradox" that many children with ADD are capable of focused work in the presence of an adult who is keeping them company and paying attention to them. This is no paradox at all, if we see the opposing roles of anxiety and attachment in influencing attention: attachment promotes attention, anxiety undermines it. When the child is not concerned with seeking emotional contact, his prefrontal cortex is freed to allocate attention to the task at hand, illustrating that what we call attention deficit disorder is not a fixed, unalterable physiological state; it's a physiological state, yes, but not fixed and unalterable. The warmth and satisfaction of positive contact with the adult is often just as good as a psychostimulant in supplying the child's prefrontal cortex with dopamine. Greater security means less anxiety and more focused attention. The unseen factor that remains constant in all situations is the child's unconscious yearning for attachment, dating back to the first years of life. Where this need is satisfied, ADD problems begin to recede.

Distractedness due to emotional turmoil and thought-storms in the mind also blight memory. Anyone with ADD has experienced, numerous times a day, going into another room or running up- or downstairs only to stand there puzzled, wondering what she came to look for in the first place, or of returning with something quite useless that she had absentmindedly picked up. The key phrase here is *absentmindedly*. The notoriously poor short-term recall is in large part due to the tuned-out, semidissociated, internally preoccupied state of ADD. "This kind of 'amnesia' occurs because attention is required to form new episodic memories," writes the psychologist Daniel Schacter, "and when our attentional resources are consumed by internal thoughts and feelings, there are few left over for dealing with the world outside."[7]

I once asked a forty-three-year-old writer with ADD to describe herself as a child. "Pepper pot, flibbertigibbet and high strung," she shot back. I loved that account, with its spirited, hyperenergetic, all-over-the-place scatter-mindedness. For the record, though, I did ask her what exactly she meant. Unpredictably explosive, intense, unfocused and always trying to engage other children in chatter, she explained.

"You see, you were focused," I countered. "You were focused on what was important to you: your relationships in the world. But nobody understood."

# 15

# The Pendulum

# Swings:

# Hyperactivity,

# Lethargy and Shame

I do not know if you have noticed that the moment you
cease to be active, there is immediately a feeling of
nervous apprehension; you feel as though you are not
alive, not alert, so you must keep going. And there is fear
of being alone, of going for a walk alone, of being by
yourself, without a book, without a radio, without talking; the fear of sitting quietly without doing something
all the time with your hands or with your mind or with
your heart.

— J. KRISHNAMURTI

**"I**'VE ALWAYS HAD THIS feeling like getting up and doing something else," says Andrew, an eighteen-year-old with attention deficit disorder. Many a time he obeys that feeling without a thought, leaving in the middle of a conversation, while the other person is speaking. Other times he talks so much that his friends can stand being with him for only an hour or so. He is always on the go but seldom productive.

Hyperactivity is experienced in a number of ways. The person with ADD feels discomfort at having to keep still for even short periods of time. There may be a physical inability to refrain from restless movements for more than a few minutes. Always, one is caught in a mental whirlwind. A seventy-two-year-old man, a geologist, called it "newsreel thinking," by which he meant the rapid shifting of his thoughts from one subject to another. (He had originally trained as an engineer but could not abide the confines of an office. He switched to geology because the work allowed him to be outdoors, on the move.) Another sign of hyperactivity may be frequent movement of the eyes, a scanning of the environment that frustrates other people. It is disconcerting to be with an individual who seems to be always on the lookout for something, or someone, else.

Hyperactivity, like other traits associated with ADD, is a normal stage in the maturation of a child. In attention deficit disorder, *stages* becomes *states*: the individual's psychological development remains static. Behaviors and emotional patterns remain at a level characteristic of the toddler. Hyperactivity and its counterpart, the lethargy of many children and adults with ADD, are both exaggerations of body states first experienced during toddlerhood, from about the end of "the second nine months of gestation" to about the age of eighteen months. They each represent the activity of the autonomic nervous system, which, in ADD, is poorly controlled. It is helpful to look closer at how that works.

The nervous system, with the brain and spinal cord at its center, has two major parts. The *voluntary nervous system* moves the muscles of the trunk, limbs and head, in deliberate actions such as speech or changes of position. The *autonomic nervous system* (ANS) is autonomous from, independent of, our conscious will, as its name implies. It controls what are called the smooth muscles, which line the walls of organs such as the gut, blood vessels, glands and airways in the lungs. It governs body states such as the release of hormones, blood flow to internal organs and to the skin and the contraction of the muscles in the intestines. Autonomic nerves also set the baseline tension level of voluntary muscles, as well as skin temperature and the erection or relaxation of hair follicles. In general, they provide the wiring for a stable internal chemical and physiological body environment.

The body's physiological states are directly influenced by emotions because the part of the cortex that processes emotions also oversees the ANS. The tummy aches of the sensitive child are muscle cramps caused by autonomic signals, triggered by unconscious fears and tensions. "Gut feelings" express the effect of emotions on the ANS, as does the common report that "my hair stood on end." Autonomic nerves are responsible for tight muscles and explain why some things make us "sick to the stomach," or give us a "pain in the neck."

The ANS has two opposing divisions: the *sympathetic*, which expends energy, and the *parasympathetic*, which conserves energy. When we are in a sympathetically aroused state, our muscles tense, our heart rate increases, blood flow goes to our limbs and adrenaline is pumped through our bodies. The firing of sympathetic nerves creates a body climate of high arousal, important in survival because it enables us to move quickly in either escape or self-defense. This is the well-known fight-or-flight response. In daily life, we experience it as the body state associated with excitement.

There are also times when the body needs to slow down, even times when being absolutely still is a matter of life and death. If flight or fight are impossible, not being noticed may be our ticket to survival. When parasympathetic nerves dominate, the body slumps, the head hangs down, the arms go limp, the eyes are averted, the facial muscles go slack. As the smooth muscle fibers encircling the arterioles in the face lose their tone, these small blood vessels dilate and the facial skin is suffused with blood. We blush. The low-arousal state is experienced in the common feeling of shame. In a chronic form, it is a characteristic of depression.

Hyperactivity is unregulated high arousal, appropriate in the young toddler. Toward the end of the first nine months of life, the infant begins an enthusiastic exploration of her universe. No longer having to rely on adults for mobility, she tirelessly examines every nook and cranny of her surroundings, every object. She tests, tastes, plays and discovers, learning the purpose and use of many things. During this phase of prolonged excitement, neural pathways are established that enable the cortex to inhibit the sympathetic nervous system—if the necessary circumstances are present. During stress, these circuits do not develop properly, and hyperactivity persists. The *stage*, meant to last only a few months, becomes a *state* that the child remains stuck in.

There is another component to hyperactivity: throughout life, it continues to be a human response during times of high anxiety. If you were told that in the next week, at some unpredictable moment, some unnamed disaster would strike you or one close to you, and that you were helpless to do anything to prevent it, your response would quite probably resemble the habitual mental and physical behaviors of the hyperactive child or adult with ADD. You would have difficulty focusing your thoughts, and your mind might feel like a squirrel on a treadmill: racing but not going anywhere. Sitting still would be a chore. A clichéd image of helpless anxiety in an adult is the father pacing nervously outside the delivery room where his wife is giving birth. I believe hyperactivity in ADD is fed by a current of permanent, subterranean anxiety.

Derek is forty-two years old. He has always had an inability to complete tasks and to continue with any particular activity for any length of time. His problems were evident right from elementary school. Despite his high intelligence, he has a very poor school record, failing or having to drop out of classes and chronically underachieving. On the odd occasion that he was in a situation congenial to his type of personality, he was capable of doing very well. In Grade 8 he excelled, making the honor roll; in Grade 9, his previous patterns recurred. Derek is restless, constantly on the go and has had many traffic violations. "It's as if I'm always trying to catch something that isn't there," he said at our initial interview.

The "trying to catch something that isn't there" is a neural memory of the way, as an anxious infant, Derek scanned his surroundings, looking for comfort, for an untroubled connection with someone. His parents had divorced when he was only four years old, following years of acrimony. After that, he barely saw his father. He has never felt quite safe in the world.

My eyes, like the eyes of almost everyone with attention deficit disorder, sweep across faces I meet as if of their own volition, seeking everyone's eyes, looking for signs of contact.[1] Strangers will suddenly catch me staring at them intently. This automatic scanning happens even when I am engaged in conversation with someone, perhaps creating the impression that I am not interested in the interaction with that particular individual. I know it now for what it is: the activation of the brain circuitry created when I scanned my mother's withdrawn or depressed features constantly, seeking contact, and even more, when I sought her very presence during the period of our separation toward the end of my first year of life. It's an expression of anxiety, a triggered memory of it. The Vancouver psychologist Gordon Neufeld calls anxiety "an attachment alarm." Its role in the survival of the human infant and child is to signal when our attachment relationships, which we are absolutely dependent on, are threatened. It is useful, unless it becomes a chronic state.

Just as inattention diminishes in the presence of a warmly supportive adult, so does the hyperactivity. Some children are very clear about this. An eight-year-old patient of mine insisted that one of his parents accompany him to the bathroom every evening when he brushed his teeth. "I get hyper when you're not with me," he told his father.

If hyperactivity expresses anxiety, lethargy and underarousal express shame. Shame, like anxiety, is an attachment emotion. "Whenever someone becomes significant to us, whenever another's caring, respect or valuing matters, the possibility for generating shame emerges," writes the psychologist Gershen Kaufman.[2] The origin of shame is the feeling of having been cut off from the parent, of having lost the connection, if only momentarily. It cannot be helped, it occurs unavoidably as part of maturing.

The toddler's hyperactive explorations are curtailed a few months after they began. A necessary outcome of exploring is the identification of limits, of boundaries. Some of these boundaries are physical, such as the curb on a street; some are social, like the pain another human being might feel having his hair pulled. The child who does not learn boundaries is in danger. There are limits not to be crossed, and the mode of learning this is the attachment relationship.

We do not find out about the boundaries of acceptable behavior by reading a manual or even by being told. The setting of limits has to begin long before we understand why those limits must be respected. We find out by the reactions of our parents, the most important of which are nonverbal. The word *no* by itself would mean nothing to the toddler unless it was said in a stern voice and with a disapproving look, along with other evidence of disapproval, such as shaking the head. Throughout life, the nonverbal messages we read between the lines of verbal communication—far more than the words themselves—define our relationships with others, either inviting us in or keeping us out.

"Even the most benign parenting," writes Allan Schore, the seminal psychological researcher and therapist, "involves some use of mild shaming procedures to influence behavior."[3] At the beginning of the stage of mobile, restless exploration, 90 percent of maternal behavior consists of affection, play and caregiving, with only 5 percent involved in prohibiting the junior toddler from ongoing activity, according to one study. In the following months, there is a radical shift. The aroused toddler's curiosity and impulsiveness lead him into many situations where the parent must express disapproval. Between the ages of eleven and seventeen months, the average toddler experiences a prohibition every nine minutes. In response to the words, vocal tone and body language of disapproval, the toddler goes into the physiological shame state: from activity to inactivity, from expending energy to conserving energy, from a high-arousal state to a low-arousal state. This achieves exactly what nature would intend—stopping a possibly dangerous activity, at a signal from the parent.

During the phase of decreased arousal, new circuits will develop so that the cortex can inhibit the other part of the autonomic nervous system, its parasympathetic division. As before, the environment has to be right for the pathways of inhibition to mature.

Shame becomes excessive if the parent's signaling of disapproval is overly strong, or if the parent does not move to reestablish warm emotional contact with the child immediately—what Gershen Kaufman calls "restoring the interpersonal bridge." Chronic stress experienced by the parent has the effect of breaking that bridge. The small child does not have a large store of insight for interpreting the parent's moods and facial expressions: they either invite contact or forbid it. When the parent is distracted or withdrawn, the older infant or toddler experiences shame. Shame postures are observed in infants in response to nothing more than the parent breaking eye contact. The demeanor of the infants of depressed mothers is one of inactivity and the averted gaze.

Past the toddler phase, there will be many times the child's behavior may trigger an angry response from the parent, the ADD child more than the average. Some parents are able to express anger without making the child feel cut off emotionally. They convey disapproval without rejection. Other parents, especially those with self-regulation problems of their own, may react with open or choked rage, punishing coldness or dejected withdrawal that signals defeat and disappointment. These were the anger responses my children experienced from me. Each time this happens, shame is evoked in the child, especially as the parent usually believes—and makes the child believe—that whatever his (the parent's) reaction is, the child is responsible for it.

The deep feelings of shame associated with attention deficit disorder are usually explained by the obvious fact that the ADD individual gets many things wrong. On the face of it, this makes sense. The adult or child with attention deficit disorder may frequently offend people or break a promise or be late somewhere. Given his inattentiveness and difficulties reading nonverbal social messages, he treads on toes—in both senses of that phrase. He carries memories of having failed at many tasks, of being deservedly criticized— so he thinks—for many shortcomings. Such events, however, can only reinforce shame or provoke it—they cannot cause it. Its origins have nothing to do with bad deeds, failures or hurting anyone. Like its opposite number, hyperactivity, shame began as a normal physiological state that escaped regulation by the cortex. It becomes wound tightly into the self-identity of the individual.

John Ratey has aptly observed that "I'm sorry" is the most common phrase in the vocabulary of attention deficit disorder. What strikes me immediately when I meet new ADD patients is how often they apologize. They apologize when I ask them to speak louder, when they cannot easily answer a question, when I interrupt their flow of speech to ask for more information, when I tell them that we will wind up the session in a few minutes as time is running out. People ask forgiveness for being in my office in the first place. Their opening words may be an apology: "I am sorry to be taking up your time. I am sure there are many people waiting to see you who need help a lot more than I do." Of course, they also apologize if they think they have too serious a problem: "I'm sorry, I know it's difficult to help me. You couldn't have imagined you would be dealing with such a basket case." These expressions of remorse, where no offense was committed, communicate a deep sense of shame. If the words did not betray shame, it could still be recognizable in the averted eyes.

In ADD, hyperactivity and a low-arousal state have become entrenched, inappropriate to the individual's age or to events in the immediate present. They are triggered too easily, and once triggered, they tend to go out of control. The cortex is not able to regulate either division of the autonomic nervous system. Physiologically and emotionally, the child or adult with ADD swings back and forth between over-the-top, purposeless excitement and a nonrestful vegetative state in which the predominant emotion is shame. Some tend to get stuck at one or the other of these opposite poles. The two states may also be present at the same time, resulting in agitated, unfocused inactivity.

Like so much else about attention deficit disorder, hyperactivity, lethargy and shame are closely connected with the neurological memories of the distant, stressed or distracted caregiver. There will be a sense of discomfort as soon as the mind becomes aware of itself, because such awareness immediately triggers responses encoded with the infant's distress at feeling emotionally alone. The mind then lapses into helpless lethargy, or races away, looking for something to attach to: some idea, some fantasy, some memory, conversation, music, reading—anything. When it cannot do so, there is intense unease—or the aversion to one's own mind, which we call boredom.

A requirement of healing, becoming whole, is circuitry in the brain that can carry different messages and a different, nonhelpless image of the self. There is strong evidence that such circuits can develop at any time in life, as can neural pathways to help the cortex to do its job of inhibition and regulation.

# PART FIVE

The ADD Child and Healing

# 16

# It Ain't Over

# Till It's Over:

# Unconditional

# Positive Regard

We now have evidence to illustrate the details of the
anatomical changes that do occur with modifications of
the environment... It is now clear that the brain is far
from immutable.

— MARIAN CLEEVES DIAMOND, PH.D., *Enriching*
*Heredity*

PEOPLE OFTEN ASK IF ONE CAN "grow out"
of attention deficit disorder—a good question, for healing is a matter of growth. And
the answer is yes. It is not curing that ADD children need: they
need to be helped to grow. What is required is not a change in parenting techniques but a change in parenting attitudes, based on a

deeper understanding of the child. The adult with attention deficit disorder needs also to gain a deeper understanding of herself, to undertake the task we will later describe as self-parenting.

The outlook is positive for the healing process in attention deficit disorder. This kind of optimism is typified by Yogi Berra's remark, much beloved by sportscasters: *it ain't over till it's over.* Nowhere is this more true than in the life history of the human brain and the human personality. We have seen that experience has great influence on the circuitry of the brain, and also that chemical changes—for better or worse—are affected by the environment. If the wiring and chemistry of the brain are not rigidly set by hered- ity, neither are they unalterably fixed in early childhood. The chal- lenge of healing later in life is identical to looking at causation in infancy. What conditions promote development? What condi- tions hinder it?

Laboratory work on the brain and clinical experience with human beings have opened up a world of possibilities. "The mam- malian brain appears to have the capacity to remain responsive to environmental enrichment well into advanced age," writes Dr. Marian Cleeves Diamond, a noted brain researcher at the Univer- sity of California's Department of Anatomy–Physiology in Berke- ley.[1] In her laboratory, rats ranging from newborns to elderly were kept in varying degrees of social isolation, stimulation, and envi- ronmental and nutritional enrichment. Autopsies showed that the layers of the cortex in the brains of the environmentally favored rats were thicker, their nerve cells larger, their branching more elaborate, their blood supply richer. Enriched rats well past midlife could still grow connecting branches almost twice as long as their "standard" cousins, after only thirty days of differential treatment. Dr. Diamond reports these results in her book *Enriching Heredity: The Impact of the Environment on the Anatomy of the Brain*. "Perhaps the single most valuable piece of information learned from all our studies," she writes, "is that structural differences can be detected in the cerebral cortices of animals exposed at any age to different levels of stimulation in the environment... at any age studied, we have shown anatomical effects due to enrichment or impoverishment."

Most encouraging was Dr. Diamond's finding that even the brains of animals deprived before birth, or deliberately damaged in infancy, were able to compensate by structural changes in response to enriched living conditions. "Thus," she writes, "we must not give up on people who begin life under unfavorable conditions. Environmental enrichment has the potential to enhance their brain development too, depending on the degree or severity of the insult."

That in humans, too, we can expect even the adult brain to be positively influenced by the environment is not surprising. The same has long been known to be true for almost any other organ or part of the body. Unused muscles atrophy but grow in size and strength if well exercised; blood supply to the heart is improved by exercise and healthy diet; lung capacity increases with aerobic training. Elderly people who remain physically and intellectually active suffer much less decline in their mental functioning than their more passive contemporaries.

Early in life, *plasticity*, the responsiveness of the human brain to changing conditions, is so great that infants who suffer damage to one side of their brain about the time of birth, even if they lose an entire hemisphere, may compensate for the deficit.[2] The other half develops so that these children grow up to have nearly symmetrical facial movements and only a mild or moderate limp. With age, plasticity declines, but it is never completely lost. Neurological adaptability even in adulthood may be seen in the recovery many people make from a stroke. In a cerebrovascular accident, or stroke, brain tissue is destroyed, usually because of bleeding. Although nerve cells that have died will not come back to life, often the patient will, in weeks or months, be able to use again a limb that was paralyzed by the stroke. New circuits have taken over, new connections have been made. "Under normal conditions 'growth' may be a characteristic of the brain throughout life," writes the physician and neuroscientist Francine Benes.[3]

One way neurological circuits change is by the strengthening or weakening of synapses, the connections between nerve cells. "Since different experiences cause synaptic strengths to vary within and across many neural systems, experience shapes the design of circuits," observes the neurologist and neuroscientist Antonio Damasio. "As a result, the design of brain circuits continues to change. *The circuits are not only receptive to the results of first experience, but [are] repeatedly pliable and modifiable by continued experience.*"[4] (Italics mine.)

The strength of synapses is influenced by many factors, including the frequency of their use or disuse, or the composition of body chemistry from one situation to the next. Circuits are also weakened or enhanced by other circuits that may interfere with their functions or assist them. We see this in attention deficit disorder when the same child is able to attend to a subject in one type of environment but is unable to concentrate on the same topic in another. This situationality of ADD reflects the input of emotions, which play a powerful role in attention.

As we know, in ADD the cortex does not exercise firm enough control over the arousal and emotion-generating centers in the lower brain areas. Dr. Benes points out that important linkages between the cortex and these emotional centers continue to mature "as late as the sixth decade.... [This] suggests that human behavior may involve, at least in part, a progressive integration of cognition with emotion." Integration of cognition with emotion—the melding of what we know with what we feel—is the very integration the healing process in ADD requires. Lack of it underlies the fragmentation of the ADD mind.

As a child psychiatrist, Stanley Greenspan has had a special interest in the treatment of autism, a form of neurophysiological and psychological dysfunction far more disabling than attention deficit disorder. Dr. Greenspan reports that some children with autism have been helped to become intelligent and emotionally healthy, with "cognitive, emotional and social skills in the normal or even superior range." He asks a pertinent question: "If large numbers of children who showed such severe physiological symptoms that they were diagnosed as autistic or retarded could be brought into interaction patterns that allowed them enormous growth, what of lesser challenges?"[5] We should view this question as a call to action for parents, teachers, doctors and psychologists concerned with attention deficit disorder, and also for adults who are themselves struggling with the effects of their ADD traits. It is no small challenge to promote the neurophysiological and emotional development of either a child or an adult with ADD, but it is far from impossible, as we shall see.

According to Carl Rogers, the healing process relies on the basic trustworthiness of human nature.[6] It is a false belief that the human child is an egotistical savage needing to be tamed. Infants do go through a phase of complete narcissism when they have no sense of any experience or point of view other than their own and see the world only in terms of their own needs. This is a natural stage, a part of development, reflecting only the wants of the helpless young human being. It is a phase we outgrow, or become stuck in, depending on circumstances. The child will attain maturity, compassion and the capacity for focused effort if the conditions for development are provided.

Many times, dealing with an ADD child seems utterly impossible. The understandable desire of parents is for point-by-point advice: What do I do in this situation? How do I handle that? Important as such questions are, they are secondary. The answers to them depend on how one interprets the child's behaviors and on what the long-term objectives are. What we want to promote is not a mere change of behavior but a transformation of inner experience leading to the development of self-regulation.

Every child with ADD has been wounded by a disruption in the relationship between the caregiver and the sensitive infant. All the behaviors and mental patterns of attention deficit disorder are external signs of the wound, or inefficient defenses against feeling the pain of it. If development is to take place, energy has to be liberated for growth that now is consumed in protecting the self from further hurt. The key factor is cementing the attachment relationship.

Science tells us that not even in rodents can the link between emotions and mental organization be ignored. In her Berkeley laboratory, Dr. Marian Cleeves Diamond found improvements in the problem-solving capacity of rats treated with tender loving care corresponding with the growth of richer connections in their cortex. "Thus, it is important to stimulate the portion of the brain that initiates emotional expression," Dr. Cleeves Diamond writes. "Satisfying emotional needs is essential at any age."[7]

In human brains, the circuitry of reason and emotion are closely connected, which is why troubled relationships lead directly to difficulties in brain processing. They are not the only cause of disorganized thinking, but they are by far the commonest cause. Restoring relationships on a healthy basis promotes mental organization. New ways of processing emotions need new neural circuits, and the wiring of new circuits requires new experiences in a favorable emotional milieu. The relationship with the parents is the earth, the rain, the sun and the shade in which the child's mental development must blossom. First and foremost, it is in the context of the family that children will have transforming experiences that nourish growth.

In his book *On Becoming a Person*, Carl Rogers described a warm, caring attitude, for which he adopted the phrase *unconditional positive regard* because, he said, "It has no conditions of worth attached to it." This is a caring, wrote Rogers, "which is not possessive, which demands no personal gratification. It is an atmosphere which simply demonstrates I care; not I care for you if you behave thus and so."[8] So the first thing is to create some space in the child's heart of hearts for the certainty that she is precisely the person the parents want and love. She does not have to do anything, or be any different, to earn that love—in fact, she *cannot* do anything, because the love cannot be won and cannot be lost. It is not conditional. It is completely independent of the child's behavior. It is just there, regardless of which side the child is acting from, "good" or "bad." The child can be ornery, unpleasant, whiny, un-cooperative and plain rude, and the parent still lets her feel loved. Ways have to be found to let the child know that certain behaviors are unacceptable, without making the child herself feel not accepted. She has to be able to bring her unrest, her least likable side, to the parent without fear that it would threaten the relationship. When that is made possible, absolute security is established. We can reliably expect emotional growth to follow.

Parents need to keep asking themselves which goal they think is more important: a desired short-term outcome, or long-term development. It's nice when that question does not have to be faced, but often the two are incompatible and even antagonistic. Choosing one means, for that moment at least, giving up on the other. If the child is to be freed to go through the necessary developmental stages, the attachment relationship with the parent has to be made paramount. Our immediate objective of getting the child to obey or to perform this or that task may need to be sacrificed. On the other hand, tactics needed to achieve short-term behavior goals may have to involve the weakening of the attachment. Especially in the beginning, the parent will be confronting those options regularly.

The unfortunate "time-out" technique of disciplining is an archetypical example of how opting for the short-term goal can harm attachment and therefore be ruinous to the long-term objective. In "time out" the small child is sent to his room or otherwise banished from contact with the parent for varying periods of time, and is supposed thereby to learn the difference between good and bad behavior. That is not what they learn. Time out requires raising as a threat the worst nightmare a young child can have—being cut off from the parent. Whatever the parent intends, the message received by the child is *If you do not do as I want you to do, if you displease me, I am quite ready to sever the relationship with you. I only want you around on my terms.* Time out may achieve its immediate goal, especially with a young child already anxious about his attachment with the parent and thus inclined to please. The effect, however, is to increase the child's anxiety and, deep down, the child's rage as well. Anxiety will diminish the child's capacity to develop self-regulation. There is, too, the danger that eventually, when he is no longer so dependent on the parent—in adolescence, for example—the child will detach from the relationship. The only justifiable use for this method is to help a parent who feels out of control to collect himself before pursuing further interaction with the child. In this case, the child is not being blamed or threatened.

A daily illustration of the conflict between the short-term and long-term objectives occurs with the ADD child who is slow as a sloth getting up and ready in the morning. The parent dutifully wakes her at seven-thirty, giving her a generous hour before it's time to leave for school. After several reminders, the child finally moves out of bed and, with a lot of cajoling from the parent, dresses for breakfast. She eats slowly, playing with her food. In the bathroom to wash hands and face, she becomes distracted by the nail clippers. She appears ten minutes later, nails haphazardly trimmed, hair unbrushed and jam around her mouth from breakfast. Her shoes are not on. She has to search for her schoolbag, misplaced the previous night. The school bell will ring in less than a quarter of an hour. The parent's sense of urgency and anger are by now rising exponentially. The more insistent his tone, the less cooperative the child. He finally yells at her to get ready "or else." The child's face darkens, she hurriedly pulls her shoes on and they silently leave the house. During the drive to school the atmosphere is funereal. When he bends toward her to kiss her goodbye before she leaves the car, she pulls away. Tomorrow some version of this will be acted out again.

The parent has, just barely, achieved the short-term goal of getting the child to school on time. But at what cost? At the cost of another disruption of his daughter's safety in the relationship. The ADD child is not capable of understanding what triggered her father's outburst, at least not at that moment. She has poor self-insight to begin with, owing to her age and owing, as well, to the developmental delay that prevents such children from being able to view the world from another person's perspective. Her psychological alarm system notes only the sudden changes in the parent's face and tone from support to hostility, and she senses in them a threat or an unfair punishment. She is far too consumed by her fear or anger to consider what behavior on her part contributed to the tense situation. Secure attachment has been undermined. So, for that reason, has the long-term goal of development.

As a parent, I have found myself in this situation many times. I have felt the frustrated helplessness of being caught between the urgency to meet some inflexible deadline on the one hand and the recalcitrant immobility of a son or daughter on the other. The temptation is to scream, to take matters physically in hand without regard to the feelings and emotional reactions thus stirred up in the child. I have gone so far as to threaten to drag my child to school in her pajamas, or semidressed and barefoot, if necessary. One can get a child to school on time by such threats and desperation tactics— on time, but frightened, angry and humiliated. Again, at what cost?

Let's replay that scene with a slightly different emphasis. The parent decides that being at school on time is not a question of life or death. There are natural consequences for a child who is chronically late, so it's not a lesson he has to drive home to her this very morning. Without that sense of urgency, the father no longer sees the situation as a power struggle to be won at all costs. Not allowing his frustration to get in the way, the parent can maintain his empathy with the child. From this change of attitude a change of technique automatically follows. He firmly but gently reminds her about the passing of time but does not allow himself to become hooked and filled with anger—it is, after all, the child's problem. He has let go of the short-term goal, so there is nothing to get angry about. His frustration does not block his loving feelings: he puts a higher value on the attachment relationship than on relieving his momentary frustration.

A child free of anxiety about a break in the relationship with her parent can gradually become more conscious of other priorities, such as being on time for school. She feels accepted even with her faults. The attachment relationship is maintained, and further room has been cleared for development. Eventually, the question of punctuality will resolve itself. The world will teach her the necessary lessons, if she is helped to become open to learning. What the parents are teaching the child is that her well-being and security are more important to them than behavioral goals, and that conflicts between people do not have to end in emotional estrangement. They also demonstrate their basic faith that the child is okay and has the capacity to deal with her problems. Nor do they need to fear that they are facing years of agonizing tardiness. A few weeks, perhaps longer, but once the attachment relationship does become consistently fixed as the fundamental value, parents will be amazed and gratified how rapidly their child responds with cooperative behavior. Even more surprising to them will be that their rigid rules and their expectations become less important as they learn to place their emotional bonds with their child above everything else.

It may be, of course, that a parent cannot avoid pressuring the child because his own work schedule simply does not allow for any lateness. In that case, he should acknowledge his stake and at least make some emotional room for the child's reactions. It is often not our children's behavior but our inability to tolerate their negative responses that creates the greatest difficulties. We ourselves may need to get to work on time, but there is no earthly reason why our anxious and sensitive child should take on that priority. School, in fact, may represent a separation from the parent that the child does not at all want. If parents learn to anticipate the child's impulsive expressions of negative emotion and are not threatened by them, the cycle of escalating anger or rejection can be broken. The parent remains firm but loving and resists becoming embroiled in emotional hostilities. It is not a war. He does not need to gain a victory over the child but only over his own anxiety and lack of self-control.

# 17

# Wooing the Child

Regardless of age, youngsters can begin working on
developmental levels they have been unable to master,
but they can do so only in the context of a close, personal
relationship with a devoted adult.

    — STANLEY GREENSPAN, M.D., *The Growth of*
     *the Mind*

BRIAN IS ELEVEN YEARS OLD, in Grade 5. His parents described the typical ADD signs of disorganization, short attention span, easy distractibility. His moods fluctuate. He can work himself into a rage or a sulk from one moment to the next. "I don't even know what sets him off sometimes," his mother said. "If I tell him to stop, he just covers his ears with his hands. He won't listen." The father said that bedtimes were impossible, school mornings a "nightmare," suppertime "a zoo." In his fits of anger, Brian could become sharply insulting toward his parents, to the point of obscenity. At such times, they could barely recognize in him the lively and engaging child they know him to be.

My advice to Brian's mother and father was that they not bring their son in for assessment just yet, but instead put the emphasis on the dynamics of their interaction with him. The kind of hostility

Brian was exhibiting has one source: an unconscious sense of being cut off from the parents, of having been abandoned. He experienced his parents' frustrated criticisms and attempts at discipline as rejection. I felt that to deal with his behaviors as "the problem" would only evoke resistance in him and that, in any case, the behaviors were only an acting-out of deep emotions of pain and insecurity. I referred Brian's parents to a highly skilled developmental psychologist for counseling. Before they could successfully embark on any effort to help their son with his ADD, they needed to reestablish their relationship with him on a much more safe, supportive and nonadversarial ground. To do that, this mother and father would have to understand just where in emotional development their son stood in relationship to them: at the maturational level of an anxiety-ridden toddler. We agreed we would meet in three months.

On their return visit, the parents reported a changed atmosphere in the home. Brian's outbursts had mostly stopped. When they did come, they were considerably milder than before and did not last long. There was significantly less resistance to getting ready to go to school in the mornings and much less of a to-do at bedtimes. Brian's attention problems continued, and he still had trouble being organized. He was far more motivated and resilient, however, and did not become discouraged nearly so easily. He was also less resistant to accepting help from his parents and able to acknowledge that he was having some difficulties, that he wasn't being criticized because everyone was against him. I suggested that medications might be beneficial. The father was in favor of trying them, but the mother was not. She preferred to continue to build the relationship and Brian's self-esteem, and to see how things went over the next half year or so.

This couple was helped by their son's sensitivity, the same characteristic that in the past gave rise to so many difficulties. Children with ADD may be highly susceptible to the negative aspects of their environment, but the other side of the coin is that they are equally responsive to positive changes. The very sensitivity that makes them vulnerable is also an asset that gives them tremendous potential for development. Just as this boy was highly reactive to his parents' anxiety-driven behaviors toward him, he was able to thrive as he felt greater security in his relationship with them. By nature a warm and affectionate child, as most children with ADD are, he soaked up the warmth his parents were now increasingly able to give him. This mother and father were surprised and delighted by how quickly, after only a few months of changing their approach, their son began to achieve important milestones of emotional growth.

Whether or not I prescribe medications, in all cases I tell the parents that what they do themselves to draw the child closer to them emotionally is far more important in the long run. In his work with autistic children, Stanley Greenspan describes this as *wooing the child into relationship*. It is the basis for everything else we try to do for the child. Learning techniques, behavioral modification and other strategies are all on a firm base only if the attachment relationship is maintained. Otherwise, they rest on sand.

The following principles help to restore and solidify the parent-child attachment. The reversal of ADD patterns in a child begins with them. They have been successfully employed by a number of parents I have worked with, and I can personally attest to their efficacy as well. Their value is not restricted to the ADD child; they are the fundamentals of working with any child, and particularly with any troubled child, ADD or not. The long-term project of promoting healthy development in a child with attention deficit disorder becomes next to hopeless without a consistent attempt to apply these principles.

1. *The parent takes active responsibility for the relationship*
*Technique: Invite the child*
*Goal: Fostering the child's self-acceptance*
The parents enthusiastically and genuinely invite the child into relationship. They do not issue declarations of love; they demonstrate day by day that they want the child's company. They think of things to do together, or they just "hang out" with the child, with an attitude of active attention. When they are with the child,

they are fully there, not just being dutiful, putting in time. They have active energy that radiates toward the child. They make sure they have space in their lives for the child.

Being wanted and enjoyed is the greatest gift the child can receive. It is the basis of self-acceptance. ADD children, without exception, harbor a deep insecurity about themselves. It is essential to demonstrate to such a child that his very *existence* is appreciated. The parent may put out this message verbally, but if she does not *live* the message by a commitment of time and energy, the child will receive mixed signals at best.

Whenever possible, the parent does the inviting. That may be a chore. A highly insecure child can be exhaustingly demanding of time and attention. Understandably, the parent may long for respite, not more engagement. The conundrum is that attention given at the request of the child is never satisfactory: it leaves an uncertainty that the parent is only responding to demands, not voluntarily giving of himself, or herself, to the child. The demands only escalate, without the emotional need underlying them ever being filled. *The solution is to seize the moment, to invite contact exactly when the child is not demanding it.* Or, if responding to the child's request, the parent can take the initiative, expressing more interest and enthusiasm than the child herself anticipates: "Oh, that's a great idea. I was wondering how we could spend time together! I'm so glad you thought of it." This will take the child by surprise and make her feel that she is the one receiving the invitation.

Woo the child, as one would woo anyone with whom one wanted a relationship.

2. *The parent does not judge the child*
   *Technique: Avoid pointing out faults, mistakes, shortcomings*
   *Goal: To increase security, reduce shame*
   Shame, as we have seen, is the physiological-emotional state resulting from the sense of being isolated, cut off. The ADD child is mired in shame. She will express it in many ways. There may be self-abusive statements such as "I'm stupid." There may also be

their opposite: a complete denial of the child's own negative contributions to her interactions with others: "So-and-so is mean. She is always starting fights." When someone's shame is deep, he may defend himself by rejecting even the slightest suggestion of wrongdoing on his own part. There is no point countering with logic either the self-putdowns or the self-protective attitude of the child. Shame does not arise in the left hemisphere of the brain; it will not be dislodged by left-brain logical and verbal means. One weakens shame by not feeding it, by not doing anything to make the child feel isolated or deficient.

Criticism from the parent is devastating to a sensitive child with low self-esteem. As parents, we sometimes do not hear the critical tone in our words. The child, on the other hand, hears only the tone, not the words. The emotion-processing centers on the right side of the brain interpret the tone as rejection and invalidation. If the parent wants to help the child improve a skill or an attitude, it's best to do it warmly, respecting the child's vulnerability. It should not even be attempted if the relationship happens to be on shaky ground. When in doubt, it is best to bite the parental tongue rather than to utter a critical comment. At all times, the child must sense that the parent's acceptance of him does not depend on how well he does something. It is not threatened by poor performance. It is unconditional.

As a child develops a stronger self-concept, she becomes more and more open to help or correction in areas of difficulty. Acknowledging that she may have shortcomings is no longer so scary if she feels that these do not threaten her relationship with the parent.

3. *The parent does not overpraise the child*
   *Technique: Give praise in measured terms; reflect back the child's feelings*
   *Goal: Reinforcing the child's confidence that achievements are not needed to earn the parent's acceptance and respect*

Too much praise can be almost as harmful as too much criticism. They seem opposite, but the underlying message is the same: the parent puts a high value not on who the child is, but on what he does. This is why many ADD children, no matter how much they crave and court attention, are uncomfortable with praise. Nature's own agenda is hindered when parents foster what the developmental psychologist Gordon Neufeld calls *acquired self-esteem*, that based on external evaluations. "We don't want to build a child's self-esteem on how pretty they are, how popular they are, how smart they are, how good they are in baseball, how well they do in school," he says. "There is a much, much truer, more solid type of self-esteem we can provide for our children than something that just follows cultural trends and approximates cultural norms. We should avoid making children believe that these things influence how we feel about them."

The parent acknowledges warmly when the child does something well or achieves a new milestone but makes his comments about the deed rather than about the child, about the effort rather than about the result. And he refers to the child's own emotions. "You really worked hard on that. Good for you. You stuck with it even though it was difficult." How the child feels about what he does is far more important than what the parent thinks about it. A positive evaluation by the parent is still an evaluation, a judgment. It leaves a question: how would they feel about me if they could not judge me favorably? People do not need judgments—they need acceptance.

4. *One does not parent from anger*
*Technique: When the parent feels anger, he refrains from criticizing, giving orders, expressing opinions*
*Goal: To avoid faulting the child for even a momentary break in the relationship with the parent*
The shame bound into the personality of any child (or adult) with ADD is easily activated. When the child is confronted by a parent's anger—face tight, voice harsh, words cutting—he immediately experiences a loss of contact with the loving mother or father. He is thrown into the physiological shame state, or into a reactive and aggressive rage meant to keep shame at bay. He feels keenly the

accusation, which the parent may or may not intend, that he, the child, is responsible for the parent's emotional withdrawal. The loss of the loving parental presence is especially frightening for an insecure and sensitive child. He also feels confirmed in his core belief that he does not deserve warm contact with anyone. He may not show this directly, and may even react with seeming indifference and arrogant dismissal. But the most defiant behavior is nothing more than a defense against overwhelming shame. The more entrenched the child's psychological defenses become, the more difficult the parent will find it to build the relationship.

Avoiding feeling anger altogether is an impossible goal for any parent, and especially for the parent of an ADD child. One should not set oneself up for failure by thinking that it is just a matter of resolutions and good intentions. The behavior and impulsiveness of the child would try the patience of saints—parents are bound to react. The parent may himself have a volatile personality. It is unrealistic to expect to be able to remain calm all the time, but when a parent feels the anger rising, he may disqualify himself from parenting for as long as it takes to cool down and regain some balance: "I'm feeling too upset right now. It's not your fault. I'm not feeling in control. I can handle it, but I need time out." Gordon Neufeld likens this to throwing the clutch into neutral when the motor starts racing too fast. It is of great help if one is able to call on a spouse or some other trusted adult to take the steering wheel at such moments.

To try to teach a child any useful lessons when cold anger seizes hold is self-defeating. In the biochemical soup of stress and shame, no learning can take place. The child's nervous system is simply not receptive; it is too concerned with survival. At best, the child adopts techniques to avoid the parent's rage. There is a type of anger that we may call warm anger, which is not damaging. This is anger under control. It addresses the deed without attacking the child, and it does not carry the threat of parental withdrawal. Children can handle this type of anger and can learn from it, especially if in general they feel secure in the relationship with the parent.

5. *The parent takes responsibility for restoring the relationship*
*Technique: Do not wait for the child to reestablish contact after a fight*
*Goal: Allowing the child to feel that the attachment relationship is*
*greater than whatever argument or disagreement may come between him*
*and the parent*

As parents, we may as well accept that we will "lose it" at times. Perfect equanimity is beyond us. Temporary breaks in the relationship with the child are inevitable and are not in themselves harmful, unless they are frequent and catastrophic. The real harm is inflicted when the parent makes the child work at reestablishing contact, as in forcing a child to apologize before granting "forgiveness." There is neither genuine remorse nor genuine forgiveness in such situations, only humiliation. Since in principle nothing the child does should threaten the relationship in the first place, he should have to do no work to restore it.

So, if the parent has lost it, it is his responsibility to restore the interpersonal bridge. This should not take the form of abject apologies, and promises not to be "mean" any more. Assuredly, we will lose it again—no point pledging not to. Restoring the bridge simply means acknowledging that we see what has happened and understand how the child might feel about it and hearing nondefensively what the child has to say. When she expresses her feelings about the negative interaction—and even if she does so in a form difficult for the parent to take—the parent does not explain himself or try to justify his behavior. He just listens with empathy.

When they give priority to the attachment relationship, parents are not only building the child's sense of security and self-acceptance. They are themselves modeling the most important lesson for the child to learn: the importance of remembering the future. They are putting the emphasis on development and healing, not on short-term—and short-lived—objectives.

# 18

# Like Fish in

# the Sea

Parents who are faced with the development of children
must constantly live up to a challenge. They must
develop with them.

— ERIK H. ERIKSON, *Childhood and Society*

N ANY COMMUNITY OF BEINGS living in close
contact with each other, the behavior of individuals can be understood only in the context of their
relationship to the group as a whole. In an ant colony, for example,
larvae are hatched with essentially identical genetic makeups. Who
becomes queen or worker or soldier is determined by the needs of
the group, not by individual predisposition. The requirements of
the community shape the physiology and functions of each ant.
The human family is not an exception to this rule. It, too, forms a
system that powerfully influences not just the early development of
its young but also their behaviors and development later on. Understanding the family system can be turned to great advantage in
promoting the healing process of the child with ADD.

At no time in life do behaviors reflect a relationship with significant others more closely than in childhood, because at no time in life are people as emotionally and physically dependent on others. We think that children *act*, whereas what they mostly do is *react*. Parents who realize this acquire a powerful tool. By noticing their own responses to the child, rather than fixating on the child's responses to them, they free up tremendous energy for growth. "If parents shift their focus off the child and become more responsible for their own actions, the child will automatically (perhaps after testing whether the parents really mean it) assume more responsibility for himself," writes Michael Kerr, psychiatrist and director of training at Georgetown University Family Center. "If parents focus on being responsible for themselves and respecting boundaries in relating to their children, the children will automatically grow towards being responsible for themselves."[1] This taking of responsibility for oneself is based on the capacity for self-regulation.

As we have said, self-regulation is the goal of development; the lack of it is the fundamental impairment in ADD. One way of describing self-regulation is to say that it is the ability to maintain the internal environment within a functional and safe range, regardless of external circumstance. On the emotional level, the self-regulation of moods means that neither despondency nor uncontrolled exuberance, neither passive submission nor blind rage, control the mind. A person can experience frustration, disappointment or sadness without being seized by despair. Happiness does not need to be euphoria or anger hostility. Moods are not controlled by the vagaries of external events or by the moods of others.

Emotional self-regulation may be likened to a thermostat ensuring that the temperature in a home remains constant despite the extremes of weather conditions outside. When the environment becomes too cold, the heating system is switched on. If the air becomes overheated, the air conditioner begins to work. Or, to use an analogy from the animal kingdom, emotional self-regulation is like the capacity of the warm-blooded creature to exist in a greater range of environments. Its blood will neither chill nor overheat, no matter what the external temperature. The cold-blooded animal can endure a far narrower range of habitats because it does not have the capacity to self-regulate the internal environment. People with ADD, especially children, are like cold-blooded animals, in this sense. Their internal balance is too easily upset by even relatively slight external variations. They are too often reacting automatically instead of acting purposefully. Many find transitions stressful because they are not flexible enough to adjust emotionally to even small changes. Others with ADD thrive on constant turmoil and change. This also is a failure of internal regulation expressed in the need to take up new activities, new relationships or new situations constantly because the interest and energy level cannot be sustained from within, without highly charged external stimuli. When circumstances make that impossible, there is chaos or emptiness.

An indispensable condition for the evolution of self-regulation in children is its presence in the nurturing adults. In families where one child or another has ADD, the parents often lack this capacity. Their moods are not independent of the child. Almost all parents with an ADD child report that their son or daughter has an uncanny power to dictate what the emotional atmosphere of the family will be. "When he gets upset," one father said of his seven-year-old son, "the climate in our house can go from fair to foul in a matter of seconds. When he is happy, it is sunshine and joy all around." Should the child become downcast, the parents feel despair; if the child is angry, they themselves fly into a rage; when the child acts out of control, they feel helpless.

In some of the families I have seen, I've sensed an invisible umbilical cord that still connected a parent to the child. "It is true," one mother said. "If my son is happy, I am happy. If he is doing poorly, I am devastated." Not only the parents but other siblings as well seem to revolve in emotional orbits around the child with ADD. They naturally come to resent the control he or she appears to wield over the family.

Parents of an ADD child will often say that their son or daughter has a "powerful" personality. Far from being powerful, the child is weak and vulnerable. It's not his "power" but the inefficiency of the parents' own emotional thermostat that enables the fluctuations in the child's moods to set the emotional tone of the whole household. A child in this situation is deeply insecure. He is made insecure by his lack of emotional self-control because there are no adults around able to maintain a steady and functioning environment, whatever his own particular internal states may be. There is no development amid such a lack of safety. It only appears that the child's moods are in control, because the parents are unaware of how profoundly their own mind states and their own lack of internal self-regulation affect the child. It's another vicious cycle. The parents need the child to be in balance only because they are not. But because the parents are not independently in balance themselves, the child cannot be.

Let's examine the all-too-familiar dinner scene more closely. The ADD child is hungry, and therefore out of sorts. He may be slow coming to the table, or may even refuse to do so. "Fine," the mother says testily, "we will just have to eat without you." The child now takes his place at the table sullenly, picks at his food and utters a stream of complaints about this or that aspect of the meal, or he may stay out of the kitchen altogether. From another room, he yells protests and insults at his parents and siblings, the message being that no one cares about him, or that he wants no part of such a selfish and unlikable collection of people. Either way, his mood will infect the entire family.

As the tension mounts, the mother casts an exasperated and defeated look at her husband. He, in turn, slams his fist on the table, leaps up and roars at his son, who is still defiantly complaining. It no longer matters who wins the ensuing yelling match, or whether it ends with the father trying to drag the boy to the table or to his room. Everyone's mood is dark, the dinner is ruined and all the rest of the family is confirmed in their belief that there is something terribly wrong with this particular child.

Some version of this story is recounted by most parents of a child with ADD at the very first visit to my office. Understandably, they are desperate for advice. They want to be given parenting techniques to help them be more effective in such distressing situations. "What are we supposed to do?" is one of the first questions. "How do we handle it when our son is so completely out of control?"

There are many books and other aids that advise mothers and fathers of children with ADD on techniques of motivating the child, helping him get organized, controlling his behavior. "We have listened to tape after tape given to us by our psychiatrist on how to do this or that," one father said, "but nothing works." Methods may fail not because they are not reasonable but because in themselves they do not address the emotional context, the emotional transaction that, unseen, takes place between the parent and the child.

What matters above all is not the technique, but the degree of parental self-regulation. The fundamental issue is not *how to parent*, but *who is parenting*? By this I don't mean which parent, the mother or the father, but the state of mind of the adults as they respond to the child. The unbearable tension that arises in scenes such as the suppertime drama we have just witnessed is only partly due to the child's behavior. It is fed and magnified out of all proportion by the anxiety the child's oppositionality provokes in the parents. Such anxiety has many roots, including the parents' fear of losing control, their exasperation at having yet another family scene ruined, their emotional pain at being so attacked by the child and a deep-seated pessimism that unless it's nipped in the bud, their child's bad behavior will be only the harbinger of much worse as he gets older. In short, the child triggers the parents' anxiety. Anxious parents revert to behaviors characteristic of young children without self-regulation: impulsiveness, rage, physical acting-out or helplessness. Approached in this manner, the hyperreactive ADD child will be propelled into yet greater anxiety, manifested in ever-escalating and seemingly impervious hostility or in fearful clinginess.

If we revisited this family, but with the parents' having developed a little more self-regulation, the outcome would be quite different. Self-regulation in this context has nothing to do with "controlling one's temper." What we call "temper" is only an automatic anxiety response. It is the reaction of a person who cannot tolerate the feeling of anxiety. Self-regulation is not the absence of anxiety, at least not in the very beginning, but *a person's ability to tolerate her own anxiety*. As the child begins his well-choreographed routine at suppertime, the parents now see that becoming tense is only one of any number of possible responses on their part. They do not then have to suppress their own anxiety by trying to control the child's moods and behaviors. They could just see him as a child who has some growing to do.

The parent who can tolerate her anxiety does not need to respond to the child with anger, emotional coldness or pleading. The child is not under pressure to change his behavior immediately in order for the parent to feel comfortable. If the parents do not react with their usual anxious manner and their voices do not convey anger or despair, the child himself will not feel further anxiety. If the child knows that the parent is okay even if the child is not okay, he feels safer. Whatever his immediate response may now be, it no longer has the power to escalate the conflict. He can relax a little.

When he does not have to put up defenses against parental hostility, the child can more easily get in touch with his deep-seated wish to be part of the family circle or with his sadness at feeling excluded from it. When the child shows even a hint of his vulnerability, in place of his defenses, the parent can immediately move in and establish contact. The child can feel secure with a parent whom he cannot reduce to his own level of functioning. When safety is established, growth takes place.

The parents of children with ADD have to strive for self-knowledge. That is the first prerequisite for nurturing the development of the child. Even with the best of goodwill, no one can long escape her unconscious. The passing on of psychological burdens from one generation to the next occurs around those issues that the parents are least aware of in themselves, and it occurs precisely when the child pushes the parent's unconscious emotional buttons. Many parents have had the frustrating experience of going into a situation with optimism and a firm idea which parenting technique to employ, only to find themselves soon yelling at the child or withdrawing from her, completely sabotaging their own best intentions. Our knowledge of parenting techniques, like all intellectual knowledge and learning, is a function of the cognitive left side of the brain, while who the parent is—what face she turns toward the child—is at any given moment determined largely by forceful emotional mechanisms governed in the right hemisphere. A struggle between hemispheres is an unequal battle. Once our deepest emotions are stirred—as they so easily are in our interactions with our children—intellect and understanding are quickly subdued.

The professional literature on ADD talks of "maintenance factors" that reinforce or trigger ADD traits. No maintenance factor is more powerful than the emotional states of the parents. Unresolved psychological conflicts between the parents, and within each parent individually, are a major source of unrest for the hypersensitive ADD child. This anxiety absorbed by sensitive children will lead to hyperactivity or other ADD-related behaviors.

Parents who put the attention on their own psychological functioning soon notice this highly interdependent relationship between their moods and the level of the ADD child's reactivity. Much of what the parent interprets as problematic or disturbed behavior represents the child's automatic right-brain responses to the parent's emotional messages. Only superficially are dysfunctional responses the results of her "disorder." They do not originate purely from within herself. The child is manifesting what the noted family therapist and author David Freeman calls the parents' "unfinished business."[2] That she does so is a sign of her immature self-regulation, but what she expresses by her acting-out says as much about her environment as about herself.

Dr. Freeman defines unfinished business as "a present emotional reaction shaped by a past experience. It is a reactive response guided by strong emotional feelings based on past experiences of anxiety.... Behaviour on the part of our spouse or children that appears critical, distant, or unloving will trigger anxiety and doubt in us and block our ability to be loving and nurturing," writes Dr. Freeman.

Children swim in their parents' unconscious like fish in the sea, in the succinct phrase of the Vancouver psychotherapist Andrew Feldmar. To create safety for their children, parents need to devote energy and commitment to processing their own "unfinished business." In this way they can do much more to further the development of their child than by any behavioral approaches aimed at motivating the child or at making him more compliant.

Self-regulation is intimately connected with a process developmental psychology has called *individuation*, or *differentiation*. Individuation—becoming a self-motivating, self-accepting person, a true individual—is the ultimate goal of development. As individuation unfolds, children are able to move more and more independently into the world, impelled by their own interests and needs. Less and less do they require that another person see exactly what they see in order to feel validated, or that another person feel exactly what they feel. They may have needs and desire for closeness, warmth and mutual support with another human being, but they do not need to be emotionally fused with the other person—they can function on their own, if need be.

If parents are to foster individuation in their children, they must also work on their own maturation. Try as they might, poorly individuated parents cannot successfully foster individuation in their children. They are likely to have unsatisfactory relationships with their partners, especially after children begin arriving to upset the fragile emotional balance between them. They are also likely to fuse emotionally with one or another of their children. There may be the semblance of a close relationship between parent and child, but in reality the child's individuation is hindered, as he grows up feeling automatically responsible for the parent's feeling states. Later the child will harbor a sense of responsibility for the whole world. Even what can be seen as selfish behaviors represent nothing more than unconscious and desperate efforts to throw off that sense of overwhelming responsibility.

"Our troubles began with the birth of our son," the mother of a young boy with ADD told me. "Then things started to fall apart." Neither partner in this couple was highly individuated when they got married, and neither could function without anxiety unless they felt loved or supported by another person. They could avoid feeling their anxiety because their closeness compensated for their lack of emotional confidence in themselves as individuals. When their son was born, the mother naturally had to direct much of her nurturing energy toward the baby. Her own needs for emotional bonding were also satisfied, in part, by the close contact with the infant. She could feel intense joy, for example, when she was breast-feeding. For the father, it was a different story. Without knowing it, he began to exhibit behavior that betrayed mounting anxiety. Increasingly he resented what he interpreted as his wife's reduced sexual interest in him, tired as she was from nights interrupted by the baby's feeding needs. He did not realize that what he imagined was sheer sexual frustration was in reality his dissatisfaction at finding himself psychologically on his own more than he could handle. He made demands, and when they were frustrated, he began to withdraw emotionally. He threw himself into his work, which helped to alleviate his need for emotional contact and therefore his anxiety, but, in turn, led to anxiety in the mother, who now felt quite alone in the relationship.

The emotional balance in the home, increasingly tenuous, was easily upset. Neither parent being sufficiently differentiated, each reacted strongly to the other and to the ADD patterns their son was showing more and more as he approached school age. The wheel of anxiety was continually kept in motion. If these parents had had the opportunity in their own families of origin to become more independent individuals, the anxiety cycle would not have begun.

Not depending so much on his wife's complete emotional availability, the father would have been able to tolerate her devoting all
her nurturing attention to the child. Nor would she have interpreted as abandonment the signs of his anxiety.

Family therapy helped this couple to realize their mutual and
interlocking emotional dependencies. No longer so threatened
each time their partner seemed a little aloof or unavailable, they
were able to tolerate a little bit more emotional space around
themselves without feeling bereft. They learned to see their son as
a separate individual rather than as an extension of themselves, no
longer feeling personally devastated when he experienced distress
or acted out in some immature fashion. Having a stronger identity
allowed each of them to put less stock on what other people
thought of them, which meant that they had less need to control
their son's behavior simply to spare themselves embarrassment.
The result was that their son felt more accepted by his parents,
which gave a boost to his self-confidence and self-acceptance. He
now demanded less affirmation from his peers, who no longer had
to keep him at arm's length because they could not handle his
neediness. Less taken up with social anxiety, he became more calm
and more attentive in the classroom.

These changes did not take place overnight. The couple experienced failures and setbacks before they could feel sure that they
were on a healing path. They had to keep in mind the long-term
goal, development, to avoid reacting with self-defeating behavior
whenever their anxiety was triggered either by their partner or by
their child. At no point could they definitively say that their son
had left all his problems behind. But as they developed, so did their
son.

As long as parents are willing to look into themselves, they will
stay on a learning curve, and their child will have the safety that
encourages development. If this challenge is taken up, the diagnosis of attention deficit disorder can be the beginning of a healing
process for the child and for the whole family; otherwise, it may
become a trap. The parents may become fixated on "treatments"

for the child's "disorder," which can contribute to the child's own sense, deeply embedded in her psyche, that there is something wrong with her. No doubt there is disorder, but it involves the entire family system. If the child is to heal, the family system must heal.

To maintain compassion toward their children, parents have to be compassionate toward themselves as well and spare themselves their own harsh self-judgments. Inevitably there will be mistakes, many times when they will "blow it." It's all right. Although sensitive, children are not made of glass and do not break that easily. They are, in fact, highly resilient. As normal human beings, we are bound to have our emotional ups and downs, our moments of greater or lesser emotional balance.

"I feel like I always have to be on," one mother complained. "If I am even slightly off, everything goes to pieces." No one can be "always on." But a giant stride forward is made when parents recognize the need to monitor their own emotional states and the level of tension in the entire household. If children swim in their parents' unconscious, it is good to make sure that the water stays clear. Or at least as clear as possible.

# 19

# Just Looking

# for Attention

The child who seeks constant attention is, of necessity, an unhappy child. He feels that unless he gets attention he is worthless, has no place. He seeks constant reassurance that he is important. Since he *doubts* this, no amount of reassurance will ever impress him.

—RUDOLF DREIKURS, M.D., *Children: the Challenge*

ADD CHILDREN, ALL TOO OFTEN even after they have been diagnosed, suffer the preconceived notions and judgments of the adult world. Common to all these is the assumption that the child's actions, and in particular how the parent responds to them, are the responsibility of the child and that he could change them at will. In this chapter, we look at five of the most damaging misconceptions applied to the ADD child.

*Myth 1: The child is just looking for attention*

There is no more common disparagement of the ADD child than that she is "just looking for attention," a phrase one hears from many an exasperated parent and teacher. "Yes," I say. "That's absolutely right. The child is looking for attention. Only there is no 'just' about it."

Attention of the right kind is the child's central need, the lack of it her central anxiety. Recognizing that transforms the meaning of the very name *attention deficit disorder*. As politicians intent on further cutbacks in public services such as health care and education are forever reminding us, a deficit is incurred when one pays out more than one receives. The child with ADD has had to pay out more attention than she has received, which is precisely how she has incurred an attention deficit.

It may be perfectly true, as many parents point out, that their ADD child monopolizes their attention to such a degree that other children in the family come to feel neglected. The trouble is, by the time ADD behaviors are present, the child is provoking much more negative than positive attention, which gets worse as she becomes older. It may seem paradoxical, but many children will go for negative attention rather than for no attention at all. They do not do this consciously, but they do it. The child acts out, partly to gain attention. The adult responds with a punishing look, act, or statement that the child's brain interprets as rejection. Her anxiety about being cut off from the adult is magnified, as is her desperation for attention. Only the adult can break this cycle. *The key to doing so is learning to give the child not the attention he is asking for, but the attention he needs.*

"Do not mistake a child for his symptom," writes the psychotherapist Erik Erikson. The attitude adults are best to adopt when it comes to dealing with the distressing behaviors of the ADD child is one of compassionate curiosity. The compassion is for the child who, beneath the surface of what so often is seen only as obnoxious behavior, is anxious and is hurting emotionally. The curiosity, if genuine and open-minded, leads us to consider exactly what message the child may be trying to communicate to us by a particular behavior, even more unbeknownst to herself than to us.

Compassionate curiosity can help us break the coded language of attention seeking. When the child is in one of his insatiable attention-hungry modes, the parent may become resentful and frustrated. She may feel trapped. She has already spent hours playing with the child, helping him clean his room, reading to him, being the audience for the child's performances. She feels she has nothing left to give at that moment, yet still the child demands more. The parent points out to the child just how much attention has already been devoted to him. The child argues, and the parent tries even harder to convince him. "You never want to play with me," says the child, hurt and angry. How can we understand this? I am worried that you don't want me around you, the child is really saying, and when I am anxious I do not know how to be on my own. One cannot successfully counter this unconscious feeling by arguing with the child, by showing him how mistaken he is. The more we try to convince him, the more he will be confirmed in yet another of his core beliefs, which is that nobody understands him and that perhaps no one wants to.

The look-at-me-ism of the ADD youngster is tiresome, insatiable and self-defeating. It represents a voracious appetite that cannot be appeased even if it achieves its immediate objective. Whatever the child receives in the emotional relationship with the parent only after demanding it has, by definition, no capacity to satisfy. Just as with unconditional acceptance, the child should not have to work for attention either by destructive acts or by look-at-me behaviors, or by "good boy, good girl" compliance. The hunger is eased by the parent's seizing every possible opportunity to devote positive attention to the child *precisely when the child has not demanded it*. "We have to satiate the child with attention, stuff her full of it until it's coming out her ears," says the developmental psychologist Gordon Neufeld. Once the attention hunger is alleviated, the "just-looking-for-attention" behaviors will lessen. As the child develops greater security in the relationship and greater confidence in herself, the motive driving these behaviors gradually weakens.

The parent has to be able to say a kind but firm no whenever he is unable to meet the child's insistent demands for attention. "I am just not up to doing that now," he may tell the child. Or, "That does not work for me right now." The statement is about the parent and does not express a judgment either about the child or about the particular activity in question. The operative word here is *kindness*. The problem is often not the parent's legitimate refusal per se but the punishing irritability with which the message is delivered.

The demand for attention, like all the child's demands, is a compensation for an unconscious emotional hunger. The parent may rightly deny some demand of the child's for attention, or any other demand, such as for the candy bar at the supermarket, but there is no reason that the child should be expected to understand that decision or to like it. The emotionally wounded child is struck by every refusal as by a rejection, even though no such rejection is intended by the parent. If the parent allows his reaction to the child's reaction to become cold and punishing, the child's anxiety will have turned into a self-fulfilling prophecy. In many situations it is fit and proper for the parent not to give in to the child's demands. The main thing is to refuse without blaming or humiliating the child for the attention seeking or for the demanding behavior. If we anticipate the child's reactions, understand their source and do not shame the child for them, the child will eventually learn to tolerate refusal. When we endure children's anger or frustration with compassion, they will often move on to the sadness of not having what they wish for, of having to give up what they think they need just then. At such moments, a parent can move in and witness that sadness with an empathy that will make the child feel understood and supported, despite the refusal.

Finally, as we consider the child's needs for attention, the parents' lifestyle has to be carefully examined. In an earlier chapter,

I mentioned my own workaholism and breakneck pace of living at the time my children were small. I observe similar patterns almost universally in the families I see for ADD assessment. One of, and often both, the parents may work long hours. Morning is rush, rush, rush, and the evening is no different. The parent comes home depleted and must put full energy into meeting the physical and emotional needs of a child who, for a whole day, may have been deprived of parental contact. And parents have often taken up other commitments—school committees, church bazaars, courses of various sorts and so on. Such extracurricular activities magnify the parent's level of preoccupation and stress, decreasing her patience with the child. Even during the time she devotes to the child, the parent's mind may be spinning with the events of the day and the chores yet to be done. Research shows that many parents spend virtually no more than five minutes, if that, of *meaningful* contact with their child each day. If that snippet of time is to grow, parents need to create some space around themselves, and in order to do so they may have to reconsider their lifestyle.

Socioeconomic trends greatly exacerbate the attention starvation of children. According to the Economic Policy Institute in the U.S., the average work year is now 158 hours longer than it was three decades ago. "An extra month has been tacked on to what in 1969 was considered a full-time job!" writes the psychologist Edward L. Deci. "It's extraordinary, really."[1] In such a society, it is only to be expected that many children would be looking for attention—looking for it, but not finding it.

Parents may need to change their lifestyles, sacrificing whatever activities can be eliminated if these diminish their availability to their ADD child. This could mean saying no and disappointing friends or colleagues, and it might mean giving up projects and involvements close to one's heart. There is a lot to be gained, however, for their child has already incurred a deficit of attention. Too, a poorly self-regulated child can hardly learn to be calm in a hyperactive atmosphere. Narrowing the range of activities is wrenching for many of us, but in terms of our children's development, the rewards far outweigh the cost. It may be a nonnegotiable condition for the healing of the child with attention deficit disorder.

### Myth 2: The child is deliberately trying to annoy the adult

"He is out to get a rise out of me, I swear to God," a father asserted of his ten-year-old son. Many parents find such motives to be a convincing explanation for their child's distressing behavior. On the face of it, this is a seemingly reasonable conclusion to arrive at: given the intelligence of many ADD children and the number of times they have been told not to do this or that, it may seem like they are misbehaving knowingly and on purpose. Fortunately, the assumption is wrong: these children are neither so cunning nor so malevolent. It is a mistake many of us make in our relationships with others, whether children or spouses, acquaintances or strangers, to imagine that we know the intentions behind the actions of others. Some psychologists refer to this misbelief as "intentional thinking."

The family therapist David Freeman once concluded a public lecture on intimacy and relationships by saying that if there was any one thing he hoped his audience would remember from his talk, it was the awareness that one does not know his or her spouse, his or her children. We may believe we have a perfect idea of why they act as they do, when in reality our beliefs reflect no more than our own anxieties. Whenever we ascribe a motive to the other person, as in "you are doing this because...," we discard curiosity and immobilize compassion. The person who knows has nothing to learn, has given up on learning. "In the beginner's mind there are many possibilities, in the expert's mind there are few," said the Zen master Shunryu Suzuki. It is good to be aware that we are beginners as we approach the ADD child.

In our interactions with children, intentional thinking gets in the way of seeing the child for who he really is. Worse, the judgments we deliver on our children become the self-judgments they will carry into adult life. "I was a bad kid," or "I was always trying to cause some trouble" frequently express the way adults with ADD recall themselves as children. The child sooner or later comes to see himself, as much as he may protest against it, through the negative opinion of the parent.

A dysfunctional search for attention underlies some of the behaviors of the ADD child, as we have just seen. Poor self-regulation, poor impulse control are also responsible for many behaviors, as are unconscious shame or rage or anxiety. All these are expressions of vulnerability and pain, not of bad intent. And even if, on a given occasion, there is consciously harmful intent, we still need to maintain the spirit of compassionate curiosity. "Why would a child want to do harm?" asked without prejudgment is a question that can provide fertile ground for inquiry. What happened to this child to make her this way? What is happening now in her life to make her act it out? There is much we can find out if we know that we don't know.

### Myth 3: The child purposefully manipulates the parent

In the category of intentional thinking is the belief that the child is manipulative or controlling. It's worth a closer look because it is another commonly held misperception that visits harsh judgment on ADD children. No child is by nature manipulative, no child by nature controlling. A child who does develop a propensity to manipulate or to control others is doing so out of weakness, not strength. Manipulation and the drive to control are fear responses based on unconscious anxieties. The truly strong person need not be so afraid that she has to direct and control every aspect of her environment. Given that children are always the weaker party in the relationship with the adult, it is natural for them to want to control at times. "I don't know why we hold it against our child," says Gordon Neufeld. "The most ridiculous thing we can say is that 'my child is trying to manipulate me.' It's like saying the rain is wet. Of course children want to get their own way, and often they can do that only if they get the adult to go along with them."

Some children rely on manipulation and control more than

others. If we can remain curious, we can explore why a child would need to manipulate. To manipulate is to subtly and covertly influence others, by dishonest means if necessary, to achieve goals that would be unachievable if we were being honest. Powerful people may do this, but only when they are in a morally weak position, as when a government hopes to induce a population to support an unjustifiable war. With children, the manipulation occurs only because the child has learned that openly expressing his needs will not necessarily bring an understanding and nurturing response. It occurs also because the emotionally wounded child may no longer be able to articulate his real needs. Lacking a completely secure sense of attachment, he tries to compensate by getting things that the adult world, quite rightly, perhaps, does not want to give—for example, another expensive toy or a candy bar at an inappropriate time. No healing would come if the adult yielded to inappropriate demands or manipulative tactics, but no healing is possible, either, if the adult insists on seeing the child's behavior as the primary problem. Excessive manipulation, controlling, bossiness are simply the dysfunctional and self-defeating acquired characteristics of a sensitive and anxious child. Just as these qualities developed in interaction with the environment, so they can atrophy when the environment becomes understanding, nurturing and supportive.

### Myth 4: The ADD child's behavior causes the adult's tension or anger

Anger, anxiety, despair: all normal human emotional states. They belong to each one of us, in proportions that reflect our individual life histories and temperaments. They are distressing states to experience. The temptation is to blame someone else whenever we feel them.

The parents of a child with ADD will often find themselves angry and upset. The parent tells the child to hurry: the child drags her feet and may even say something insolent. The parent flies into a rage, and he imagines that his rage has been caused by the child's behavior. The child is chastised not for what she has done but for the unpleasant feelings experienced by the parent. In reality, the child cannot cause the parent's rage. She may have inadvertently triggered it, but she is responsible neither for the capacity for rage in the parent nor for the existence of the trigger. The parent acquired them before the child was born. The uncooperative behavior may belong to the child, but the rage belongs to the parent. It is only one among many potential ways the parent could have responded to the child's procrastination. In fact, when he later thinks about it, he recognizes that his reaction was quite out of proportion to the stimulus. On another day, had he slept better, perhaps, he would have responded quite differently—with non-hostile impatience, with mild annoyance, possibly even with humor.

Parents need to be aware of the wide range of their emotional responses, from the functional to what may be called the dysfunctional. They are then much less likely to insist that the child take responsibility for how they feel, regardless of what the child may or may not have done. An enormous emotional burden is lifted off the child's shoulders once the parent learns to acknowledge within himself the sources of his reactions to the child.

That other people do not cause our reactions is a difficult concept, so automatically have we come to associate our feelings with what someone else is doing. The confusion is only natural. When we were very small children, other people did, in fact, cause us to feel this way or that, depending on how they treated us. To the extent that this still remains true for someone as an adult, it reflects the failure of self-regulation to develop. A simple example is the way I might react if someone accidentally stepped on my foot, say, on a crowded bus. I might address the offender politely or in a fit of rage or, if I felt intimidated, I might not even say anything. Although the stimulus in each case is the same, the reaction depends not on the stimulus but on my particular state of mind. Even the same person will react differently to the same stimulus from one moment to the next, so the stimulus cannot be said to cause any one particular reaction. We cannot blame the trigger for the shotgun blast. A person can squeeze the trigger all he wants, but if there is no bullet, the gun will not fire.

The parent who learns to observe herself carefully will soon recognize that greatly complicating many situations is not what the child is doing as such but the degree of anxiety that the child's actions set off in the parent. When the child "misbehaves," the parent could react with curiosity and attempt to understand exactly what is being acted out, which would make for a much more effective parental response. When, instead, we as parents are flooded by anxiety, we move immediately to control the behavior, which is to say, to control the child.

### Myth 5: Children with ADD are lazy

Beneath the surface of the so-called laziness ADD children are often berated for is also emotional pain. When we consider the word *lazy*, we realize that it does not explain anything. It is only a negative judgment made about another person who is unwilling to do what we want them to do. The so-called lazy individual will be a whirlwind of energy and activity when faced with a task that arouses interest and excitement. So the laziness and the procrastination are not immutable traits of a person but expressions of his relationship with the world, beginning with the family of origin.

An exasperated couple related that their twelve-year-old son rejected with outrage and indignation their demand that he contribute to the housework—for example, by emptying the dishwasher. "I always have to do everything," he complained. The reality, of course, was that when it came to household duties, the parents found it easier to wring water from a stone than any cooperation from their son. All they could do was to engage him in unwinnable verbal battles or give up. This child, too, was speaking in code language that could be deciphered by using the key of compassionate curiosity. From early on, I have had to work too hard on my relationship with you, he was saying. I am tired of doing that. I don't want to do any more of the work that you should have been doing all along. The solution came not from the parents trying to coerce their son into doing his share, or to bribe him, but from their work on reconnecting with him emotionally. As they did so, he spontaneously became more ready to help out. Eventually he needed hardly any reminders at all. What allowed the parents to achieve this was their newfound ability to understand the code. Once they deciphered their son's messages, they became far more supportive of his needs and less threatened by his seeming indifference to responsibility.

Another aspect of what is seen as laziness is the child's automatic resistance. Probably the most frustrating and dispiriting aspect of dealing with ADD children is their virtually routine negative and defiant refusal of almost any demand, expectation or suggestion the parent puts forward. This resistance serves an important purpose and tells an important story. It, too, has meaning.

# 20

# The Defiant Ones:

# Oppositionality

And one may choose what is contrary to one's own interests and sometimes one *positively* ought... One's own free unfettered choice, one's own caprice, however wild it may be, one's own fancy worked up at times to frenzy... What man wants is simply *independent* choice, whatever that independence may cost and wherever it may lead.

   – FYODOR DOSTOEVSKY, "Notes from the Underground"

STEVEN, A THIRTY-EIGHT-YEAR-OLD labor relations officer for a large company, was referred to me for ADD assessment. He was respected as a creative man who brought original and innovative thinking to his work. A skilled negotiator, he was able to approach any situation from new angles and unique perspectives that could break a logjam when everyone else was stuck. "I do things nobody else would dream of doing, but I feel I could be doing a lot more," he said. At times he would impulsively take on problems and responsibilities beyond his experience or control. This propensity for risk taking had brought him and his company near the precipice of disaster more than once.

As I wrote in my consult letter to his family doctor, "It is a tribute to Steven's daring, acumen, and creativity, and thanks to some good luck, that so far he has avoided catastrophic consequences to his original and idiosyncratic approach to his work."

In this and in every other way, the diagnosis of ADD was self-evident. As he related his life story, Steven expressed one major regret. He had been an extraordinarily gifted classical musician in his childhood and adolescence. An international solo career had been widely predicted. In his midteens, however, he had given up his instrument, the clarinet, and completely severed his involvement with music. My consultation report noted:

> The parents were both artistically inclined. The mother was an actress, the father a talented musician. Steven himself was introduced to music at an early age and was apparently something of a child prodigy on the clarinet, being invited as an adolescent to play with the ... National Youth Orchestra. He was at one time considered to be a great prospect. He quit the clarinet at age sixteen for what he says were reasons of spite and defiance toward his father, who forced him into practicing and would beat him when he refused to do so. He was made to practice four hours a day. He continues to love classical music and deeply regrets not having continued with his musical studies.

Steven has for a long time considered his abandonment of a musical career as a perverse, boneheaded misjudgment. "It was the stupidest thing I have ever done," he said.

He was surprised to find that I did not agree with him. "It was one of the most necessary things you have ever done," I told him. "To have continued under those circumstances would have been to surrender your soul to your father. Psychologically, you might not have survived that."

The mistake, if we could speak of it as a conscious act, was not committed by the son but by the father. The force he had exerted on his son produced its own counterforce, resulting in the impulse that finally sent Steven in the direction exactly opposite what his father had wished. Sadly, it also went against Steven's interests and contrary to the choice he probably would have made, had he been truly free to make a choice. He did not have that freedom. Steven had not *acted*, which would have meant autonomy, but *reacted*, which reflected psychological subjection—not to his father but to the unconscious defenses he had built up against his father. Quitting music was not an act of will, it was an expression of what the Vancouver developmental psychologist Gordon Neufeld calls *counterwill*.* Distinguishing will from counterwill is important for any successful parenting. Understanding counterwill is particularly crucial for the parenting of the ADD child and for the self-understanding of the ADD adult.

Children with attention deficit disorder are often characterized as stubborn, oppositional, cheeky, insolent, spoiled. *Willful* is a description almost universally applied to them. Parents worry that the difficulty is rooted in some deeply embedded negative trait in their child's personality that will impede her future success in life. The truth is more complicated than that, and it leaves more ground for optimism. Oppositionality cannot arise on its own. By definition, it has to develop in response to something. It is not an isolated trait of the child's but an aspect of the child's relationship with the adult world. Adults can change the relationship by changing their own role in it.

ADD children can hardly be said to have a will at all, if by that is meant a capacity that enables a person to know what he wants and

---

* The term *counterwill* was originally coined by the psychoanalyst Otto Rank. The description of the concept in this chapter is based on the synthesis arrived at by Gordon Neufeld and is, by his kind permission, adapted from Dr. Neufeld's lecture series on counterwill.

to hold to that goal regardless of setbacks, difficulties or distractions. "But my child is strong-willed," many parents insist. "When he decides that he wants something, he just keeps at it until I cannot say no, or until I get very angry." What is really being described here is not will but a rigid, obsessive clinging to this or that desire. An obsession may resemble will in its persistence but has nothing in common with it. Its power comes from the unconscious, and it rules the individual, whereas a person with true will is in command of his intentions.

The child's oppositionality is not an expression of will. What it denotes is the *absence of will*, which—like Steven's abandonment of music—only allows a person to *react* but not to *act* from a free and conscious process of decision making.

Counterwill is an automatic resistance put up by a human being with an incompletely developed sense of self, a reflexive and unthinking opposition to the will of the other. It is a natural but immature resistance arising from the fear of being controlled. Counterwill arises in anyone who has not yet developed a mature and conscious will of her own. Although it can remain active throughout life, normally it makes its most dramatic appearance during the toddler phase and again in adolescence. In many people, and in the vast majority of children with ADD, it becomes entrenched as an ever-present force and may remain powerfully active well into adulthood. It immensely complicates personal relationships, school performance and job or career success.

Counterwill has many manifestations. The parent of a child with attention deficit disorder will be familiar with them. Most obviously, it is expressed in verbal resistance—"I don't have to," "You can't make me," the constant arguing and countering whatever the parent proposes, the ubiquitous "You are not the boss of me." Like a psychological immune system, counterwill functions to keep out anything that does not originate within the child herself. It is present when the four-year-old puts both hands over his ears to keep out the parent's voice, or when the older child pins up an angry Keep Out sign on her door. It is visible in the body language of the adolescent and teenager: the sullen look and the shrugged shoulder. Its signs drive some adults around the bend, as in the futile "I'll wipe that smirk off your face" of many a parent or teacher. Counterwill is also expressed through passivity. Every parent of an ADD child has had the experience of feeling intense frustration when, being pressured for time, they have tried to hurry their son or daughter along. The greater the parent's anxiety and the greater the pressure he puts on the child, the more sloth-fully slow the child seems to become. Passivity begins to look like almost second nature to some of these children, although when she is highly motivated, the child will perform many tasks with alacrity. This passivity, what people may call laziness, can signal a strong internal resistance.

Counterwill is a natural inclination and does not mean there is anything intrinsically wrong with the child. It is not as if the individual *does* it; it happens to the child rather than being instigated *by* him. It may take the child as much by surprise as the parent. "It really is simply a counterforce," says Dr. Neufeld. "The counter-will dynamic is simply a manifestation of a universal principle. The same principle is seen in physics, where it is considered fundamental to keeping the universe together: for every centripetal force there has to be a centrifugal one; for every force, a counterforce." Like all natural phenomena and all stages in the child's life, counterwill has a positive purpose. It first appears in the toddler to help in the task of individuating, of beginning to separate from the parent. In essence, the child erects a wall of no's. Behind this wall, the child can gradually learn her likes and dislikes, aversions or preferences, without being overwhelmed by the far more powerful force generated by the parent's will. Counterwill may be likened to the small fence one places around a tender young shoot to protect it from being eaten. The vulnerable little plant here is the child's will. Without that protective fence, it cannot survive. In adolescence, counterwill serves the same goal, helping the young person loosen his psychological dependence on the family. It comes at a time when the sense of self is having to emerge out of the cocoon of the family. It is a defense mechanism to protect this fragile, threatened sense of self. By keeping out the parent's expectations and demands, counterwill helps to make room for the growth of the child's own self-generated motivations and preferences.

Figuring out what we *want* has to begin with having the freedom to *not want*. "Far from being depraved, counterwill is bequeathed by nature, to serve the ultimate purpose of becoming a separate being," says Dr. Neufeld. "Counterwill, the dynamic, should not be identified with the child's self. This is really important. It is not the person that we are getting to know when we get to know the resistance. Nature designed the child that way. It is really Nature that has a purpose, not the child."

The great importance of understanding counterwill in attention deficit disorder stems from the extreme sensitivity of the ADD child who in this, as in many other things, is affected by environmental stimuli more than the average. Any force or pressure of whichever sort, no matter how good the intention, will be experienced by the ADD toddler, child or teenager to a highly magnified degree, and will generate counterwill of greatly heightened intensity. The tendency of the ADD child is to behave in ways that provoke disapproval and attempts at parental control. Disapproval makes the child feel more insecure and promotes acting-out, and the parent's controlling responses deepen the child's automatic resistance.

Emotional hypersensitivity in ADD is coupled with psychological underdevelopment. The weaker the child—or, for that matter, the adult—is psychologically, the more automatic and rigid the counterwill response becomes. A strong unconscious defense indicates a weak, undeveloped will, which is what is reflected in the oppositionality that seems intrinsic—but only *seems* that way—to the ADD personality. A strong defense is there only because there is threat, and the child is threatened only because a strong sense of his own self has not developed sufficiently. So the root of the problem is that rather than being too powerful, the inner core of self, the true will, is stunted. This is why the various epithets such as *stubborn, willful* and so on indicate not a strong will but the *lack* of one. An emotionally self-confident person does not have to adopt an oppositional stance *automatically*. She may resist others' attempts to control her, but she will not do so rigidly and defensively. If she opposes something, it is from a strong sense of what her true preferences are, not a knee-jerk reflex. A child not driven by counterwill does not automatically experience any advice, any expression of the parent's opinion, as an attempt at control. Registering deep in her psyche is a sense of solidity about this inner core, this nucleus of the self, so there is no necessity to defend the will against being overwhelmed. I will be able to hang on to myself, an inner voice reassures her, even if I listen to what somebody else thinks, or do what someone else wants me to do. I won't lose my identity, so I don't have to protect myself through resistance. I can afford to cooperate. I can afford to heed. In contrast, the counterwill of the child with an underdeveloped self asserts itself ferociously. A parent meekly suggests that the child may wish to do her homework, only to get the automatic and combative "You're always telling me what to do!"

In the ADD child, the underdeveloped circuitry of self-regulation reinforces the counterwill reaction. Because the child with attention deficit disorder is unable to disengage impulse from action, his automatic negative responses are expressed immediately and dramatically, in ways the adult world usually interprets simply as deliberate rudeness.

Further magnifying the brazen outbursts of oppositionality is another feature of underdevelopment, the one-dimensionality of the ADD child's emotional processing. In a manner characteristic of infants and toddlers, children with attention deficit disorder are unable to hold simultaneously in their minds two different images of themselves or of others. For the preverbal child, the "me" is either happy or miserably upset. Mommy is either good or bad. "When a twelve- to fourteen-month-old gets angry at someone he may have no sense that just moments ago he was playing happily with that person," writes Stanley Greenspan. "If he had a gun, one suspects, he'd shoot without remorse. By fifteen months or so, however, a dawning awareness that a relationship of trust and security can coexist with anger has often begun to moderate his temper."[1] For ADD children (and for ADD adults), it's all or nothing. When anger arises, all feelings of attachment and love are banished. Since counterwill grows as attachment weakens, the child who is upset and angry may, in that moment, resist the parent with the emotional fury one would feel toward a despised enemy.

In the literature of child rearing, counterwill is sadly neglected because so much of the emphasis has been placed on behaviors. If specific behaviors are the goal, then threats, punishments, promises and rewards may work very well—for a while. That, unfortunately, characterizes much of the advice parents of ADD children receive. With counterwill, as with every other aspect of parenting, it is far wiser to put the emphasis on long-term development. The long-term objective here is the growth of a healthy and robust sense of self.

Counterwill becomes maladjusted, as it does in ADD, only when adults do not understand it and try to overcome it by some sort of pressure, be it physical or emotional, be it inducement or threat. Counterwill is triggered whenever the child senses that the parent wants him to do something more than she, the child, wants to do it. It arises not just when the child absolutely does not wish to do that something but also when she does wish it, but just not as much as the parent. Many parents find out to their chagrin that there is no better way to kill a child's interest in music than to force him to practice, even if by methods much milder than the brutality Steven's father employed. All one ends up with is the child's resistance.

The use of rewards—what might be called positive coercion—does not work in the long run any better than threat and punishment, or negative coercion. In the reward, the child senses the parent's desire to control no less than in the punishment. The issue is the child's sense of being forced, not the manner in which the force is applied. This was well illustrated in a classic study using magic markers.[2] A number of children were screened to select some who showed a natural interest and inclination for playing with magic markers. Those who did were then divided into three different groups. For one group, there was no reward involved and no indication what to do with the markers. Another group was given a small reward to use the markers, and the third was promised a substantial reward. When retested sometime later, the group that had been most rewarded showed the least interest in playing with the magic markers, while the children who had been left uninstructed showed by far the greatest motivation to use them. Simple behaviorist principles would suggest it ought to have been the other way around, another illustration that behavioral approaches have no more than short-term efficacy. At work here, of course, was residual counterwill in response to positive coercion. In a similar experiment, the psychologist Edward Deci observed the behaviors of two groups of college students vis-à-vis a puzzle game they had originally all been equally intrigued by. One group was to receive a monetary reward each time a puzzle was solved; the other was given no external incentive. Once the payments stopped, the paid group proved far more likely to abandon the game than their unpaid counterparts. "Rewards may increase the likelihood of behaviors," Dr. Deci remarks, "but only so long as the rewards keep coming... Stop the pay, stop the play."

We have seen that the very first step in helping the ADD child is to strengthen the security of her relationship with the parents. The process of making the child feel safer, more secure in the relationship, becomes much smoother and less frustrating if the parents understand counterwill and do what they can to relax its chronic hold on the child.

# 21

# Defusing

# Counterwill

Even though you try to put people under some control,
it is impossible. You cannot do it. The best way to
control people is to encourage them to be mischievous.
Then they will be in control in its wider sense. To give
your sheep or cow a large, spacious meadow is the way
to control him. So it is with people: first let them do
what they want, and watch them. This is the best
policy. To ignore them is not good; that is the worst
policy. The second worst is trying to control them. The
best one is to watch them, just to watch them, without
trying to control them.

— SHUNRYU SUZUKI ROSHI, *Zen Mind, Beginner's
Mind*

P ARENTS UNAWARE OF HOW counterwill works may see oppositionality as originating in the child, as a deliberate challenge to their authority or a testing of limits. A power struggle ensues. When such conflicts are frequent, counterwill becomes established as the child's automatic response to any sort of parental expectation. Chronic counterwill will complicate and negate many of his relationships with other people, as will the rebellious stance against all authority and all rules reported by many adults with ADD.

There are ways of *counterwill-proofing the relationship*, in Gordon Neufeld's phrase, of drawing the sting out of the counterwill dynamic.

### 1. *Keep attachment foremost*

The importance of the attachment relationship has been the underlying theme of this book. Counterwill is greatly increased when the child's attachment to the parent diminishes, and decreases as the attachment bond improves. The child is much less likely to oppose someone whose proximity and contact she greatly cherishes than someone she is at odds with.

### 2. *Do not mistake acquiescence for voluntary "good behavior"*

We can create the *appearance* of close attachment by threatening the child or treating him harshly, but what really happens is that the child clings to the parent for fear of rejection or punishment. Counterwill will roil underground to surface later.

Compliance does not necessarily mean effective or wise parenting. In cases of divorce or separation, for example, a mother may complain that her child acts out with her but is well behaved with the father. One psychologist's report in a custody case I was asked to review even concluded that the father was the better parent because the young child—a five-year-old with clear signs of hyperactivity—seemed better mannered in the psychologist's office with the father than in the presence of the mother. The mother also reported that the child was especially uncontrollable in the day or two immediately following overnight visits with the father, further proof in the mind of the psychologist of her ineptitude as a parent. This psychologist seemed not to have understood that the child's supposed bad behavior with the mother really represented a sense of greater security. Since the mother did not treat the child as harshly as the father, who, as he proudly explained, would hit the child's fingers as a method of discipline, the child's counterwill reactions were not suppressed in her presence. On the contrary, the suppressed counterwill built up when the child was with the father erupted with all the greater force in the safety of the mother's care.

The children most at risk for problems later in life are those who feel so threatened that their counterwill falls completely silent. Many a good little boy or good little girl grows up to be a depressed and troubled adult.

### 3. Do not take the child's recalcitrance personally

Parents who do not take the child's opposition as a personal challenge to their authority will avoid the contests of power that make everyone a loser. Not taking counterwill personally, as if it was directed against them, they will not participate in the cycle of pressure–counterwill–greater pressure–greater counterwill. They will not demand that the child justify behavior she herself has no way of understanding. They will not set themselves up for frustration and blame.

### 4. Make room for some resistance in the relationship

Sometimes opposition must just be anticipated. When the parent simply has to exert more control and coercion than usual, a counterwill reaction can be predicted. The parent can remain focused on what must be done without being surprised or shocked by the child's resistance. This does not mean that the child must get her way, only that the parent does not react with rage or help-lessness that add to the conflict. There is room for the child to express her resistance without the relationship being threatened.

### 5. *Engage only in those fights that parents must win*

I have on numerous occasions engaged in pitched battles with one or another of my children over matters that, in retro-spect, seem completely unimportant. Many disagreements between parents and children occur over minor issues—such as which coat to wear, when to take out the garbage, whether an apple or a piece of toast will be the bedtime snack. When I thought about these scenes, I realized that they were caused mostly by my own inflexi-bility. Such unnecessary set-tos over trivial differences do nothing but entrench counterwill and undermine parental authority. The child's automatic opposition will be magnified, and for no good purpose.

### 6. *Encourage verbal expression*

Instead of trying to overcome the child's counterwill, help him find more acceptable ways of expressing resistance.

Say a child responds to a parental command with rude, unac-ceptable language. Instead of punishing the *expression*, the wise parent shows some empathy for the resistance. "You didn't feel like being bossed around today. It made you want to do the oppo-site of what I said. I can see that. But next time, I want you to tell me without using those insulting words." In this way, parents invite the child's expression of resistance in forms that are socially appropriate. They do so by helping the child *symbolize* feelings by putting them into words.

Feelings that are expressed directly do not need to be acted out in destructive physical behaviors. As children start to use words, they become less victims of their own impulses. They can now put the feeling out there, outside themselves, where they can see it. We, the parents, can come alongside. At least we can say, "Yeah, I know. It's understandable. I don't expect you to feel like it."

"It's a lot easier for a child to comply," Gordon Neufeld points out, "when they know at least you understand what they experience."

### 7.  Parents recognize that they, too, can be recalcitrant at times

Very often when my children have asked me for this or that small favor or privilege, my answer has been an automatic no. For many years now, I have had immediate second thoughts. Why exactly am I saying no, when there is nothing really wrong with what's being asked of me? I see now that my own counterwill reaction was engaged, a sign that my own sense of self was not completely developed. When a parent feels controlled by a child, it's her own automatic resistance she is experiencing instead of conscious choice. Many parents will respond irritably to a demanding child, which is not at all the same as making a conscious and loving decision not to give in to some unacceptable request. Faced with a parent's intractable resistance, a child becomes even more anxious and demanding.

### 8.  Mend fences after the fact

Inevitably there will come times when parents lose control, times when the child's resistance feels like more than we can handle. We react, we blame, we are frustrated, we attack. "At such times," says Dr. Neufeld, "we can counterwill-proof in retrospect. There is such a thing as patching up relationships, mending fences, immunizing the child against the impact of our reactions, in the past and in the future." This process is much the same as what in chapter 17 was described as the parent's taking responsibility for restoring the interpersonal bridge.

"We can debrief," Dr. Neufeld advises. "Even after situations, even long after situations, but preferably right after, when things have cooled down." The parent can state what happened, draw out the child's fears, show we understand how she would have felt, say what happened to us and acknowledge that it was we, the parent, who lost control. The message is that the child's impulsiveness and the parent's reactions are not the substance of the relationship; neither will cause a rupture.

"I don't have as much control over myself as I would like," the parent acknowledges implicitly. "I am not a perfect parent, but that means we will build a stronger relationship, you and I. We will make it so strong that it will be able to take a lot of your resistance and a lot of my reactions." One fence-mending tactic I have developed is to promise my daughter as an absolute rule that no punishment I pronounce in a state of anger will ever be carried out.

Counterwill-proofing in retrospect is very important. "Not to do that," cautions Dr. Neufeld, "leaves the child with fear that he can blow this relationship apart by his instinctive, impulsive outbursts and negative responses—and that gets very confusing and makes him very insecure."

### 9. Encourage self-discipline instead of controlling the child

Too often parents confuse discipline or good parenting with control. They are supported in this misbelief by their relatives and neighbors, or by voices in the media, who say that the only problem with the behavior of ADD children is that parents are too lax with their discipline, too weak to control their son or daughter. If that were true, children treated harshly should be the best behaved and should grow up into the best citizens. As a survey of the population of any foster home or prison would show, the contrary is true.

The issue is not how to control the child but how best to promote the child's development. By the time it becomes an urgent matter of control, as with aggressive or destructive behaviors, the relationship with the parents is usually in tatters and the counterwill dynamic has grown immense. One *prevents* having to control by maintaining the relationship and defusing counterwill. In the end, of course, the resolution of counterwill-driven oppositionality comes from the development of the child's core self.

As a sense of an independent self gains strength, the child is able to accept the advice of the parent without feeling controlled, the teenager can follow the directions of a teacher without feeling demeaned, and the adult can absorb the instructions of a foreman without a sense that he is being treated like an imbecile. They will also not be afraid to stand up for themselves when the demands on them truly are unreasonable and unfair. Unlike my patient Steven who gave up music, they will make decisions out of a clear sense of their own values and preferences.

# 22

# My Marshmallow

## Caught Fire:

## Motivation and

## Autonomy

The truth is that there are no techniques that will motivate people or make them autonomous. Motivation must come from within, not from techniques. It comes from their deciding they are ready to take responsibility for managing themselves.

—EDWARD L. DECI, PH.D., *Why We Do What We Do*

I N HER EXCELLENT PRIMER for parents, the psychologist Natalie Rathvon describes the unmotivated child as follows:*

- Performs well when given one-to-one attention but is restless and unproductive when required to work independently
- Has trouble beginning and completing tasks
- Withdraws attention when parents or teachers give instructions
- Becomes distractible and distracting when not the centre of attention
- Has difficulty relating to peers (may be revealed in complaints that others are "bothering" the child)
- Has difficulty relating to siblings
- Displays frequent temper outbursts or abrupt mood changes
- Makes incessant demands but is never satisfied with anything for very long
- Requires caretaking on some tasks beyond the age when it is appropriate
- Has difficulty organizing school materials and belongings at home [1]

The description is, of course, a textbook list of characteristics associated with attention deficit disorder. Although not all unmotivated children have ADD, all ADD children are unmotivated. Their absence of motivation is evident not only when it comes to activities and tasks expected of children their age but even in their

---

* The book is *The Unmotivated Child*, and every parent of an ADD child should have it. My only disagreement with Dr. Rathvon is that she seems to make a distinction between the ADD child and the unmotivated child, a distinction that is unnecessary and unwarranted in most cases of attention deficit disorder.

approach to projects and plans that originally aroused their interest and enthusiasm. A lack of inner-directed purpose also typifies a large number of ADD adults.

Not surprisingly, one of the most frequently asked questions by parents of children with attention deficit disorder is, "How can I motivate my child?" The answer, if we understand the dynamic of counterwill discussed in the previous chapter, is that *you can't.* More exactly, you may succeed in activating the child temporarily with a threat or with the promise of immediate reward but at the expense of the child's self-motivation in the long run.

The more helpful long-term goal is to foster the development of motivation that arises intrinsically from the child's own nature. This truer form of motivation reflects the genuine inclinations of the individual, not the values and expectations of significant figures in her life. Trying to motivate a child by coaxing or pressuring her to accept what the parents want of her is worlds away from promoting the growth of her natural, self-generated motivation. The first is done *to* the child. The second happens *within* the child and is a process she actively participates in.

There are, as Edward Deci points out, universal human needs for self-determination, to feel competent and to be genuinely connected with others. These needs and the drive to satisfy them do not have to be instilled in people: they exist, even if in undeveloped form. Allowed to unfold, they will motivate. The problem is not that parents and other important adults, such as teachers, do not know how to motivate children. The problem is that our parenting styles and teaching methods in many cases fail to support the child's natural drive for discovery and mastery. Encouraging development to unfold is based on the knowledge that nature has its own positive agenda for the child: it has given the child, every child, all the potential and capacities required for full maturation. Attempting to motivate from the outside betrays a lack of faith in the child and in nature. It reflects the anxiety of the parent, not the limitations of the child. It's unfortunate but true that while we may not be able to transplant genuine motivation into our children, we are altogether too successful when it comes to sowing in them the seeds of our own anxiety.

A child who must meet only parental expectations will likely acquire a chronic sense of incompetence as she fails over and over again to live up to them. Or she may function well enough as viewed from the outside but will have to pay a grievous price internally. She will be unable to experience the joy and satisfaction of acting from her own free choice and may not learn what her own genuine preferences are. Her self-esteem will hinge on *what* she does, not on *who* she is. Even if she succeeds in the eyes of others, she will be mercilessly critical of herself.

True motivation is knowing that I do what I do not because someone else wants me to do it, or because I believe someone will respect or like me for doing it, not because some inner voice tells me I "should" do it, and not because I am asserting my independence by defying someone who forbade me to do it. What I do satisfies me, regardless of what others may think. As long as I am not deliberately injuring someone else, knowingly causing them harm, I will honor my preferences and inclinations, even if others will feel disappointed in me.

As with every aspect of the development of the ADD child, the growth of true, internal motivation requires a secure attachment relationship with the parent. Without the safety of the attachment relationship, the small child will be too anxious to focus his attention on a meaningful exploration of the world around him. By school age, he will automatically be guided by what he perceives to be the values and opinions of others. "How can this be true," parents of the ADD youngster may protest, "when my child is completely defiant and refuses to accept any direction or opinion from me?" The child has transferred his conscious striving for acceptance from his parents to his peers. Recalcitrant at home, he is desperate for the approval of his playmates, a desperation more often than not met with rejection. The weakness of his core self relative to his playmates makes him a natural target for ostracization. Parents are often baffled by the apparent paradox of seeing their rebellious and fiercely contrary child submit to various humiliations in school or on the playground, continuing to seek favor with his tormentors. It is not a paradox. At home his counterwill is being manifested, while with peers he openly displays his lack of self-esteem and need for inclusion at any cost. Both behaviors bespeak an underdeveloped autonomous will. He cannot develop his own true motivation when he is too busy fending off the pressures coming from his parents and, simultaneously, working overtime to gain the acceptance of his peers.

Along with attachment, the other necessary condition for the development of motivation is autonomy. "People need to feel that their behavior is truly chosen by them rather than imposed by some external source," writes Edward Deci, "that the locus of initiation of their behavior is within themselves rather than in some external control." Supporting the child's autonomy, Dr. Deci points out, means "being able to take the other person's perspective and work from there. It means actively encouraging self-initiation, experimentation and responsibility, and it may very well require setting limits. But autonomy support functions through encouragement, not pressure."[2]

It is worth recalling here that the injudicious use of rewards and praise can be pressure tactics no less than verbal or physical coercion. As we have seen, there are three dangers with motivating by means of reward and praise. First, they feed the anxiety that not the person but the desired achievement is what is valued by the parent. They directly reinforce the insecurity of the ADD child. Second, since children can sense the parents' will pushing them, even if under benign disguises such as gifts or warm words, counterwill will be strengthened. Third, praise and reward will themselves become the goal, at the expense of the child's interest in the actual process of what he is doing. Children thus motivated will sooner or later learn to get by with the least amount of effort necessary to earn the praise or the reward. Short cuts and cheating often follow.

Accepting the child's reference point, the parent gives her as much choice as possible. Without some choice, autonomy is not possible. "You don't feel like doing your homework now. When would be a better time?"

The choices offered have to be realistically on par with the child's maturity, and within boundaries the child can handle. It is unrealistic to expect, for example, that the ADD child will sit for a long time by herself, immersed in mathematics problems, even if she is free to decide when to begin her homework. Recognizing this, parents need to structure their time so that they can be present when homework is being done. This does not mean hovering over the child and correcting her every mistake, but simply being around so that the child's attachment anxiety does not interfere with her motivation to do the work. As attachment security and competence in handling the work improve, the child will have a growing ability to function independently. One family I know has approached this problem by having the child do his homework in the kitchen, with one of the parents always around, engaged in kitchen work, available to help when the child asks for it.

True autonomy allows the child to make choices the parent may not like. With the middle-grade child, and especially with teenagers, the option must be left open, for example, *not* to complete homework. It is for the school to decide what the consequences of homework left undone will be, not for the parents to impose arbitrary outcomes. If the parents put the emphasis on attachment and autonomy, the child will eventually be able to learn from the natural consequences of his actions. Schools on occasion will contact parents, trying to recruit them to pressure the child. As much as parents may share the school's objective that their children become productive, they should resist adopting the role of enforcer. They can communicate their concern to the child *as their own concern*, not as an ultimatum.

True autonomy requires that the parents provide a supportive structure. It is futile to expect a child to do self-motivated and organized work if the parents' lives express a near-desperate frenzy to keep up with their own responsibilities, which is what I often see in the families of ADD children. Without structure that involves the whole family and is not just forced on the child alone, there cannot be autonomy. For the child's choices to mean anything, he has to know that the atmosphere in the family will be calm and supportive, that meals and other group activities will be at regular times so that schedules can be adhered to, and that the parents will be available and present both in body and spirit.

A supportive structure must include the setting of limits, boundaries demarcating where the autonomy of one person ends and that of another begins. Supporting autonomy, therefore, is not the same as permissiveness, which, by definition, allows children to infringe on the rights of others or leaves in their hands decisions and choices they are not equipped to handle. The latter is very much an issue of age. It is unwise to leave a two-year-old to decide how many hours he can spend in front of the television each day, but—regardless of the parents' own views on the matter—an older child who is highly aware of control issues and who sees that his peers are not under strict control needs to be allowed greater latitude. The setting of limits works much better if the boundaries are defined as generously as possible, allowing maximum reasonable scope for individual choice. The rationale for the rule needs to be clearly articulated, so that the rule itself rather than the parent's will is seen as authoritative.

As always, attachment needs to be attended to, especially when we have to impose limits the child will not like and may resist. "Keep in mind that rapport and limit setting go hand in hand," Stanley Greenspan advises. "As you increase limit setting, you need to increase empathy."[3] Extrasensitive children, which is to say all ADD children, need more empathy and understanding in direct proportion to the need for more structure and limit setting. These must all go hand in hand to be effective in promoting development. Without parental empathy, the child shuts down and hides behind the wall of emotional defenses; without structure, he becomes lost, uncertain and anxious. "The key is to empathize with the child's feeling even if it is a feeling you don't like," writes

Dr. Greenspan. "Often parents think that if they empathize with the child's feeling, they will somehow encourage that feeling in the child's mind or intensify it. But recognizing what a child is feeling will help *her* recognize and label that feeling rather than experience it as a vague sensation."[4]

Helping the child to label her feelings in words is what was referred to as *symbolization* when we discussed counterwill. It is also an important step in promoting autonomy. Words are symbols. They stand for feelings and actions. Without the capacity to put things into symbols, children are driven to act out every strong feeling and every urge—it is the only way they can express themselves. They are thus unable to take charge of themselves, impelled as they are to act by emotions they cannot identify. Without learning to symbolize emotions they are also likely to experience everything in terms of simple and opposing categories: people are alternately mean or nice, good or bad. It's either "I love you, Mommy" or "I hate you." The child has greater autonomy, a greater choice of possible responses, when she can say, "I didn't like what Mrs. So-and-so said to me in class today," than when she is restricted to "Mrs. So-and-so is mean." Language supports freedom, including freedom from one's own impulses.

Finally, in supporting autonomy, we address the child, not the deed. A parent can get angry at a four-year-old who spills some milk, or she can say, "You were trying to do it yourself. That's great, but this bottle is just too heavy and big." Especially with ADD children, not a few of whom have problems with motor control, parents can avoid painful scenes if they learn to respect the motive instead of fixating on the outcome.

Actions have their own consequences in the world; we don't need to create them. For instance, if a boy is late for school every day for a week, his teacher may require him to stay after school— the parent does not need to add some arbitrary sanction, such as, for example, a denial of permission for the child to play with his friend on the weekend. There is no logical connection there. Many so-called "natural consequences" taught in parenting courses are, in fact, arbitrary punishments that undermine the child's security and autonomy. Punishments are designed to control behavior rather than to encourage learning and development in the child. They are, according to all the relevant research, bound to backfire. They sabotage learning from consequences and hinder the ability to take responsibility. Punishments substitute the parent's feelings and judgments for the lessons taught by reality.

In a Gary Larson *Far Side* cartoon, four Old West cowboy types are ranged around a campfire by their wagon, roasting marshmallows. One of them is lying in the classic cowboy death pose, boots stiffly raised toward the heavens. A second man, smoking gun in hand, addresses the other two in a tone evidently dripping with righteous indignation. "You are my witnesses," he says. "He laughed when my marshmallow caught fire." There is quite often not much more natural connection than that between the consequences we as parents impose on a miscreant child and whatever it is the child may have done to provoke our ire.

Artificial consequences devised by parents intensify resistance and reinforce the child's already negative view of herself. This is especially true for the underproductive and underachieving ADD child. "Although punishment is ineffective in making [the child] try harder," writes Natalie Rathvon, "it is highly effective in solidifying her view of herself as unlovable and her view of others as unhelpful. If treatment by punishment continues, it is likely to motivate her to act out her image of herself as bad and dumb by misbehaving in school or at home or by performing even more poorly academically."[5]

Will is like psychological muscle, says Gordon Neufeld. Parents cannot do anything directly to develop the child's will, any more than they can make the child's muscles grow. What they can do is to provide the nurturing, the right conditions and the proper direction. Like muscles, will needs exercise to grow. "Parents can provide lots of exercise," Dr. Neufeld says. "Exercise is basically making choices—that is how we exercise our will."

Parents may worry that if they support the child's autonomy, she may grow up to be selfish, unmindful of others. It is a common fear, but unfounded. It is based on the completely erroneous view that children are wild creatures needing to be tamed by any means necessary. The process of becoming connected with other people and learning appropriate human interactions, of developing into a social creature, is called *socialization*. Children don't have to be *trained* into socialization. Because it is a fundamental human drive, we naturally develop connectedness and compassion if our own basic needs have been respected. Socialization is at the apex of a pyramid. The base is formed by secure attachment and autonomy. We often make the mistake with our children of putting socialization—the rules of social conduct, what is called "good behavior"—ahead of attachment and individuation. We try to make our kids act as truly socially responsible people at the expense of their emotional security and their autonomous sense of self. This may result in compliance, but not in the internal, organic growth of true morality and social responsibility. We can no more foster genuine socialization this way than we can balance a pyramid on its apex, upside down.

# 23

# Trusting the Child,

# Trusting Oneself:

# ADD in the

# Classroom

What, after all, does it mean to provide an *appropriate education* to a student? Frankly, nobody knows. Appropriate education is relative. It depends on the kid. Some seventeen-year-olds need to be able to factor polynomials and deconstruct *Ivanhoe*; other seventeen-year-olds need to learn to recognize common visual cues: *skull and crossbones mean poison, do not touch, stay away.* And there are a lot of seventeen-year-olds in between. It's hard to tell who requires what.

— ALLYSON GOLDIN, "The Incoherent Brain"[1]

THERE IS A BUILT-IN contradiction in North American education that particularly affects students with attention deficit disorder: the tendency to teach everyone as if their brains all worked the same way, when the reality is that they do not. The social crisis of the growing number of children whose educational needs the present school system simply does not meet is translated into a medical problem—at best. Even worse is when the ADD child is reduced to a problem of discipline and behavior control.

The goal is to teach children to take responsibility for their own learning in a positive way. In attempting to do so, teachers have no easy task. With hyperactive children especially, teachers face almost ceaseless disruption of the classroom order. They are up against the ADD child's attention difficulties, low self-esteem, ingrained oppositionality and deep social anxieties. They may also be up against their own lack of preparedness.

Before I returned to university to study medicine, I taught high school for three years. My teaching style was influenced by my ADD traits: I was a gifted improvisational artist but did virtually nothing to plan lessons, units, course outlines. The results reflected my methods. Some students were inspired by the freely inquisitive and good-humored, relaxed atmosphere in my classes; others who needed more structure and direction felt quite lost. I certainly did not ask myself how my teaching should adjust to the various needs of the students under my charge—it all came from me; it was teacher centered. I believe this to be a weakness of schooling throughout North America, though in most classrooms the problem may present itself from the opposite angle than in mine: too much imposed structure and discipline, not enough freedom for individuality and self-expression. The lesson plans are based on what the teacher has been told to teach, not necessarily on who the students are and what, at any given stage of their lives, they need to learn. Teaching methods do not take into account the emotional and cognitive realities of the student. Many children are left out of the loop; the ADD child is almost guaranteed to be.

I did have experience with an entire classroomful of ADD pupils as a student teacher at West Vancouver Secondary in 1969. Although nobody then had identified them as such, in retrospect it is clear to me who most of these teenagers were and it is clear to me, too, why I felt such a special affinity for them. Early in my first practicum during my teacher training year, I was thrown into the lion's den of a classroom of students everyone had quite given up on—the "school rejects" was how they spoke of themselves. All other student teachers had broken their teeth trying to bite on this particular apple, and the regular teachers, too, had been defanged. I had to teach this Grade 9 class map making. On a complete whim, I brought every musical instrument within my reach to school the very first morning I was to teach them: my guitar, castanets, recorders, harmonicas, pots and pans, bongo drums. I also brought a candle. I asked my supervising teacher—a straitlaced but very decent man—where in the school we could make noise. I then marched the class out to the woodworking shed, distributed the instruments, lit the candle and began strumming my guitar. They all immediately and spontaneously joined in. "The rule is," I said to my supervisor, "that you can't be an observer. You either play an instrument, or you leave." He left. For a whole hour the music/cacophony went on. By the end, they were dancing on top of the shed. We whooped and shouted. Not a word was said. When the bell went, I collected the instruments. Next day, I began the unit on map making. They lapped it up. My supervisor could not believe it.

I now see that I instinctively resonated with the suppressed energy of these kids, recognized that it needed expression. Moreover, I liked them, enjoyed them and did not feel threatened by them.

The following general principles will help all teachers who have ADD children or teenagers in their classrooms. The distinction between *principles* and *techniques* needs to be kept in mind here. I have no expertise to offer teachers techniques. I do believe these principles, however, are essential, no matter what technical approach one may choose. They are distilled from what has been said about the nature of attention deficit disorder in the rest of this book.

### 1. *Do no harm*

Foremost among the Hippocratic injunctions regarding the practice of medicine is *primum non nocere*: first, do no harm. The same ought to be the primary rule in teaching as well.

Teachers sometimes forget their immense power to wound. How deep classroom-inflicted emotional hurts can go, how long-lasting their sting potentially is, may be gleaned from the histories ADD adults give of their school years. Many still cringe as they recall humiliations, the cutting and sarcastic remarks of their teachers, the punishments for misbehavior they did not deliberately initiate and for inabilities they did not know how to overcome. Teachers need to remember that the ADD child, by definition, has suffered the pain of feeling cut off from emotionally significant adults, has a profound sense of shame and has—underneath whatever defiant behavior—weak and precarious self-esteem. Moreover, odds are he also suffers from some degree of social rejection. Shaming ADD children for their mistakes, inattention, slowness at grasping instructions and sloppy handwriting only reinforces their negative self-image and undermines their emotional and intellectual growth. "The class will now wait until Karen returns to earth" is a relatively mild comment a Grade 3 teacher made about an inattentive ADD child in my practice. The child came home that night, sobbing helplessly. "Mrs. N. hates me," she said. "All the kids laughed at me." Painful for any child, an experience of that sort is devastating for the sensitive, insecure ADD child.

In his novel *In a Glass House*, the Canadian writer Nino Ricci renders poignantly the private despair of a young student struggling to keep focused in an intimidating school environment. Perhaps it ought to be required reading in faculties of education:

When we did assignments my exercise book was always filled with the same hopeless errors, though Sister Bertram had explained them a dozen times, so that sometimes she'd take the ruler in hand and simply rip out the pages with a single swift jerk. And I didn't pay attention: even though I knew that Sister Bertram would catch me out, that I wouldn't learn if I didn't pay attention, still I couldn't stop my mind from wandering, because the moment Sister Bertram began to talk I'd feel the classroom slipping away from me the way a dream did in the first moments of wakefulness, and I couldn't force myself then to hold the world in focus.

Sometimes our own responses to an individual may give us important clues about the other person. Whenever a teacher notices in himself a tendency to speak sarcastically, irritably and in a blaming way to any particular child on a repeated basis, he would be well advised to consider what behavior of the child invokes those responses. Unless he is so troubled personally that irritability and sarcasm are his general style with children—in which case he needs help either to grow emotionally or to leave the profession—the teacher might well consider whether the particular child who triggers his irritability might have ADD.

### 2. Working with the parents

Teacher training has neglected a systematic study of attention deficit disorder, just as medical training has. How ADD is handled in the classroom parallels its fate in the medical system in unevenness: skillfully here, with uninformed incomprehension there. And yet the classroom teacher is in a front-line position to identify the problem and to initiate the task of organizing help for it. It is not up to teachers or school psychologists to confront parents with the diagnosis as a given, as in "Your child has ADD," but they can bring the behaviors and the study difficulties to the parents' attention as a mutual challenge calling for the partnership of school and family. The parent should be seen neither as the villain who caused the problem nor as a gendarme to enforce the school's dictates. Needless to say, I think it entirely inappropriate for schools to pressure parents to have their children medicated. If the question is to be raised at all, it should be done only as a suggestion so that the parents may consider exploring the issue with competent medical personnel. Medications must never be a precondition for a child's right to attend school.

*Who are we trying to teach* must precede *what are we trying to teach* as a fundamental consideration. Teaching methods must reflect the first of those questions at least as much as the second. If the student population is to include a sizable number of ADD children—as is increasingly becoming the case throughout North America—creative minds working in education need to apply themselves not to trying to fit the students into the schools but to fashion the schools around the needs of the children.

### 3. ADD *specialists*

Not every family doctor, pediatrician or psychiatrist can be up on attention deficit disorder, although all should at least be able to recognize it and not to mistake it for something else. Similarly, it may be too much to ask that all teachers become proficiently familiar with the condition. Outside the ledgers of bottom-lining politicians, however, there is no excuse for school districts not employing resource people—teachers, psychologists, special education consultants and teachers' aides—who are trained to assess the needs of the ADD child and to assist their colleagues. There have to be people in the schools who can support the classroom teacher, for example, by working one-to-one with ADD children when required. Hyperactive children often settle down when given one-to-one attention, and may need to be gradually integrated into the classroom. The immediate financial costs will be more than compensated for in the long term, not to mention the avoidance of years of emotional stress for school personnel, parents and—far from least—for the children.

#### 4. Keep attachment needs in the foreground

The teacher who can maintain warm, nonthreatening contact with the ADD child will be rewarded with less disruption and longer attention spans, except in the most severely affected cases. Just as at home, the relationship with the child, not any cognitive goals, has to be kept foremost.

Of necessity, the teacher's ability to provide for any one child's attachment needs is going to be limited. No teacher will "cure" a child of ADD. But each teacher, properly informed and motivated, can make a tremendous difference in easing the path in school of any ADD child just by paying attention to the relationship. Difficult as it is for the overworked teacher in the hubbub of the busy classroom, reaching out to the child each day, even for a brief moment, will go further than any number of sternly delivered instructions.

#### 5. Allow time for play and creative expression

It should be superfluous to point out the importance of play in childhood, except for a frightening trend in North American education to forget the value of play. A *New York Times* article in 1998 reported that some new schools in the U.S. are being built without playgrounds, on the theory that recess and play are a waste of time that divert the students' attention and energy from important learning tasks.[2] "We are intent on improving academic performance," the superintendent of schools in Atlanta, Georgia, told the *Times*. "You don't do that by having kids hanging on the monkey bars." This mind-set ignores decades of research in education and in developmental psychology. Specifically in managing ADD, the problem is to introduce more play—more physically unstructured time, more freely flowing creative expression—into the classroom, not less.

As my experience with the Grade 9 class of "school rejects" demonstrated, ADD students have a volcanic amount of pent-up kinetic energy. Allowed some creative outlet, even if at first without a specific outcome in mind, much of this energy can be channeled constructively. The problem, again, is not so much how to motivate the child as to find the way to unlock his intrinsic motivation. To foster creativity, the main thing is to honor the intention and the effort rather than to evaluate the result. The student encouraged in following her own creative inclination and secure in her relationship with the teacher will, sooner or later, want direction and correction, will want to learn how to improve her work by means of disciplined effort.

In these days of cash-register approaches to education funding, the first subjects to be dropped—after teachers' aides, school psychologists and other essential personnel are declared redundant—are the creative courses: music and art. A CBC radio phone-in program in British Columbia recently devoted an hour to the question of whether the creative arts in public schools are expendable. That the question is even raised as a matter of public discussion is a sad commentary on the times, given how close to the human heart and soul aesthetic and musical expression are, how meaningful they are in most people's lives and how important they are to healthy psychological and even neurological development. On the social level, the denial of arts education simply helps foster a culture of consumerism rather than of self-expression. Especially for the ADD child, impoverishing arts programs means blocking an essential channel for emotional growth and creative outflow.

### 6. Adjust examination and home assignment expectations

An ADD student being examined under time pressure is not necessarily being tested on knowledge as much as on his ability to write examinations. A poor mark may reflect not a lack of knowledge, only a prefrontal cortex malfunction under conditions of examination stress.* A failure under such conditions predicts nothing about the student's ability to apply his knowledge in real life. The exam situation may therefore need to be rendered flexible for him: he may need more time, or he may need to write the

---

*For a fuller explanation of the prefrontal cortex shutting down under examination pressure, see chapter 25.

test under single supervision, away from the distraction of the classroom or examination hall. In this way, what he really knows will be tested. In many jurisdictions in the United States, such conditions are already mandatory for ADD students, up to university level. The Canadian system is far behind in this regard, and seems stubbornly intent on staying that way.

With homework too, the special needs of the ADD child must be kept in mind. The long-term goal of fostering her ability to do applied, consistent work need not be sacrificed, but if this child must complete assignments early in her school career the same way as her classmates who are not neurophysiologically tuned out and distractible, she will experience only failure, discouragement and a chronic sense of inadequacy. If exceptions cannot be made for a particular few children in a classroom, perhaps a more general relaxation of rigid rules and expectations is needed. There is little to suggest that this would do the long-term development of children any harm.

The role of the parents in structuring a calm, supportive and organized home environment is crucial. Without that, the school will be facing a constantly uphill battle. On the other hand, the school cannot wait for the parents to resolve all their home problems before embarking on its own efforts to help the child.

### 7. *Trusting the child, trusting oneself*

"Your book has helped me see more clearly what schools can and cannot do," Mary Watson, a specialized early childhood educator from San Francisco wrote to me after reading the manuscript. "A teacher cannot really replace a parent in her ability to give unconditional positive regard. The classroom situation just doesn't work that way—teachers have to judge, to encourage, and they feel the need to criticize. Nevertheless, I do think that understanding the student is itself transformative. Sometimes just the attentive attention to the student is helpful. First, I have to have trust in people—in the children to do what they need to do. But also, we need to trust ourselves and our own experience. I don't think we can be with others, really, without that. I think somehow this is also the basis of what you are saying. It takes tremendous trust to let go the 'shoulds' or the wanting to be 'cured' or the wanting to 'cure' others of all the troubles in life. A teacher who understands ADD can best help students by supporting them to find their own unique way."

Nature has its own positive agenda, which is at work in all of us. The point in education, as in medicine, is not just in knowing how to interfere with nature, but—most important—how to observe it without interference, how to help it unfold.

# 24

# Always on My Case:

# Teenagers

A lot of people, especially this one psychoanalyst guy
they have here, keeps asking me if I'm going to apply
myself when I go back to school next September. It's
such a stupid question, in my opinion. I mean how do
you know what you're going to do until you *do* it? The
answer is, you don't. I *think* I am, but how do I know?
I swear it's a stupid question.

— J.D. SALINGER, *The Catcher in the Rye*

ADOLESCENCE AND ATTENTION deficit
disorder make for a volatile mix. As the
teenager begins to loosen his ties with his
family, he drifts more and more toward his peers for understanding, validation and values to identify with. Because his needs for
attachment are now partly satisfied by the peer group, he can
afford to take a more rebellious stance toward the parents. Counterwill asserts itself with a vengeance; the exaggerated oppositionality that has become second nature to many ADD children receives

a powerful boost. Parents find themselves disobeyed and their opinions rejected with disdain.

Exactly at this time parents tend to become more and more fed up with their offspring's ADD patterns. They begin to have higher expectations, to lose all patience with the uncooperativeness, seeming indifference and disorderliness of their children. It is frustrating enough having to pick up after a smaller child, but it feels intolerable to have to play valet and chambermaid to a near-adult human being. With only a few short years before their son or daughter graduates into the real world of work, study and responsibility, the parent feels an urgency to correct matters. What we are anxious about we try to control, and when we can't control we may throw in the towel. Parental attitudes move between controlling and permissiveness, rarely finding a middle point. The stage is set for confrontation, mutual distrust and, increasingly, parental despair.

Desperate is not too strong a word to describe many parents with teenage children who visit my office for ADD assessment. They are at their wits' end. In their day-to-day interaction with their teenage daughter or son, they feel that their wisdom is evaporating just as rapidly as the demand for it is increasing. They grasp at the diagnosis as at a life raft.

Having parented two sons with ADD who are now past their teens, I understand the alarm parents feel. I no longer share it. Families do face serious problems around this time, but the solutions are well within the capabilities of committed and open-minded parents. As bad as things may look, there are in families deep sources of healing beneath the strife and the pain. In this, as in all tasks, we find in nature a reliable ally.

The apparent rejection that teenagers exhibit toward their parents is deceptive. Underneath their defiant demeanor is a desire and need for love and acceptance from their mothers and fathers. If this is offered with no strings attached, it is a far more powerful attraction than the siren song of the peer culture. Contrary to appearances, this is especially so for the emotionally sensitive teenager with ADD. The young person willingly maintains his ties to the family and accepts the authority of the parents *if* he is not confronted by pressures to conform that he finds threatening to his sense of self. He will bridle at the authority of parents who are authoritarian.

Issues of autonomy and control surface time and again as I interview teenagers and their parents. The common complaint of parents is that their ADD teenager "doesn't listen to a thing we say." The reality is that what teenagers hear very often drives them in directions quite other than what the parents would want.

Many teenagers are wary of the diagnosis of attention deficit disorder. They do not want to be different, or to be regarded as if something was mentally wrong with them. They sense very strongly that the parents see the attention deficit disorder as the root of all the conflicts and clashes that erupt each day. "They're just trying to pretend that the only thing wrong is in my head," the very first teenager I assessed said to me. Lara, as I'll call her, was a vivacious sixteen-year-old. Her biological father had disappeared from her life years before, and her mother had remarried. There was a two-year-old brother from this second marriage. Lara liked her stepfather but she complained that "he is too much on my case. He is not even my dad and he makes all the rules." Lara was constantly embroiled in arguments with her mother and stepfather. The parents found her impossible to manage, while for her part, Lara felt that everyone was against her. When I interviewed Lara's mother, it became obvious that she deferred to her husband's way of disciplining, which consisted of very strict rules and quick punishments. Lara was "grounded" for relatively minor infractions of these rules. When push came to shove—which at times it literally did—the mother found it easier to side with her husband than to support her daughter or even to hear out her point of view. For fear of jeopardizing her relationship with her husband, she tried to make her daughter tone down her personality and suppress her natural resistance to feeling controlled. Mother and daughter fought a lot. Lara was somewhat depressed, felt quite isolated in the family and worried that her mother would choose her new family over her relationship with Lara. At the same time, Lara was too feisty to be fearfully compliant, which, as I pointed out to the mom, was actually a tribute to the warm parenting she had given her daughter over the years.

Lara clearly met the criteria for the diagnosis of ADD. Since her earliest school years, she'd had difficulties concentrating, was impulsively disruptive in class, was forgetful when it came to her school work and other responsibilities and had poor study habits. She was not willing to concede, however, that these amounted to any significant problem in her life. With the marked lack of self-insight that characterizes young people with ADD, she was unable to recognize that her troubles were in any way connected with her own behavior. Of course, in this she was only mirroring the attitudes of the adults around her—parents and teachers—who, in turn, also did not realize to what extent their approach to Lara triggered and defined her responses.

I felt there were other issues far more important than how Lara did in Grade 10 and whether she could focus on her homework. To have simply delivered the verdict of ADD would have made me appear in Lara's eyes as just another authority figure blaming her particular shortcomings for everything that was going wrong in her life and in her relationship with her parents. Explanations to the effect that "it's not you, it's the circuits and chemicals in your brain" do not mean very much to the insecure and defensive teenager who already worries that she is somehow different and craves all the more to be seen as normal, like everyone else. I told mother and daughter my opinion that Lara did indeed show signs of ADD and that dealing with these would potentially help her. I also explained that the acrimony between Lara and her parents was not a result of her ADD but of troubled interactions in the family, which she was only in part responsible for. I said that the rules Lara was having to live under needed rethinking. They were more a cause of her problems than a solution to them. The most urgent changes to be made were not to improve Lara's attention span or behavior but to improve understanding and communication in the family. When those issues had been addressed, we could revisit the question of diagnosis and specific treatment. Subsequently I met with Lara's mother and stepfather. I urged them to have a greater appreciation of Lara's needs for autonomy. I also suggested that their relationship could use some work so that during moments of conflict the mother would not feel she was having to choose between her daughter and her spouse. The parents were open to this approach, much to Lara's surprise. "It's the first time," she said, "that anyone has ever listened to me."

Three months afterward, she was already more willing to talk about her own ADD-related problems. Eventually she chose to try a psychostimulant medication to help her concentrate and act less impulsively. As it happened, her first experience with medication was not successful. There were side effects, and Lara did not wish to continue trying. Now, two years later, she is at the top of her class in her favorite subject, a position she never before had been even close to achieving. According to her mother, in some other areas Lara still has difficulty concentrating, but she is much more motivated and is eagerly planning to go to college. The family is continuing with counseling on a regular basis, and the atmosphere at home has greatly improved. Now that Lara has less to resist, she also knows that help is available whenever she feels she needs it— for example, if she should experience problems with her studies in the future, or in her personal life. As I told her parents, it doesn't matter when that time comes, whether now, or two or five years from now. The point is that when she is ready to seek help, it will be on her own initiative, with a much greater likelihood of success than when she felt pushed into it.

There are a number of lessons to be learned from Lara's case, confirmed time and again with every other teenager referred to me for ADD assessment. First and foremost, teenagers with ADD have an immense need to be heard. Until they feel that their point of view has been listened to and that the legitimacy of their feelings has been accepted, they will simply not move toward any examination of themselves. These young people have a deep sense of being misunderstood, deeper than they realize. Every criticism they hear, every blaming word—anything they interpret as at all judgmental—activates in them feelings of shame, which they try to defend themselves against with all their might. It is easy for parents to fall into the trap of arguing with their teenager, trying to be "logical," pointing out to him the many times they did try very hard to respect his feelings; heatedly explaining that they, too, have feelings; that if anybody doesn't know how to consider others' point of view it is not them but he, the teenager; that things would be a whole lot better if he came to realize finally that he is not the only person in the world and so on. This approach, unfortunately, only locks the two sides into fixed positions.

I have in the past spoken to or about my children with the bitterness of someone wronged by an equal. Many parents similarly complain about their ADD teenagers. Parents need to understand that it is not yet a matter of fifty-fifty. Helpless and bewildered as they may feel, there is in the emotional relationship a power imbalance, and they hold the upper hand. Not only is the teenager dependent on them financially and in many other practical ways, but he is also still yearning for their love and acceptance, his offputting behavior being only a mask behind which he hides his vulnerability from himself and from them. Having more power, the parents also have more responsibility. If anything is to shift, they have to make the first move, which means hearing not just the words their son or daughter throws at them but grasping their meaning, recognizing the mind-set and the feelings behind them. If they can do that nondefensively, the emotional deadlock is broken. Parents need not fear that they are enabling or rewarding unacceptable behavior. To hear someone's point of view and to recognize the legitimacy of his feelings is not the same as necessarily agreeing with everything he says or approving of everything he does. My experience with ADD teenagers is that they are quite open to looking at themselves more realistically and to reach out for help once they see that their parents are willing to see and accept them for who they are, and to respect their feelings and their autonomy. That has to be the first step. As we saw with Lara, a professional can hardly even reach the stage of "treating" anything unless parents first assume responsibility for their own role in the interaction.

My first interview with the parents of ADD teenagers almost always ends with advice that they relax the rules and regulations they have imposed in the hope of inducing better work habits and behaviors in their child. When it comes to rules and regulations, less is more. Until they understand the counterwill dynamic, this seems paradoxical to some parents. Why should we give our daughter more privileges, they ask, when she is showing such irresponsibility with the privileges already granted? The answer is that we are not talking about privileges here. The issue is autonomy, which is not a matter of privileges but of rights. A teenager should have the right to decide when and if to clean her room. If parents are appalled at the unsightly mess, they can shut the door to avoid seeing it. As long as she is not inconveniencing others, it is up to the older teenager to decide how long and with whom she talks on the phone, or what time she goes to bed. A distinction needs to be made between what is simply personal to her, affecting only her, and what affects others as well. Her own room is strictly her business, but participation in housekeeping chores is a family affair, and a mess in the kitchen inconveniences everyone. If we want the adolescent to see such distinctions, we as parents must be able to see them first. A person becomes open to respecting the boundaries of others when her own rights and boundaries are respected. We have to grant autonomy for the inescapable practical reason that without it, no psychological growth will take place and none of our long-term goals will be achieved.

Homework and school work in general are points of daily conflict between the ADD teenager and his parents. The poor concentration skills that characterize attention deficit disorder around activities of low interest, the procrastination and the difficulty getting motivated mean that many teenagers with ADD underperform in school and that few of them are working anywhere near their potential. "He will flunk out if we don't do something," parents say, or "It's heartbreaking to see such a bright kid doing so poorly." My advice is that parents back right off the homework issue if there are more important problems to be tackled. Nobody ever dies of failing Grade 10. It's not a disease. "That may be true," some parents have said, "but what about the blow to the teen's self-esteem that would cause?" I can only respond that such a teen already has low self-esteem. If self-esteem is to grow in the long term, the individual has to heal psychologically, has to feel accepted unconditionally, has to be able to make his own choices. Failing school is not a desired outcome, but the emotional ties within the family and the teen's sense of autonomy are more important than short-term academic setbacks. If school performance and good family relationships can both be preserved, so much the better. If one would come at the cost of the other, the parent again has to choose between long-term or short-term goals.

It's essential to find a path here that does not veer toward either control or permissiveness. A younger child can take more direction than an older one, but no child, teen or pre-teen, will take direction without coercion when the attachment relationship with the parent is shaky. Younger children will simply resist, perhaps passively, while the teenager may find ways of rebelling actively and dramatically. Parents need not abandon their concerns for their teenager's progress in school, but any possible intervention has to be considered in the context of the relationship and of the child's emotional state. The repetition of injunctions and warnings that many of us as parents tend to deliver day after day in tones of criticism and exasperation become tiresome even to ourselves. They only frustrate and alienate the teenager even further.

"If all the pleading, cajoling, persuading, forcing, urging, arguing, convincing, or begging you do would lead your son or your daughter to perform one iota better in their studies than they otherwise would, there might be a case for that sort of an approach," I point out to parents, "although even then, the long-term harm would outweigh any temporary gain. In fact, none of that works, even in the short run. It doesn't advance what we are trying to accomplish one little bit; it only makes matters more difficult." It is useful, on the other hand, to consider with the teenager what her goals are for school, what factors may hinder her ability to achieve them and how they may be remedied. When the relationship is trusting and the motivation is there, the input and support of the parent are invaluable.

Unless the situation is drastic, care must also be taken that we don't intrude in areas where we have granted autonomy, even when we don't approve of what the teenager is doing. A person whose failures are the result of decisions she makes freely is far more capable of learning from consequences than someone whose actions and reactions come from succumbing to the demands of others, or from resisting them. Eventually the young man and woman will have to find his or her individual path in the world. We can't save them from their own mistakes, nor would we be doing them any good if we did. I advise parents of an ADD teenager to practice biting their tongues until it hurts—and, I can attest, sometimes it hurts quite a bit. "But how will I teach my son self-discipline if I don't make him do his homework?" asked the mother of a seventeen-year-old.

"You won't," I said. "Neither will you at this stage teach him *self*-discipline by pressuring him. You may be able to force him to be disciplined, but only temporarily at best, and even that would not be self-discipline. Respecting his autonomy will at least clear some ground for the development of self-discipline within him."

Lara's statement that her parents are always on her case is the predominant complaint of every ADD adolescent and teenager I see. Sometimes we forget teenagers have their own take on life. They look at things differently. They see many of our attitudes and concerns as irrelevant or, like Holden Caulfield in *The Catcher in the Rye*, even absurd. Their priorities are not ours.

That much was evident in an illuminating conversation I had with Angus, a highly gifted sixteen-year-old in my practice. I have known him all his life, having been the attending physician at his birth. I saw him grow up. I saw his parents' marriage fail as his father—a very personable and clever man, an accomplished juggler—sank deeper and deeper into alcoholism. Angus has ADD, and until he participated in a very demanding outdoors course this past year, he also had a heavy-duty drug problem. He was expelled from no fewer than five schools in the two years between Grades 9 and 10. I quote him at some length because he articulates very clearly the ambivalence many teenagers have toward the diagnosis of attention deficit disorder. Parents are best to respect that ambivalence, not to try to force the issue. Angus also voices the teenager's demand to be accepted as he is.

"I love history and English," Angus said, "but in my other subjects the teachers are always saying that 'Angus doesn't pay attention. Doesn't concentrate. Talks too much.' I don't take notes."

"Why don't you want to try medications?" I asked.

"It's just the way I am. It might sound strange, coming from an ex–drug addict, or however you want to phrase it—a clean addict now, a sober drunk—but I don't want to alter my mind with drugs as behavior control. I am the way I am as a result of my upbringing, the influence the world has had on me, what I have seen, my experiences. I am not about to try to change because some people say I've got a problem. And maybe I do."

"If you don't think it's a problem for you," I said, "there is no reason you should take medications."

"It's not that it's not a problem," Angus replied. "I can see how it is, but I don't care. I'm not going to change myself in that way for others. I may be extremely selfish in that respect, but I'm not going to put myself on pills so that I'm more—what's the word—more controllable…"

"Manageable," I suggested.

"Yeah, that's it, so that I am more manageable for my teachers. I wouldn't, 'cause that's not me. If you can't accept me for me, I think, then what are you looking for? What are you asking for from me?"

I pressed the point a little: "But wouldn't you like to be able to concentrate better, to be more focused in some of these other subjects besides just your favorite ones?"

"Nah," said Angus. "I think ADD in itself isn't that bad. It's when you put it on top of a broken home, or alcoholic parents, or bad crowds you get in with and you have trouble getting out of, you put it on top of not a lot of self-confidence, then you get a serious problem. And then Ritalin isn't going to take away everything. It's just going to take away the ADD, not relieve all these other problems you have."

# PART SIX

The ADD Adult

# 25

# Justifying One's

Existence:

## Self-Esteem

If you persist in throttling your impulses you end by
becoming a clot of phlegm. You finally spit out a gob
which completely drains you and which you only
realize years later was not a gob of spit but your inmost
self. If you lose that you will always race through dark
streets like a madman pursued by phantoms. You will be
able to say with perfect sincerity: "I don't know what
I want in life."

    — HENRY MILLER, *Sexus*

      **"I** HAVE WASTED MOST of my life," said Andrea,
a fifty-year-old unemployed woman. "I have
achieved nothing. I have no excuse for existence. I haven't justified my existence yet."

Guilt, shame and self-judgment are commonly heard in interviews of adults with attention deficit disorder. While features of many other chronic and troubled psychological states, such as depression, for example, low self-esteem and merciless self-criticism are so much part of the ADD personality that it would be difficult to know where ADD ends and low self-esteem begins. Many of the traits thought to be caused by attention deficit disorder are, I am convinced, not the expressions of the specific neurophysiological impairments associated with ADD but of low self-esteem. Workaholism, drivenness and inability to say no—all endemic in the adult ADD population—are some of the examples discussed in this chapter.

In the ADD child, low self-esteem is manifested not just by the self-putdowns he may utter, such as "I'm dumb." Above all, it is apparent in the perfectionism and in the dejection and discouragement he experiences when he fails at a task or loses in a game. Nor can he accept not being in the right. The fragile and self-rejecting ego is unable to endure any reminders of its fallibility. Many people with attention deficit disorder retain that fragility into adulthood.

Where do self-judgment and lack of self-respect originate? The conventional view is that the low self-esteem of ADD adults is a natural consequence of the many failures, lost opportunities and setbacks they have experienced since childhood, owing to their neurophysiological deficits. Plausible as it sounds, this explanation accounts only in small measure for why people with ADD think so very little of themselves.

Andrea, like so many others I have seen, would never judge anyone else as severely as she does herself. That people do judge themselves so harshly reflects low self-esteem, not low achievement. Self-esteem, we must realize, is the quality of self-respect that is evident in a person's emotional life and behavior. A superficially positive self-image and true self-esteem are by no means necessarily identical. In some cases, they are not even compatible. People who have a grandiose and inflated view of themselves on the conscious level are lacking true self-esteem at the core of their psyche. Their exaggerated self-evaluation is a defense against their deepest feelings of worthlessness. The professionally successful workaholic suffers from low self-esteem, no matter what his conscious and projected self-image may be. Some years ago a Toronto study purported to have determined that men had higher self-esteem than women by asking people whether they ever felt despondent, vulnerable or lonely. Male respondents tended to deny such feelings, hence the study's conclusions. It appears not to have occurred to the researchers that what they might have been measuring was not, in fact, self-esteem but the denial and suppression of negative emotions—hallmarks of low self-esteem!

There are some adults with attention deficit disorder who exhibit great self-confidence in specific areas of functioning and are high achievers according to social standards. Many others are low achievers who bring little confidence to any field of endeavor. *What they share is low self-esteem.* The low achievers may believe they would gain self-esteem if their ADD impairments could be eliminated and they could perform better in society's eyes; the high achievers would tell them otherwise. The wide chasm that may yawn between success and self-acceptance is illustrated by a diary fragment shown to me by a forty-three-year-old professional with attention deficit disorder who enjoys a high income, the good opinion of his clients and public recognition. The diary is typical of attention deficit disorder in its format, written on dog-eared scraps of paper filed in no particular order, months and years separating individual entries. It is typical, too, in the deep dissatisfaction with the self it reveals:

> I have not achieved enough in life. I feel that my abilities exceed my attainments. I feel I could do more.... I vegetate, my ambitions like rotting weeds around me. I want to paint. I want to study languages: French, German, Spanish.... What else? I want to exercise. I want to meditate. I want to read. I

want to see people. I want to take in more culture. I want to
sleep enough. I don't want to watch junk television any more.
I want an end to the binge cramming of food into myself every
evening.... I want to live!*

Characteristically, what this man did not think to write was *I want
to learn to accept myself.*

What are some of the markers of low self-esteem, besides consciously harsh self-judgment? As mentioned above, an inflated,
grandiose view of oneself—frequently seen in politicians, for
example. Craving the good opinion of others. Frustration with
failure. A tendency to blame oneself excessively when things go
wrong, or, on the other hand, an insistence on blaming others: in
other words, the propensity to *blame* someone. Mistreating those
who are weaker or subordinate, or accepting mistreatment without resistance. Argumentativeness—having to be in the right or,
obversely, assuming that one is always in the wrong. Trying to
impose one's opinion on others or, on the contrary, being afraid to
say what one thinks for fear of being judged. Allowing the judgments of others to influence one's emotions or, its mirror opposite,
rigidly rejecting what others may have to say about one's work or
behavior. Other traits of low self-esteem are an overwrought sense
of responsibility for other people in relationships and, as we will
discuss shortly, an inability to say no. The need to achieve in order
to feel good about oneself. How one treats one's body and psyche
speaks volumes about one's self-esteem: abusing body or soul with
harmful chemicals, behaviors, work overload, lack of personal
time and space all denote poor self-regard. All of these behaviors
and attitudes reveal a fundamental stance towards the self that is
*conditional* and devoid of true self-respect.

Self-esteem based on achievement has been called *contingent*

---

* This entry was written before the man knew he had ADD. I quote by permission.

*self-esteem* or *acquired self-esteem*. Unlike contingent self-esteem, *true self-esteem* has nothing to do with a self-evaluation on the basis of achievement or the lack of it. A person truly comfortable in his own skin doesn't say, "I am a worthy human being *because* I can do such and such," but says, "I am a worthy human being *whether or not* I can do such and such." Contingent self-esteem evaluates; true self-esteem accepts. Contingent self-esteem is fickle, going up and down with a person's ability to produce results. True self-esteem is steadfast, not adventitious. Contingent self-esteem places great store in what others think. True self-esteem is independent of others' opinions. Acquired self-esteem is a false imitation of true self-esteem: however good it makes one feel in the moment, it does not esteem the *self*. It esteems only the achievement, without which the self in its own right would be rejected. True self-esteem is *who one is*; contingent self-esteem is only *what one does*.

ADD adults don't have low self-esteem because they are poor achievers, but it is due to their low self-esteem that they judge themselves and their achievements harshly. It is also, in part, due to low self-esteem that people do not reach their full potential, do not strive to locate within themselves fonts of creativity and self-expression, do not venture to embark on activities and projects where success is in doubt. They feel safer not trying, because their poor self-regard is terrified at the risk of failure. Much of my initial counseling with people is to help them recognize that in many ways the problem is not in what they have done in life but in how they view themselves. There live human beings afflicted with far more debilitating impairments who do not necessarily hold the low opinion of the self prevalent among ADD adults.

The deep shame of adults with attention deficit predates any recollections of poor achievement. The association between low self-esteem and attention deficit disorder is not that the first arises from the second, but that they both arise from the same sources: stress in the parenting environment and disrupted attunement/ attachment. Healthy development of self-esteem needs the atmosphere of what Carl Rogers called "unconditional positive regard."* It requires that the adult world understand and accept as valid the child's feelings, from which kernel the core self will grow. A child taught to disregard or mistrust her innermost feelings and thoughts assumes automatically that there is something shameful about them, and therefore about her very self.

Absolutely universal in the stories of all adults with ADD is the memory of never being comfortable about expressing their emotions. When asked whom they confided in when as children they were lonely or in psychic pain, almost none recall feeling invited or safe enough to bare their souls to their parents. They kept their deepest griefs to themselves. On the other hand, many recall being hyperaware of the parents' difficulties and struggles in the world, of not wanting to trouble them with their own petty and childish problems. The sensitive child, writes the Swiss psychotherapist Alice Miller, has "an amazing capacity to perceive and respond intuitively, that is unconsciously, to this need of the mother, or of both parents."[1] When I explore with my clients their childhood histories, emerging most often are patterns of relationships that required the child to take care of the parent emotionally, if only by keeping her inmost feelings to herself so as not to burden the parent. ADD adults are convinced that their low self-esteem is a fair reflection of how poorly they have done in life only because they do not understand that their very first failure—their inability to win the full and unconditional acceptance of the adult world—was not their failure at all.

Although low self-esteem springs originally from the disrupted attunement/attachment relationship with the parent, the belief that it is exacerbated by poor achievement is not wrong. Only, the link is not a direct one. In the majority of adults I have interviewed, it was evident that the inability to accept themselves was heavily reinforced throughout childhood by their parents'

---

* See chapter 16.

expectations of better performance, and by their disappointment and disapproval at the absence of it. Superimposed on the parents' anxieties were the contemptuous judgments and shaming that, throughout their childhoods, many of these ADD adults had experienced in school. Not performance as such but the attitudes of the adult world toward performance defined how many children learned to value themselves.

At our second session, I asked Andrea, the fifty-year-old self-confessed failure at the game of existence justification, if she had truly never done anything worthwhile in her life. She was silent for a while. "I have tried to be kind to people," she finally replied. "I have tried not to hurt people. I am creative in crafts. I teach people. I do a bit of gardening. But to me those things come easily. That's just who I am. I didn't have to work at them much. I mean, I'm not an accountant or a lawyer."

"Would you want to be an accountant or a lawyer?"

"It's not that I feel like doing those things," Andrea said, again after a moment's pause. "It's that I think I should feel like doing them. I am still trying to get my father's approval."

Andrea's dismissal of her own talents resonated with me. In my undergraduate years and even beyond, I had little respect for my ability to write. I could use it to advantage—for example, my capacity for relatively elegant verbal flourishes inflated the value of some pretty thin essays—but I had little regard for it precisely because I felt it came naturally to me. "I don't trust my words," I would say. "They come too easily." It never occurred to me that possessing a vein of talent did not mean that one could not work diligently at mining it. If I had a facility with something, or if I enjoyed it, it could not be worth much. Unless it was pure blood, sweat and tears, it could not have value. Much the same has been said to me by many adults with ADD. A few have even butted their heads against the wall trying to become accountants, which, in my estimation, must be the profession least suited for anyone with attention deficit disorder. As far as I could see, they were working to convince themselves of their own self-worth by striving to achieve something completely contrary to their nature.

Debra, a woman in her early thirties with a bachelor of science degree in zoology, wanted help with her difficulties remembering and concentrating. "I feel so dumb," she said. "I can never keep up with discussions. People talk about politics and current affairs and I have no head for those things. I try hard to remember facts and names and dates from the newspaper, but it doesn't stick. I tune out." What Debra does have a mind for is seeking the emotional truth in people's lives, what their existence is like underneath the surface of social niceties. Her desire to be more adept at social conversation was not an unreasonable goal. It struck me, though, that she seemed to place value on a facile awareness of facts, which she did not have, above insight, empathy and understanding, all of which she was gifted with.

One of the barriers faced by adults with attention deficit disorder in their quest for self-esteem is that they do not really know who exactly that self to be esteemed is. "It drives me nuts when someone asks me what my feelings are," a student in his midtwenties said. "I have no idea what my feelings are. I'm lucky if I figure out what my feelings *were* hours or days after something happens, but I never know what they *are*." Since having a strong core self relies on acceptance of feelings, being out of touch with the emotional side puts a person out of touch with herself. What then remains to be esteemed? Only a false self, a concoction of what we would like to imagine ourselves to be and what we have divined others want us to be. Sooner or later, people come to realize that this false self—wanting what they think they should want, feeling what they think they should feel—does not work for them. When they look inside themselves, they discover a frightening emptiness, a vacuum, an absence of a true self or of intrinsic motivation. Many a time I have heard ADD adults say, "I don't know who I am," or, "I don't know what I want to do in my life."

Women with ADD are especially prone to give a higher priority to protecting the needs of others than to respecting their own. "I don't know how to say no. I'm always so worried about what the other person is feeling," said Diane, a forty-three-year-old high school teacher. "I don't know why. I guess it's my second nature." As always, people's language is revelatory. Diane was uttering a deep truth when she spoke those words: suppressing her own feelings in preference to those of others was *second* nature to her. It had never been her *first* nature. It was acquired. Human infants are born with no capability whatsoever to hide or suppress any feeling, be it hunger, fear, discomfort or pain. Healthy newborns are skilled at communicating anger and have a superbly articulate talent for saying no, as anyone can attest who has witnessed the rage of a frustrated infant or who has ever tried to feed some unwanted substance to a baby. She shouts out her responses to the world, loud and clear. Given the survival value of emotional expression, nature would not have us give up that capacity unless the suppression of emotion was demanded by the environment. When we forget how to say no, we surrender self-esteem.

The adult with ADD is buried under a mound of yeses, many of which are not true yeses at all, only no's he dared not say. Life is one long exercise in trying to tunnel out from under them, a frustrating task since one keeps adding to the stack faster than one can take away from it. As busy as I ever was, I always found it almost impossible to refuse whenever anyone asked to become my patient. My addiction to serving the world got so out of hand that in one memorable month thirteen years ago, the very time we were to move to our new house, I ended up delivering fifteen babies. Most of these were first pregnancies, which meant that labor tended to be long and almost inevitably took up at least part of the night. I became more wan and bedraggled by the day, precisely when Rae needed the most help with packing, organizing and parenting. With the addict's typical shiftiness, I had not told her what I had taken on. She just noticed me disappearing day in, day out. I was dutiful when at home, as dutiful as a person could be whose mind was buzzing with the self-imposed duties and responsibilities that kept me endlessly busy. I could feel myself becoming more and more hollow, a nonpresence for my family. Behind the image of the empathetic physician—a true reflection of some essential aspects of myself—was also someone who, in his desperation to be needed, was willing to sacrifice his personal life. And a person who felt so alienated from his own self that he had to keep running away from any awareness of it.

The need to be needed at all costs comes from one's earliest experiences. If the child does not feel accepted unconditionally, he learns to *work* for acceptance and attention. When he is not doing this work, he feels anxious, owing to an unconscious fear of being cut off from the parent. Later—as an adult—when not doing something specific, he has a vague unease, the feeling that he *should* somehow be working. *The adult has no psychological rest because the infant and child had never known psychological rest.* He has a dread of rejection and an insatiable need to have his desirability and value affirmed by others. Being wanted becomes a drug. Self-esteem is preempted by its false shadow, contingent self-esteem. What one does and what others think of it take precedence over who one is.

The driven and hyperfunctioning workaholic tries to delude himself that he must be very important, since so many people want him. His frenetic activity numbs him to emotional pain and keeps his sense of inadequacy out of sight, out of mind. During a group psychotherapy session a few years ago, I heard one of the leaders say that a truly important person is one who considers himself worthy enough to grant himself at least one hour each day that he can call his own. I had to laugh. I realized I had worked so hard and made myself so "important" that I couldn't beg, borrow or steal a minute for myself.

There is one major respect in which the specific neurophysio-logical impairments of ADD do hinder the development of a core sense of self and the attainment of self-esteem. It is appropriate here to speak of a *sense* of self, because from the neurophysiological point of view the self simply does not exist. There is no neurobio-logical "self circuit" in the brain, no little gnome pulling all the levers. What we see as the self is really a construct, akin to the optical illusion that makes us believe that a series of photographic images projected onto a screen in rapid progression are people and objects in the real world. The "self" we experience is an unimaginably rapid series of firings of countless neurological circuits. "At each moment the state of self is constructed, from the ground up," writes Antonio Damasio. "It is an evanescent reference state, so continuously and consistently reconstructed that the owner never knows it is being remade unless something goes wrong with the remaking."[2] It is the relative consistency of the repetitious neurological activities of the brain that convinces us there is a solid self. We might say that in ADD this consistency lacks consistency. The fluctuations are greater and more rapid than most people experience. It seems there is less to hold on to. Self-esteem does require a degree of self-regulation, which the neurophysiology of ADD sabotages. The child or adult easily flung into extremes of emotion and behavior does not acquire the mastery over impulses that self-esteem demands.

It is ironic, but despite her poor impulse control, the ADD adult has persistently throttled her impulses, to use Henry Miller's phrase. Submerged beneath a surface rippling with superficial and childish impulses are truer impulses for meaningful activity, the assertion of her autonomy, the pursuit of her own truth and human connectedness. The deeper these have sunk, the less one knows who she is or in which direction her path lies. Attaining self-esteem begins with finding our true impulses and raising them to the light of day.

# 26

# Memories Are

# Made of This

This scant reliability of our memories will be
satisfactorily explained only when we know in what language, in what alphabet they are written, on what
surface, and with what pen...
  — PRIMO LEVI, *The Drowned and the Saved*

"I LOST IT TODAY, BIG TIME," said Elsa, a
twenty-seven-year-old office worker, distraught
over an incident on the bus on her way to my of-
fice. She witnessed a group of teenage girls ridiculing and taunting
a very overweight man, giggling among themselves but speaking in
voices loud enough to be easily overheard by the other passengers.
"Something came over me," Elsa related. "As I was getting off I
heard myself screaming at them. 'You girls are sick!' I yelled.
'You're immature and mean and sick! You shouldn't be allowed on
this bus!' Some other people got off at the same stop. When the bus
left, I just stood there, still in a rage. They looked at me as if I was
crazy—and I felt that I was crazy, too."

David, a forty-year-old artisan, told a similar story. He was walking down his street when he saw two policemen handcuffing an elderly Italian woman who had, apparently, been yelling at the neighbors and threatening them over some incident. "They were so rough with her," David said. "There was no gentleness, no understanding showing on their faces. She was just a problem to them. When they pushed her into the van, I wanted to scream at them to stop, but I felt paralyzed. My mouth was dry, and I couldn't have said a thing. I felt ashamed later of being such a coward. I could have made a phone call at least when I got home to complain to somebody about it, but I was too upset even to do that."

Both Elsa and David have attention deficit disorder, and the stories they told echo experiences and feelings I have heard from many others with ADD: a painful hyperconsciousness of injustice, accompanied by ineffective rage or by shamed silence. Time after time, adults with ADD relate how sickened they are at seeing someone weak hurt or humiliated—how sickened they are, and how helpless they feel at intervening. I use the word *sickened* literally: there is a churning, nauseating feeling in the pit of the stomach and the head spins.

In some of the popular literature on ADD and on some of the Internet websites, there is a celebration of attention deficit disorder as a condition that bestows a special kind of human empathy on individuals affected by it. "The world needs us people with ADD," I heard a speaker declare at a major conference, to enthusiastic applause. There is some truth in that way of seeing attention deficit disorder, but not enough insight. The stories of Elsa and David speak of something more painful than empathy and something less effective, too: they speak of *identification*. When a person *empathizes*, he can understand another's feelings and even share them, but he is conscious of himself as a separate individual, capable of taking independent and useful action. When he *becomes identified*, that boundary disappears. He reacts as if he was himself the victim. He feels the victim's humiliation, his helpless rage, his shame. This is not a state of adult human fellow feeling from which he can act effectively: *it is a state of memory*. He is gripped by the past.

As the Harvard psychiatrist Judith Lewis Herman has pointed out, "To some degree everyone is a prisoner of the past."[1] Without knowing it, we often relive the past. What we take for present-day reality represents, in many situations, reactivated early memories stored in the *implicit memory system*, a vast and infallibly accurate record of past experiences. Implicit memory happens, according to the psychologist and memory researcher Daniel Schacter, "when people are influenced by a past experience without any awareness that they are remembering."[2] Unconscious emotions and conscious feelings, rapid shifts in mood and dramatic physiological changes in the body can occur under the impact of implicit memory.

It is now known that memory does not function like a video camera, storing all the information from an experience on a single, previously blank tape. Retrieving memories is not like searching a file to locate some desired item. Not only are there many components to the recording, storage and reactivation of each memory, but also scientists and psychologists who study the subject speak these days of more than one type of memory process. "The brain clearly has multiple memory systems, each devoted to different kinds of learning and memory functions," writes the neuroscientist Joseph LeDoux.[3] The ability to bring consciously to mind specific events, feelings or ideas is only one form of memory, named *explicit memory*. Explicit memory is recall: facts, images and impressions of the past that we can "call back" more or less at will and describe verbally.

For short-term memories to fix in the brain for storage in long-term memory, they have to be *encoded*. There are many components to any experience, Daniel Schacter points out, physical and emotional: sights, sounds, words, actions, feelings. Each of these is analyzed by different sets of circuits in the brain. Encoding occurs as the connections between the various circuits involved in the experience are strengthened. (We can recall here the principle that "neurons that fire together, wire together.") These circuits are located in many separate parts of the brain, which is why there is no single neurological filing cabinet for memory storage. Each new memory is a new pattern of strengthened connections between widely distributed brain circuits. A memory happens when the circuits that participated in the original encoding are simultaneously reactivated by some stimulus in the present. The connections between these circuits can be strengthened or weakened with time. They are very much subject to emotional influences that can either reinforce or sabotage them.

The implicit memory circuits carry the neurological traces of infancy and of childhood experiences. Encoded in them is the emotional content of those experiences, but not necessarily the details of the events themselves that gave rise to the emotions. There may be at least three reasons for this. First, as we saw in the chapters on brain development, the infant's initial interactions with people are based more on feelings than on conscious awareness of the environment. Second, the brain structures that encode explicit memory, or recall, develop later than those involved in implicit memory. Third, emotions may have been disassociated or repressed even as the events that first caused them were unfolding. No conscious awareness is necessary for the encoding of implicit memory, or for its being triggered. A tone of voice or a look in another's eyes can activate powerful implicit memories. The person experiencing this type of memory may believe that he is just reacting to something in the present, remaining completely in the dark about what the rush of feelings that flood his mind and body really represents. Implicit memory is responsible for much of human behavior, its workings all the more influential because unconscious. Whenever we experience ourselves caught up in feelings that seem to overwhelm us, we are likely in the realm of implicit memory—as we also are when we find ourselves quite cut off from feelings. "[The] implicit effects of past experiences shape our emotional reactions, preferences, and dispositions—key elements of what we call personality," writes Daniel Schacter.

"...While our sense of self and identity is highly dependent on explicit memory for past episodes and autobiographical facts, our personalities may be more closely tied to implicit memory processes."[4]

The episodes involving Elsa and David are implicit memories. Their emotional and physical reactions to witnessing the humiliation and rough handling of another human being are the reactivation of sensations first encoded during a much earlier time of their lives when they themselves were helpless and felt shame and humiliation. David, I already knew, grew up in a home with an alcoholic father who had an unpredictable temper and a bent for violence. Being the youngest child, he was also the target of his older sister's verbal and physical abuse. Elsa's biography, though less overtly traumatic, was emotionally just as wrenching. She was the eldest of four children and always felt outside the family circle. Her mother was critical of her because she saw herself mirrored in the child's sensitive and highly reactive nature. Elsa was hit sometimes, but mostly she suffered from her mother's inability to connect with her emotionally, and from her cutting words. "I don't understand how I could have ended up with a daughter like you," her mother once told her. The emotions that arose in Elsa and David in response to the injustices they each witnessed recently were those of small children: impotent rage, helpless shame. Because in order to maintain their relationships with their parents they had to dissociate their emotional reactions from conscious awareness, these emotions did not come up as they recalled these facts of their childhood, only when some event in the present triggered them. The events stayed in explicit memory, the emotions survived as implicit memories. In other cases, only the implicit memory may endure, the physical events themselves completely lost to recall.

Of course, not in every case of attention deficit disorder is there parental dysfunction to the degree that Elsa and David had to live with. *There does not have to be severe trauma for neurological circuits to be encoded with emotions of exclusion, injustice and humiliation.* It can happen in loving families, if a sensitive child has unconscious or even preverbal experiences of feeling alone and cut off, misunderstood and shamed. From that arises a close identification with the powerless, with the underdog—the people Dostoevsky called "the insulted and the injured." The goal for the ADD adult is to move from the helplessness of identification to the empowered state of empathy.

Other well-known features of attention deficit disorder can be understood when interpreted in the light of implicit memory, notably the trouble with authority figures reported by most ADD adults. This trouble can present itself in three ways: fear, rebelliousness or a combination of both. There is always at least an inner rejection of authority, a perhaps unspoken sense that people with power are unseeing, unknowing and unfair. This is simply the implicit memory of the adult who, as a sensitive child, saw through the pretensions and weaknesses of the adult world. Around authority figures such as employers, doctors, teachers and policemen, the ADD adult will experience a nervousness and lack of confidence that cannot be explained by the actual power relationship that exists in the present. As influential as any of the above personages can be, under normal circumstances none of them have the power to evoke nearly so much fear. In the interaction with authority, the implicit memory system becomes activated. One is again a child, facing powerful adults. "Like a child" is precisely how many ADD adults describe their sense of themselves in relationship to authority.

ADD reactions to authority are not always due to implicit memory. Sometimes they come from counterwill, which, as we have seen, is a sign of an underdeveloped sense of self. "I was always rebellious," said Mary-Lynn, a thirty-six-year-old mother of two. "Any sign of authority, and I just want to stick it in their face." Such automatic resistance to rules, regulations and authority simply means that the adult is not yet an adult. It does not smooth one's way in the world. I have always felt, in almost any situation, a compulsive urge to expose the feet of clay, the chink in the armor, the flaws of those in charge. It is only too true that often authority does totter along on feet of clay. But one always has much to gain from an open mind, much to learn if one parks automatic oppositionality at the door.

Counterwill coupled with implicit memory can deeply affect someone's relationship to society and politics. As a student radical during the Vietnam era in the late 1960s, I used to be infuriated at psychologists and psychiatrists who explained away the antiwar activism and political rebelliousness of the young generation as a displaced, wet-behind-the-ears, unconscious adolescent rebellion against parents. Now when I look back, I can see what truth there was in that view—and what obtuse blindness as well. The style and tone of the student opposition certainly owed much to adolescent acting out and to unresolved and inchoate anger that did not originate with the war. The critics were right: the sometimes reflexive and unthinking lashing-out at authority carried the hallmarks of unconscious, implicit memory and immature rebelliousness. To the degree this was so, it was also less effective than it might have been, more likely to alienate others. Where the learned doctors and mind experts were wrong, however, was in their disregard for the reality of the issues raised by the antiwar opposition. They identified, correctly enough, the psychological flaw. Their mistake was to believe that thereby they had discredited the clear-sightedness that outrage had granted to antiwar youth. It is the same with attention deficit disorder. Sharing the perspective of the downtrodden may originate in implicit memory, but to say so is not to invalidate the truth thereby seen. In this sense, the conference speaker was right: humanity does need people capable of seeing past the official line, unwilling or unable to obliterate their conscious awareness of what is wrong in the world.

Implicit memory tends to be much less forgetful than explicit memory, especially of emotional conditioning. "Conditioned fear learning is particularly resilient," Joseph LeDoux suggests, "and in fact may represent an indelible form of learning."[5] The implicit memory of early fear conditioning probably contributes to the specific neurophysiological impairments of ADD. An example would be the loss of mental clarity, to the point of mental paralysis, experienced during situations of emotional stress. It would account for the well-known "examination amnesia" of many students with attention deficit disorder.

While explicit memories are being retrieved—when we recall something—there appears to be increased blood flow to the frontal lobe of the brain. Radioactive brain scans, by contrast, have shown in some ADD brains slowed frontal lobe activity and *diminished* blood flow to this part of the cortex during stressful mental effort. What we may be seeing here are implicit memory circuits imprinted with fear overwhelming explicit memory.* The student enters the examination room having studied and knowing his subject full well, only to find himself completely unable to answer the questions put in front of him. I believe what happens is that the experience of having to prove one's worthiness and the fear of failure give a strong emotional shock to the ADD mind's ability to activate recall memory. The circuits are sabotaged by the neurophysiological and neurochemical effects of anxiety. A massive shutdown occurs. Having to prove herself in the examination setting, within a restricted time, would trigger in the mind of the sensitive student—adult or child—deep fears of rejection buried in the unconscious. Since what is being tested here is not just knowledge but also the ability to activate memory in the face of rejection anxiety, the ADD student is at a great disadvantage. Implicit fear memory, acquired much earlier than intellectual memory, dominates.

Others with ADD may have the intellectual confidence to do well during examinations. Nevertheless, they can be reduced to the helpless inarticulateness of a semiverbal toddler in other situations, superficially trivial, if anxieties imprinted in their implicit memory system long ago are triggered. To give a personal example, my voice quickly falters when someone as much as averts his eyes from me while I am speaking with him. My words lose connection and dry up, like water trickling into sand. "For the rest of our lives,"

---

* These research findings were discussed in chapter 5.

writes Stanley Greenspan, "the seemingly trivial gestures first understood in late infancy serve to anchor both our human relationships and our thought processes... Should someone stare at us blankly, gaze off into space, or remain mute, we begin to feel confused, rejected, perhaps even unloved. Very sensitive individuals may even find their thinking becoming disorganized, their sense of purpose gradually dissolving."[6] My experience, precisely.

# 27

# Remembering What

# Didn't Happen:

# The ADD

# Relationship

The child who is deprived or rejected will tend to over-
react to successive separations throughout life.

— ROBERT W. FIRESTONE, PH.D., *The Fantasy Bond*

"I'M CONFUSED ABOUT MY relationships
with women," said Trevor, a thirty-six-year-old
stockbroker, diagnosed with ADD in his early
thirties. "It's sick that you want someone so bad when they are
cold to you, then when they warm up you start finding things that
are wrong with them."

Trevor's one marriage ended when his wife divorced him after five years, following which he lived with another woman for four years. He had cheated on both of them. He has dated and slept with dozens of women but has not had any other relationships lasting longer than a few months. At the time of our discussion, he was seeing three women, keeping each in the dark about the others. He ended many of these liaisons soon after they began, quickly growing tired of them. By the same token, he feels devastated if ever a woman begins to withdraw from him. "I just hate being left," he said. "I can't even stand it when a woman wants to end a telephone conversation. I deliberately start prolonging things, bringing up new topics I'm not even interested in, just to keep her on the phone." A year ago, Trevor spent the summer with a young woman from another country, a sudden and casual acquaintance. "It was strange," he said. "She never told me she loved me or that she would miss me when she went back home. In the end I was resenting it."

"Did you tell her you loved her?" I asked. "Did you feel that you did?"

Trevor shrugged. "That's what's so strange. I wouldn't have cared, except for the fact that she was going away. Toward the end, I was getting pretty nasty to her. I feel sad about it now. She was always very nice to me. I can't understand what was with me."

Ironically, in the midst of his jumping from one brief fling to another, Trevor yearns for a monogamous relationship. He hopes someday to have a family and is distressed by his inability to become deeply committed to any one of his female partners. As his forties approach, he worries that time is running out. "Is it that I haven't met the right one?" he asked. "Or am I just incapable of settling down?" My guess was that he'd probably met at least half a dozen "right ones."

He agreed. "My wife was wonderful, and Melanie [the four-year live-in partner] was a very good person too. It's sick, isn't it. I mean, I was brought up in a Christian home and believe in the Judeo-Christian tradition. There are some real solid values there. I'm just too weak to live up to them."

*Sick* and *weak* are not useful entries in the dictionary of self-understanding. I suggested that a little compassionate curiosity about what might be driving Trevor's fear of intimacy and commitment would yield us more insight than his self-accusations.

Fear of intimacy is universal among ADD adults. It coexists with what superficially would seem to be its opposites—a desperate craving for affection and a dread of being rejected. The reflexive shrinking away from intimacy undermines the ability of the ADD adult to find what he would find most healing: mutually committed loving contact with another human being. Trevor may be an extreme example of the relationship nomad, but the issues that trouble him are, to one degree or another, present in every relationship in which either or both of the partners have attention deficit disorder.

Trevor has tried therapy here and there in the past. These efforts usually ended after a few sessions spent trying to identify the traumatic events that would have led to his confused and conflicting emotions around relationships. The problem was that he could not recall anything traumatic. No one had abused him, neither of his parents were alcoholics and there was no violence in the family home as he was growing up. It's not that memory failed him; it was, in fact, accurately telling him exactly what he needed to know, but he had not learned to recognize the many vivid memories he was experiencing each and every day of his adult life.

There are memories, the psychiatrist Mark Epstein explains, "that are not so much about *something* terrible happening, but, in the words of D. W. Winnicott [the great British children's psychoanalyst] about 'nothing happening when something might profitably have happened.' These events are more often recorded in the soma, or body, than in the verbal memory, and they can be integrated only by subsequently experiencing and making sense of them."[1] When Trevor finally came to recognize and make sense of the memories encoded in his body states and emotional reactions, he saw that his present-day troubles arose not from what had happened in his family, but from what had *not* happened. He found that he had been living a memory each time anxiety gripped him when a woman seemed to cool toward him or even when she tried to end a late-night telephone call. His fear of intimacy was itself a reliving of long-ago events, *a precise marker of what had never occurred.* It was a function of implicit memory.

We saw in the previous chapter that implicit memory is the imprinting of brain circuits with the emotional content of early experiences. These circuits become activated without the person's having any awareness that what he feels in the present really belongs to the past. "In a situation like this," writes Joseph LeDoux, "you may find yourself in the throes of an emotional state that exists for reasons you do not quite understand."[2] LeDoux, quite aptly, refers to implicit memory also as *emotional memory.**

How can we understand Trevor's reactions to his female lovers as implicit memory? In chapter 10 we saw how a portion of the frontal gray matter on the right side of the brain—the orbitofrontal cortex, or OFC—is dominant in processing emotions and interpreting emotional stimuli. It responds to tone and body language rather than to the specific meanings of words. Its interpretation of the present is heavily influenced by the past—by the traces of early childhood emotional interactions encoded in its circuitry, what we have called the footprints of infancy. Let us assume that in Trevor's formative years there were stresses in his parents' lives that prevented his needs for attunement and attachment from being met. (There is, in fact, plenty of evidence to support that from details that he is able to recall of his later childhood years.) The emotion a sensitive infant would experience when he feels cut off from his primary caregivers would be a deep anxiety of being abandoned, which is precisely what Trevor experiences at the slightest intimation that a woman whose attention he wants is withdrawing from him, if only on the telephone.

Trevor's anxiety is not over the ending of the relationship—he

---

* The road rage example given in chapter 10 was an instance of implicit or emotional memory. Road rage always is.

is serially ending relationships—but over being the one who is left by the other. When mother and infant are rapturously gazing into each other's eyes, the infant at some point will look away, to avoid being overstimulated. He has no anxiety over doing so. Should the mother be the one to break eye contact, however, the infant is mortified and is immediately swept into the physiological state of shame. Trevor's desperation to avoid that state is based on his implicit memories of it. The circuits activated whenever he fears being left are those encoded with the emotions Trevor first experienced when, as a highly sensitive infant, he did not receive the unqualified and undivided loving attention he needed and craved. In this way he remembers what did *not* happen.

The fear of rejection is not unique to the ADD personality—no single psychological feature of attention deficit disorder is unique. Its importance in attention deficit disorder comes from the hyperreactivity of temperament everyone with ADD was born with. In the ADD adult, as in the child, this hypersensitivity magnifies the impact of every emotional stimulus. The fear of rejection is never far below the surface. People with ADD are exquisitely sensitive to the merest hint of it, even if the hint is only a figment of their fearful imagination. It is triggered by any stimulus that ever so vaguely resembles rejection, even if no rejection is intended. The trigger can be a wife declining to have sexual intercourse with her husband on a given night, but it can also be as minor as a glance, an inadvertent comment or an averted look.

The ADD adult does not know the difference between refusal and rejection. When he hears no from a lover, a friend, an employer, it's as if the universe is negating his right to exist. In the above example, the wife may or may not have rejecting feelings toward her husband, but his implicit memories make it impossible for him to feel anything other than rejection. Poor self-regulation also disables him from responding like an adult, no matter whether his partner feels rejecting or only uninterested.

The emotions associated with implicit memories of feeling rejected may be strong enough to bring up thoughts of life not being worth living. "My husband looks so lost when I say no to him," a woman reported during a family therapy session. "He looks completely defeated and crushed. It makes me feel so guilty." The husband's response is that of the sensitive infant when the parent is emotionally unavailable, because for the infant life truly seems impossible without contact with the nurturing parent. The other, the one who did the "rejecting," is seen and thought of as all-powerful and cruel; the self is experienced as isolated and helpless, utterly unable to escape from emotional pain. One man who felt unwelcome in the marriage bed spoke bitterly of his wife as the ice queen—by implication, he was the abject underling.

We can recall now that the orbitofrontal cortex is also thought to play a major role in emotional self-regulation. It helps to inhibit the powerful emotions, like fear—and fear's offspring, anxiety—that are generated in the amygdala and other brain centers below the level of the cortex.[3] As we have seen, in ADD the ability to inhibit powerful emotions is impaired because the connections of the OFC with the lower brain centers did not develop optimally. *Just as hypersensitivity magnifies the sense of being rejected, so deficient self-regulation due to impaired inhibition by the cortex exaggerates the response to rejection.* With this in mind, we can understand what comes next. The response of the infant to the fathomless anxiety of physical or emotional separation from the parent is either rage or withdrawal, or a combination of both in sequence. This is how I have many times reacted in similar circumstances. Being activated, I am sure, was anxiety and rage from my first year of life when my mother was emotionally dissociated, and particularly from our three-week separation just around my first birthday.*

In the second volume of his trilogy on attachment, John Bowlby describes what was observed when ten small children in residential nurseries were reunited with their mothers after separations lasting from twelve days to twenty-one weeks. The separations were in every case due to family emergencies and the absence of other caregivers, and in no case due to any intent on the parents'

---

* See chapter 11.

part to abandon the child. "On meeting mother for the first time after the days or weeks away every one of the ten children showed some degree of detachment. Two seemed not to recognize mother. The other eight turned away or even walked away from her. Most of them either cried or came close to tears; a number alternated between a tearful and an expressionless face."[4] After periods of briefer separation the infant around one year of age will exhibit rage.

Bowlby also points out that the parent can be physically present but emotionally absent due to stress, anxiety, depression or preoccupation with other matters. From the point of view of the infant, it hardly matters. His encoded reactions will be the same, because for him the real issue is not the parent's physical *presence* but her emotional *accessibility*. The withdrawal dynamic has been called *defensive detachment* by Bowlby. It has one meaning: *so hurtful was it for me to experience your absence that I will encase myself in a shell of hard emotion, impervious to love—and therefore to pain. I never want to feel that hurt again.*

As a result, ADD adults find it difficult to trust in relationships, to make themselves truly open and vulnerable. Depending on the degree of early sorrow they experienced, the very idea of commitment may make them anxious. Especially men with ADD will, entering deeper into a relationship, keep half an eye on possible exits. "I am always on the lookout for a parachute relationship," one thirty-year-old man said. No matter who his current partner was, he felt safer if he could think of another woman to take her place should the need arise. The criticalness toward his partners that Trevor experienced once he felt they had "warmed up" to him was really an expression of his fear of intimacy.

The other aspect of Trevor's criticality arises from boredom. Many adults with ADD report that they quickly become bored with relationships, as with much else in life. They imagine this boredom of theirs to mean that something is lacking in their partner: the reality is that they are bored with themselves. A person not in contact with internal sources of energy and interest in the world has to search for outside sources, believing that fulfillment can come only from someone else. This is the implicitly remembered state of the infant hungry for emotional nourishment, lacking the capacity to satisfy his own needs and having to look to the parent. The demand placed on the partner in the love relationship is that he or she—the other—fills the emptiness within oneself. But such nourishment is found only through psychological and spiritual growth, through self-discovery. So long as I expect another person to provide what I am lacking in myself, I am bound to be disappointed. The temptation then is to look for another partner, a new relationship in which, perhaps, I will find what I feel is missing. In the absence of personal development this quest is doomed, as the relationship nomad keeps discovering.

The fear of intimacy is also a fear of the loss of self. There is the well-known paradox that the person with ADD craves real human contact, feels like an outsider and wishes to belong—but at the same time is reclusive, often preferring his own company to that of others. The paradox is due to his oscillating back and forth between two fears: the anxiety of loneliness and abandonment, and, opposing that, a parallel sense of danger that if he commits to a relationship, he will be overwhelmed, swallowed up. "It's only when I am alone that I can really be myself," said Frank, a fifty-year-old writer who came to see me in the immediate aftermath of yet another abortive relationship. Such a person is presented with a choice between two alternatives, neither of which is satisfactory: one either choses the relationship and gives up the self, or retains the sense of self but gives up on the relationship—and, in some cases, on almost all social contact. The unsolved problem is *how to be oneself in contact with other people.* People desperate for a relationship will surrender their sense of self, their true feelings, for fear of being rejected; when they have gained the relationship they may pull back, as Trevor repeatedly has, in order to reconnect with that precarious sense of self. This dynamic is often seen after the most intimate act of all, sexual intercourse, when following deep attraction and union, there is an alienation and a drive to separate which men, particularly, may experience. One may be in a long-term relationship, lasting even decades, without ever feeling completely committed to it. The ambivalence is an intrinsic memory of childhood emotions when a choice had to be made between staying with oneself, with one's real feelings, and thereby jeopardizing the relationship with one's parent, or going for the relationship, at the cost of suppressing parts of oneself.

One gauge of persistent problems with intimacy in an ADD relationship is the couple's sexual life—or the lack of it. "Non-existent" and "What sex life?" are two of the common replies my questioning around this subject tends to bring. The lack of sexual intimacy is in most cases an unmistakable sign of mutual emotional shutdown. Interestingly, I see this not only in families where one of the adult partners has ADD, but also where one or more of the children has it, even if neither parent does. In the latter case, this marker of absent intimacy between the parents speaks volumes about the emotional alienation and tension in the midst of which the child exists.

Also dampening sexual ardor is the propensity of the ADD adult, the male especially, to behave like an irresponsible child. This may lead his spouse to act like his mother—organizing his life, taking care of his emotional needs. Many a wife of an ADD husband has complained to me of feeling as if she has an extra child in the house—five foot ten, perhaps, balding and with a graying beard. Along with that mother role, unfortunately, may come an ever-increasing component of scolding and nagging—which I have heard many a man complain of. The response to feeling that another person is trying to control him—even if it's a spouse, and even if she has legitimate reasons to be anxious—is to resist. Counterwill, described in chapter 20, mostly in regard to children and teenagers, is also a major dynamic shaping the responses of the ADD adult. It is a powerful factor in the ADD relationship. The couple find themselves chronically caught in the dense shrubbery of anxiety, control, resistance and oppositionality. One of the problems with such a mother/son relationship is, of course, that no mother in her right mind wants to sleep with her son; nor do reasonably healthy men fancy going to bed with their mothers. I have frequently advised couples that if they truly want adult intimacy, they mutually need to give up the parent/child roles toward each other.

"People gravitate toward their emotional mirror images," Michael Kerr points out.[5] It is well recognized now that people will form relationships with others exactly at the same level of psychological development and self-acceptance as their own. "People tend to sort themselves by levels of emotional development for many purposes, not just marriage," writes Stanley Greenspan, "because those functioning at different levels are practically speaking different languages... People widely separated developmentally in fact have very little to talk about."[6] What we might call the law of equal development holds true even if the partners themselves buy into the mythology that one of them is more emotionally mature than the other. Such an illusion may be created because one may seem to be functioning in the world more successfully than the other. Usually it is women with ADD who tell me that their husbands are better adjusted than they are. By certain criteria, it may seem so. The man may be working, be earning a good income and have much more confidence than his wife when it comes to worldly affairs. When such a relationship is examined, it becomes apparent that though the financially rewarding work is being done by the husband, the invisible division of labor charges the wife with all the emotional responsibility. Not only is she the linchpin holding the family's emotional life together, but she also has the secret and mutually unconscious assignment of absorbing her husband's anxieties, protecting his fragile ego, enabling him to function in the belief that his strength is purely intrinsic to him. His anxiety can be noticed, however, as soon as she becomes unavailable, for whatever reason. The cause can be something as minor as a three-day flu. Many wives report their husbands to be unaccountably tense and sullenly unhelpful whenever they are ill, which signifies the man's anxiety—his implicit memory of finding his mother, or perhaps father, inaccessible.

An individual with ADD choosing a partner on the same plane of psychological growth as herself is unavoidable. Since ADD by definition implies underdeveloped emotional intelligence, any such relationship, also by definition, will begin with two people who have both been stuck at fairly early stages of emotional development. Although, as with every other aspect of ADD, there will be a broad range of variation, no ADD relationship will avoid the problems arising from the mutual lack of maturity. By maturity, I mean here the degree of individuation, the capacity of the person to *genuinely* sustain herself emotionally during difficult times without having to be mothered or fathered by someone else. I interpose *genuinely* because many people pretend to themselves and to others that they are capable of taking care of themselves emotionally, but they do so only at the cost of suppressing their anxiety. The buried anxiety will not be denied but will assert itself in the form of psychological symptoms or direct physical illness.

Another rule with almost no exceptions is that our choice of relationship partners is patterned on our interactions with our parental caregivers. This is so even if it may appear superficially that the differences far outweigh any possible resemblance. "Many people have a hard time accepting the idea that they have searched for partners who resembled their caretakers," writes the family therapist and educator Harville Hendrix. "On a conscious level, they were looking for people with only positive traits—people who were, among other things, kind, loving, good looking, intelligent, and creative... But, no matter what their conscious intentions, most people are attracted to mates who have their caretakers' positive *and* negative traits, and, typically, the negative traits are more influential."[7] In neurophysiological terms, our choice of mate reflects the early relationship patterns stamped in the neural circuits of the right prefrontal cortex, especially its orbitofrontal portion. The OFC will recognize and hone in on someone who, on the unconscious level, activates its familiar reactions. This person, after all, will most resemble the persons whose love one so desperately craved all one's life.* We are inexorably drawn to marry the individual who is, of all potential partners, the very one most likely to trigger in us the most painful and confusing of implicit memories—as well as the warmest, happiest ones.

Relationships have to change if one is to create the conditions for growth. "I must be a very strong person," Jennifer, a thirty-three-year-old woman with attention deficit disorder said to me. "I must be, otherwise I could not have put up with what I have had to in my marriage." Her husband was well-meaning but domineering, emotionally absent and completely closed to getting any joint counseling or therapy. She felt very alone. I agreed that she had a lot of strength to carry on under such circumstances, holding down a job and taking the main responsibility of raising their children, one of whom has fairly marked ADD. She also exhibited emotional strength in recognizing, unlike her husband, that she needed help. There is, however, an important and oft-overlooked difference between being strong and being powerful. Strength is an inner quality; power is a matter of relationship. I may have strength, yet at the same time I may be powerful in one relationship and utterly powerless in another. "Which partner in a marriage has to 'put up' with stuff?" I said. "The less or the more powerful one?" Jennifer's willingness to accept an unfairly heavy share of the burden was, as always, a reenactment of her childhood status in her family of origin. As long as she continued to shoulder those burdens unquestioningly, she could make little headway toward her goal of development and the diminishing of her ADD patterns.

One of the most perplexing problems for the non-ADD partner is what John Ratey has called "the ahistorical memory" of the ADD mind. In other words, the ADD adult (and also of course the

---

* This is also why such a surprisingly large percentage of women abused in childhood end up choosing abusive male partners. Sometimes they call themselves "stupid" when the painful reality declares itself. Stupidity has nothing to do with it.

ADD child) functions at times as if previous events, even the most recent ones, had never taken place. Your ADD partner may have insulted you the night before but this morning greets you with a warm smile, the offer of a hug and the expectation of warm reciprocal contact. You are in absolutely no mood, the wounds of the previous night still being fresh. You refuse, predictably stimulating in your partner the rage-or-withdrawal response to feeling rejected. Another aspect of ahistorical memory is its either-or nature. When, for example, a person recalls the good times in a relationship, it is almost as if nothing bad had ever happened. Unfortunately, the reverse is also true: when one is remembering the bad, the good may as well not have occurred. The feeling of the moment dominates the memory. In this regard, the ADD mind is much like a television screen: you can't have two channels on at the same time; when one has been selected, the other is inaccessible. This trait is characteristic of the all-or-nothing mind states of young children and is another marker of incomplete development in the adult.

Of course, the neurological impairments of ADD also impose some extra nuisance. It is difficult to live with a partner who may be messy and disorganized, does not remember promises, tunes out in the middle of conversations, forgets events and anniversaries, has a short fuse and in moments of crisis may lack self-insight. But all that adds up to only a thimbleful of trouble when compared with the turmoil brought to the relationship by the anxiety and pain stored in the implicit memory circuits of the ADD brain.

# 28

# Moses Saved

# by the Angel:

# Self-Parenting (I)

To become what one is, one must not have the faintest
notion *what* one is. From this point of view even the
blunders of life have their own meaning and value—the
occasional side and wrong roads, the delays, "modesties,"
seriousness wasted on tasks that are remote from *the* task.
   — FRIEDRICH NIETZSCHE, "Ecce Homo"

WHEN PARENTS COME seeking treatment
for their ADD child, my main concern is
to help them see that they are the ones
best positioned and best equipped to guide and assist their son or
daughter along the road of development. The principles and
approaches by which they may do so were the subject of several
chapters. Similar principles apply to the adult. The question still is,

What are the conditions necessary for the development of self-regulation, intrinsic motivation and self-esteem in this grown-up man or woman? The difference, of course, is that building these conditions is no longer the task of a caregiving parent. An adult faces the daunting responsibility of offering herself the very support and nurturing attention that ADD has always prevented her from being able to summon up.

The ADD adult, like the child, needs more than organizational tools and behavior modification techniques. Although these do have their place, they will not address the fundamental problem, which is not how the person manages this or that duty or self-appointed task but in what relationship he stands vis-à-vis his own self. The issue still remains one of relationship, but this time parent and child are combined in one and the same person.*

The first of the self-parenting duties I suggest people engage in is the all-important one of self-understanding and psychological support. The others—issues of physical care: simple, straightforward and almost always neglected—will be discussed in the next chapter.

### 1. Compassionate curiosity in the search for self-insight

Throughout this book, I have emphasized the importance of understanding as the necessary basis for any technique or treatment approach we employ to promote healing in attention deficit disorder. Parental love is such a wise and powerful force of nature that when parents extend themselves in an effort to understand who their children are and why they do what they do, the right words and actions will follow almost of their own volition. An open mind, compassionate curiosity toward the child, letting go

---

* People sometimes wonder if I am referring to the proverbial "inner child." Not exactly. The phrase strikes me as maudlin, making it sound as if one were the living tomb for some entrapped and pitiable little creature. It has something of reality about it, however, if we take it as referring to one's unmet psychological needs, underdeveloped emotional faculties, and the neurological circuits imprinted with implicit memory.

of the idea that one "knows" what the child thinks and feels and a striving to accept the child unconditionally will go a long way toward binding wounds inflicted by past mistakes, misjudgments and the parent's own emotional blockages. Such attitudes are just as important when the ADD adult embarks on the journey of self-healing.

Developing a new view toward oneself is no easy task, for it goes against the grain of a lifetime of conditioning. It is not a matter of so-called positive thinking or the naive affirmations exemplified by vows like "Today I will be kinder to myself." It requires the shedding, gradually, of defenses constructed long ago out of sheer necessity, defenses maintained out of the anxieties embedded in implicit memory. Needed are both a desire to accept the self and the courage to look honestly. Beyond that, the ADD adult also has to acquire the skills of self-understanding, the first of which is the capacity to *notice* each time she makes a critical, judgmental comment against herself, to *notice* whenever she is seized by anxiety, to *notice* when her behavior does not jibe with her long-term goal. She notices, and asks—as parents need to ask regarding their child—what the meanings are, what is being acted out, what messages the Morse code of her behavior is trying to convey.

One notices, and gradually learns not to judge the behavior but to accept the feelings that drive it. "I am my worst enemy," a person will complain. "Why do I care so much what others think?" Or, "Why would I do something like that when I know it never works anyway?" Asked in a tone of compassionate curiosity, such questions can help to illuminate much that has been murky and dark. Too often they are not questions at all. They are *statements*, impatient and self-condemnatory. "Why do I care so much what others think" was in this case a judgment: "There is something terribly wrong with me. I should know better than to be so afraid of others' opinions." A 180-degree shift in tone and only a slight shift in words would make it into a fruitful inquiry: "I would very much like to understand why I feel so much anxiety about displeasing others." Always there is some valid reason, or *was* when the particular attitude or behavior was first adopted. We can let go of what we understand; we cling most ferociously to aspects of ourselves that remain hidden to us and whose power we do not comprehend. A person learns to become aware of the tone in which he addresses his inquiries to himself: am I conducting an inquisition against myself or a helpful, insight-oriented interview?

This sort of work is not accomplished overnight. "How long would you say it took you to develop your problems and to reach your present state?" I ask the ADD client who, typically, is in a hurry to fix everything all at once, preferably before leaving the office. Three, four decades comes the usual answer. "Can we accept that it may take at least some reasonable fraction of that time to turn things around?"

### 2. Self-acceptance: tolerating guilt and anxiety

Self-acceptance is not a pie-in-the sky abstract concept, because there is no abstract self floating around, begging to be accepted. The self is as we experience ourselves: happy one moment, anxious the next; confident in the morning, guilty and ashamed in the afternoon; giving now, needy then. The problem is not that we have these shifting and conflicting feelings, the problem is that we take a very conditional attitude toward them. We wish to hold on to some, drive away the others. In this we mirror perfectly the way, when we were children, the adults in our world preferred to see only those aspects of our personalities that did not trigger discomfort for them. So self-acceptance does not mean self-admiration or even self-liking at every moment of our lives, but tolerance for all our emotions, including those that make us feel uncomfortable.

Guilt is a prime example of an emotion ADD adults would crawl through jungles to escape. It is sometimes difficult for people to understand that their psychological safety does not lie in avoiding the feeling of guilt at all costs but in learning to live with it. "I'm a people pleaser" is the routine self-description of ADD adults. "I'm always so conscious of what the other person might need

from me. I feel guilty if I disappoint someone. I can never say no."
Or, "I am the kind of person whom everyone calls to tell their
troubles to. I can't do that myself, though. I would feel guilty,
thinking of all the people in the world who have suffered much
more than I can even imagine. I shouldn't need help."

To illustrate the inadvisability of striving to banish guilt, I find
it helpful to recall an ancient Jewish legend of the infant Moses,
not found in Scripture.[1] According to the familiar biblical story of
the Exodus, Moses was destined to lead the Hebrew slaves out of
Egyptian bondage. In divine mockery of a cruel decree of the
Pharaoh's, the newborn Moses is adopted into the royal court by
Pharaoh's daughter. According to the legend, the imperial sooth-
sayers prophesy that the child will one day challenge royal authority. It is decided to put him to a fatal test. An onyx stone,
emblematic of kingly ambition, is placed in front of him, as is a
glowing coal of fire. Should he grasp the stone, he will be slain.
Invisible to everyone, the angel Gabriel stands as his guardian
behind him. "Moses stretched forth his hand toward the onyx
stone and attempted to seize it, but the angel Gabriel guided his
hand away from it and placed it upon the live coal, and the coal
burnt the child's hand, and he lifted it up and touched it to his
mouth, and burnt part of his lips and part of his tongue, and for all
his life he became slow of speech and slow of tongue."

People readily see that the angel was savior to Moses. Even
though he caused his ward to be maimed, under the circumstances
Gabriel had no alternative. Guilt plays the same survival role. It is a
guardian. When the adult world requires, even if inadvertently,
that an infant or child suppress parts of her true self—her own
desires, feelings and preferences—she has to develop some internal
mechanisms that would automatically force her to comply. The
penalty of not doing so is to suffer the anxiety of disappointing the
parent, of feeling cut off from the parent. Guilt comes along as one
of these internal mechanisms. It guides the child's hand away from
the onyx stone, her own core impulses, and has her bring to her
mouth the coal of fire—feelings acceptable to the parent. The

child is hurt, but the indispensable relationship with the parent is preserved.

Guilt is obsessively single-minded, knowing only one stimulus and only one response. The stimulus is this: *you, child or adult, wish to do something for yourself that may disappoint someone else.* This could be a true misdeed, such as stealing, or a human desire to act in accordance with your core impulses, perhaps by expressing a genuine feeling the parent cannot tolerate in you. Guilt does not know the difference. It hurls at you the same epithet for both misdeed and self-expression: *selfish.* It also cannot discriminate between past and present. In place of your present-day interactions—with spouse, friend, doctor, butcher, baker, computer maker—it sees only your early relationships with your caregivers.

Guilt cannot grasp that its services are no longer required. It just hangs around, making us feel uncomfortable. Our problem is that we fear it. We want to get rid of it. *I will obey. Anything to make you disappear. Just get out.* If we saw in guilt the well-meaning friend it was—doggedly faithful, to a fault—we would make room for it. We would listen to its one-note song of warning, *don't be selfish,* but decide for ourselves consciously whether we need to dance to its tune. *Yes, thank you, I see what you mean. By all means stick around if you wish, but I will let my adult brain circuits judge whether I am really hurting someone else or merely serving my legitimate needs.*

Better if people learned to accept the guilt but to judge its message for themselves. It can't help being there. It speaks the voice of intricately wired implicit memory circuits. A person cannot forcibly get rid of it, and can only temporarily buy its silence by obeying. She might as well welcome it as a sign of growing self-nurturance. At least in the beginning of growth, if she does not feel guilt, she is probably ignoring her truest self.

Anxiety around self-assertion operates similarly for people with ADD. John, a gay man in his forties who lives with his partner of nearly twenty years, has been taking medication in treatment of his ADD for about six months. The psychological work John has done since being diagnosed is helping him feel more and more independent of his partner. "I never used to think about what I wanted to do," he says. "It was always whatever George wanted. Now I have my own thoughts, but whenever I want to act on them or even just to express them, I feel myself getting so anxious. My breathing gets shallow and my muscles tense." I congratulated him. In the relationship with George, he had not been conscious of his anxiety for nearly two decades only because he had never permitted himself to take so much as an independent breath. His anxiety, an automatic consequence of self-assertion, marked a giant stride forward in his efforts to discover himself. If he can endure being with his anxious feelings,* welcoming them instead of fleeing them, John will continue to grow.

It may seem contradictory to acknowledge that in fact many people with ADD do act in selfish ways, particularly when it comes to their addictions and compulsions of various sorts. How does that square with what has been said just now about the inhibiting effect of guilt and anxiety? I can attest that in some important aspects of my life—not all—I have always been a people pleaser, suppressing my truest self. I have also often behaved with narcissistic self-regard. The more the core self—the deepest impulses—is suppressed, the more compulsive are the attempts to compensate by satisfying superficial, infantile, instant-gratification impulses and desires.

### 3. You don't punish yourself for where you find yourself

If you want to go further in the direction of healing, you do not chastise yourself for wherever you happen to be along the road. You don't berate yourself for not having got there faster.

"I cannot believe how much time I have wasted in my life" is a

---

* I am not referring here to a state of chronic anxiety, nor to acute panic attacks, but to specific and identifiable anxious feelings John automatically experiences around self-assertion. I would not advise anyone to welcome these other more severe anxiety states as positive signs of development.

refrain often heard in the litany of self-judgments uttered by the ADD adult. "Here I am finding out in my forties what I should have known as a teenager." I, too, have gone through wishing I had known ten, twenty, thirty years ago what I have learned since—much of it relatively recently. But I didn't. If I could have, I would have. It's that simple. I have no reason to see myself as a victim, but I did not choose the circumstances that shaped my neurophysiology or my personality, which are one and the same thing. One can make choices when one becomes aware and awake, not before.

The awakening is not sudden. It is gradual and occurs in stages. Someone may have meandered down side paths, sleepwalked into many dead-end corridors. He pays for each mistake and, unfortunately, so do others. None of that could have been avoided, all of it had to happen not only for him to find the right direction, but to *know* that he has found it. The journey is not over even then, and he may yet find himself lost once more. To paraphrase Nietzsche, even the wrong turns and side roads have meaning and purpose, if only to teach us which way the path to oneself does not lie.

### 4. Choosing a guide: psychotherapy and counseling

The person with ADD, whatever her age at diagnosis, has lived with low self-esteem and emotional pain all her life. Many of her behaviors are futile and not very cleverly disguised attempts to kill the pain. But pain cannot be killed; it needs to be listened to. It has a story to tell and lessons to teach. In the project of self-parenting, this is one essential service the adult cannot, without the greatest difficulty, provide for herself. A loving mother and father can make themselves available to spend time with their child, to hear her story, to help her express her feelings, to mirror her emotions, but the adult needs to find a parent substitute. The people trained to do such work are counselors and psychotherapists. Adults who hope their ADD-related problems can be addressed without psychological work under the guidance of a professional are, in most cases, setting themselves up for failure.

The purpose of psychotherapy and counseling is not that the therapist either heals the "patient" or advises him what to do with his life. The goal is to mature and to individuate, to become a self-respecting person in his own right. In other words, the goal is not to be "cured" but to develop. The role of the therapist is, in part, that of a talking mirror in which the individual can see himself more clearly reflected, helping him to reflect on himself. Until he acquires the necessary skills, without a mirror he can no more see his psyche than his own eyes. The therapist must be able to extend to the client the attitude Carl Rogers called unconditional positive regard. "When a person is encouraged to get in touch with and express his deepest feelings," writes the British psychiatrist and psychoanalyst Anthony Storr, "in the secure knowledge that he will not be rejected, criticized, nor expected to be different, some kind of rearrangement or sorting-out process often occurs within the mind which brings with it a sense of peace; a sense that the depths of the well of truth have really been reached."[2]

To whom should one turn? Unfortunately, the problem of finding competent and compassionate counseling is as acute throughout the North American continent as it is in the corner of it where I live and work. To begin with, there is people's confusion about the differences between psychologists and psychiatrists.

While they both deal with problems of the mind, the education the two professions receive is markedly dissimilar. The academic training of psychologists is more likely, but far from guaranteed, to include material on the development of the human mind from childhood onward, on the roots of its potential disorders, as well as practical experience of counseling. Not being physicians, psychologists cannot prescribe medications, and their services are not usually covered by medical plans, although some forms of insurance do include psychological services in their extended coverage.

The financial side of therapy is complicated. It is perfectly true that the fees charged by psychotherapists may be high for many budgets, even prohibitively so. For many other people, it is a matter of choices and priorities. I know for myself that when I was resistant to recognizing that I needed psychotherapy, the financial argument loomed much larger than when I accepted the value of it. Resistance is compounded by denial that one has a problem, by not placing a high enough value on personal emotional needs and psychological growth and by a pessimistic belief that therapy will not do any good.

Except when dealing with severe depressions needing hospitalization or other complex mental disorders, I am reluctant to refer my patients to psychiatrists. It is not the abilities or intentions of individual psychiatrists that are in question but the very nature of what psychiatry has become and the type of training psychiatric residency provides to future practitioners. As a U.S. psychiatrist wrote in a 1996 issue of *Psychiatry News*, "Many of today's psychiatry residency graduates haven't a clue about understanding the human organism in the context of environmental and relationship stresses." The emphasis is, instead, on a narrow understanding of biology and of its manipulation by pharmacological means. "It is astonishing to realize," remarks Antonio Damasio, "that [medical] students learn about psychopathology without ever being taught normal psychology."[3]

Psychiatry tends to accept the medical model of disease and cure. Despite many visits to psychiatrists, people often report that none of the very basic issues in their lives that have led to their depression or attention deficit or anxiety or panic problems were touched on, or only in a superficial fashion. In the medical model, the patient presents the doctor with the symptoms; having elicited the necessary information, the doctor makes the diagnosis and prescribes, administers or performs the cure. This approach works for a broken bone but not for a wounded psyche, for an inflamed appendix but not for inflamed emotions. For a complex developmental problem such as attention deficit disorder, the medical model is inadequate and inappropriate, except in the narrow area of pharmacological treatment.

Does it follow, then, that no psychiatrist knows how to pro-

vide psychotherapy or that all psychologists do? No such general-
ization can be made. I have myself been counseled by a psychiatrist
whose approach I found helpful and, on the other hand, know of
psychologists whose competence I cannot respect. No formal
training and no diploma can by itself inculcate the requisite qualities of a good psychotherapist: empathy, integrity, compassion,
honesty, insight and skill. There are some excellent psychotherapists who are neither doctors nor psychologists.

Further compounding the problem for adults with ADD is that
among the commoner impairments of the brain and mind, attention deficit is probably the least understood and most often
ignored or unrecognized. It is the one about which there exists the
least consensus, the smallest commonly spoken vocabulary and the
most controversy.

Everything being equal, it helps if the prospective therapist, of
whatever professional background, is knowledgeable about ADD.
More important, though, is that he or she know about people—
and first of all, about him- or herself. The most well-accredited
academic learning remains dangerous nonsense issued from the
mouths of mental health professionals who have not dealt with
their own unfinished psychological business. Worse yet if they
deny to themselves that they have any. No one does not have any.
Certainly no one who enters the mental health field as his or her
chosen area of work is free of emotional problems.

Of all types of professional training, the one I consider most
likely to be of benefit in ADD is family therapy. The skilled family
therapist is not fixated on people's dysfunctions and their difficult
feelings. She helps clients acknowledge painful emotions but also
helps them to see their problems in the context of the multigenerational family system that they are part of. She encourages people
to take responsibility for their own feelings rather than imagining
that these feelings arise from the failures or ill will of their partners,
friends, or co-workers—a liberating perspective that allows a
client to shed the garb of victimhood.

Family therapy also helps individuals to see the invisible wires that connect their emotional experiences to those of the significant others with whom their lives are intertwined, but it doesn't necessarily mean that the entire family attends—in fact, it is usually not productive for parents to take their children along. Family therapy refers to the approach of the therapist, the training he had. A single adult can see a family therapist by himself; in the case of couples, both would attend.

The best guide to good psychotherapy is probably word of mouth. In many places, finding such professionals is, by all accounts, as difficult as finding needles in haystacks, but there is help if one keeps looking.

In the end, it comes down to how one feels in the presence of the therapist. People with ADD tend to have trouble recognizing, let alone respecting, their gut feelings. And yet, gut instincts are the best guides. I have often seen clients who had stayed on with a particular psychiatrist, psychologist or other therapist for months or years, long after they became aware of feeling that they were not being helped, or even that they were having a negative experience. Their fear of those old servants guilt and anxiety kept them there. Better to have stayed with the guilt and the anxiety and left the therapist.

# 29

# The Physical

# and Spiritual

# Environment:

# Self-Parenting (II)

Some development of the capacity to be alone is
necessary if the brain is to function at its best, and if the
individual is to fulfil his highest potential. Human beings
easily become alienated from their own deepest needs
and feelings. Learning, thinking, innovation and
maintaining contact with one's own inner world are all
facilitated by solitude.

    – ANTHONY STORR, *Solitude*

T HE ADULT WITH ATTENTION deficit disorder who hopes to do more than control her symptoms with medication has to learn to take care of herself, as a parent would take care of a child. Caught up by the swirling currents of her brain, she has coasted on automatic pilot all her life, engaged in the details of daily existence, giving little thought to what her needs would be for a saner, more self-connected existence. Time is scattered like sunlight through a sieve.

A good parent does more than get her child through the day. She is mindful that the child is a life-in-development, with needs dictated by the future as much as by the present. Adults with ADD cannot remember themselves in the future, as John Ratey has said. Usually they have not considered what conditions they need to grow and develop in accordance with their true nature. When I ask adults to rate themselves according to a simple scale gauging the parenting skills and attention they devote to themselves, the scores tend to be low—so scandalously low that I have advised many of my clients that if they truly were the unfortunate child being parented by them, I would have had little choice but to alert the child protection authorities. (Restraining me was only that first I would have had to blow the whistle on myself.)

As we saw in the previous chapter, self-understanding and self-acceptance are the first responsibility of the adult who wants to foster his own growth, which really is no different from what any parent owes a child. The other aspects of self-parenting also parallel the care conscientious parents extend to their children. The adult with attention deficit disorder has not lost the inborn temperamental sensitivity he carried into this world. No less than for children, conditions in his environment continue to have a direct and major impact on his emotions and thought processes—even if he has become adept at carrying on as if he were a creature liberated from reality, with no needs for nurturing body and soul.

Without the right conditions, the brain cannot develop new circuits or the mind new ways of relating to world and to self. A person cannot become sane in the midst of the chaos she perpetuates around herself. What, then, are the environmental conditions needed for development?

### 1. *The physical space*

First, make a conscious choice about how to live. A man may look at the disaster zone in his room and decide *consciously* to do nothing about it. There is no *should* here, nor should there be a should. Counterwill, the automatic resistance to pressure, will arise in response to dictates from himself as readily as to the commands of others. He needs to allow himself at least the same degree of autonomy he would grant to a teenager. It is not a *duty* to clear some physical space so that his mind is not oppressed by the clutter, but it is a sensible thing to do if the long-term goal is development. If he chooses not to, it still helps to keep aware of the consequences of the choice.

The adult with attention deficit disorder needs to know that the physical space she occupies can help to either harmonize or disorganize her mind. Although many ADD adults assert that they function well in the midst of the physical chaos around them, the fact is that they are too sensitive not to be affected by it. Neglecting to honor their physical environment is to neglect themselves.

If necessary, she may set herself small, incremental goals. It is discouraging to try to accomplish something that may be beyond present capacities. The ADD brain is overwhelmed by a multipartite task. She does not know where to turn, and the all-or-nothing mind-set demands that everything be done at once. Nothing needs to be done at once. The best plan, I find, is not to insist that any one task be finished but to impose a strict time limit in which to work. When the appointed time period is over, stop. This will eventually lead to a better appreciation of what one actually does with time when carrying out strange and unnatural rituals like picking clothes off the floor or sorting out dusty magazines in a corner.

This task, like all others, requires learning to tolerate failure. The many setbacks of the ADD adult have not necessarily taught him to endure failure but only to be permanently frustrated by it. Maintaining physical order may not be a difficult chore for other people, but the ADD adult might as well accept from the beginning that he will keep failing at it for some time to come. That does not matter. The effort itself, in the long term, has an organizing effect on the mind.

### 2. Sleep hygiene

The ADD adult is often a night owl. The origin of the propensity to stay up late is not clear, but I believe we can learn something from observing ADD children.

A child with attention deficit disorder may be difficult to rouse in the morning, but in the evening there is no getting him off to bed. I believe the problem is separation anxiety, because I have seen the same child be much more cooperative about bedtime when he feels more secure emotionally. I noted curiously my own experience over the years that at the times when I felt less tension and anxiety about my relationship with my wife, I had less tendency to stay up late.

Something in the ADD adult dreads going to bed and turning the light off. The fear is of being alone with one's urgent mind for even a few short minutes. I used to read until the book would drop from my hands and would wake hours later, still wearing my glasses and the lamp still burning. Many others with ADD have described the same bedtime routine. The fear of being alone with the mind is, I believe, an implicit memory of finding oneself, in infancy, cut off from contact with the parent. An infant in that situation would feel intense distress and would cast about for some other mental or physical object to relate to so as not to feel that distress. This is why small children begin to hold on automatically to their body parts, such as hair or genitalia. The unconscious fear of reactivating that implicit memory is what leads to the adult's aversion to lying down to sleep without any diversions.

A contributing factor is that the distractible ADD mind does find it easier to focus when the noises and intrusions of the day have abated, and everyone else has gone to bed. Many adults have told me this is when they get their best work done, or when they feel at peace enough to read or to rest.

The problem, of course, is that sleep is essential for the brain to regenerate the sensitive neurological apparatus of alertness and attention. During sleep also, the mind integrates events from the waking hours. "Entering the mad world of dreams each night probably promotes mental health in ways we do not fully understand," suggests Anthony Storr. "It seems clear that some kind of scanning or re-programming takes place in dreams which has a beneficial effect upon ordinary mental functioning."[1] This much is perhaps self-evident, but the ADD adult tends to regard his undisciplined sleep pattern as a "symptom" of the disorder rather than seeing it as undermining his emotional state, his alertness and his capacity for attention.

### 3. Nutrition

The parent wishes to provide the child with nutritious and attractive meals, served in an atmosphere free of tension and meant to be consumed in a leisurely fashion. Challenged on this point of self-parenting, most ADD adults throw up their hands in exasperation. Meals are not regular, not planned with nutrition in mind and tend to be wolfed down rather than eaten.

The child or adult with ADD is exquisitely sensitive not just to the external environment but also to the internal one. If we are concerned about the brain's biochemistry, so we ought to be concerned about the biochemistry of the body: to the health of both, proper nutrition is indispensable. The ADD child completely falls apart when his blood sugar is too low, becomes hyper when it is too high, showing how directly nutritional states affect the brain. Once more, it is a matter of what the goals are. If the long-term development of mental balance is to supersede charging through the day as the objective, the internal environment cannot be ignored.

### 4. Physical exercise

"Is your 'kid' getting enough exercise?" I ask ADD adults. Well-toned muscles and a healthy cardiovascular system are essential for everyone, of course. Lack of exercise leads to an internal sluggishness that undermines alertness and attention. Exercise releases substances in the brain that are necessary for mood stability, motivation and attention and, in the long term, makes the chemical apparatus that manufactures these substances more efficient. I recommend that people set a goal of vigorous exercise every day.

To balance the muscle-contracting effect of physical activity, some time must be devoted to stretching exercises before and after the workout. Stretching is important even for someone unable to do cardiovascular exercise. People with ADD, habituated lifelong to self-generated tension, tend to have tight muscles and stiff joints and ligaments. Simple stretching exercises done for a few minutes daily are tremendously freeing physically and psychologically. They are an excellent way to begin the day, and a good way to release accumulated tension before going to bed.

### 5. Nature

The parent who never takes his child out into nature, away from the city, is depriving him not only of wonderful experiences but also of a powerfully harmonizing influence for the mind. There is matchless unity, harmony and peace in nature—all that is lacking, in other words, in the ADD mind. Many parents will note that the hyperkinetic brain or body or mouth of their son or daughter will gradually slow down after a few short days away from the hurly-burly of everyday urban life. The adult, too, neglects an important need if she deprives herself of regularly experiencing the outdoors. "Nature," writes the reclusive and hypersensitive author Marcel Proust, "by virtue of all the feelings that it aroused in me, seemed to me the thing most diametrically opposed to the mechanical inventions of mankind. The less it bore their imprint, the more room it offered for the expansion of my heart."

Andrea, the self-declared incompetent mentioned in chapter

25, related a wonderful concentration exercise taught to her by a Native elder practiced in her people's healing techniques. "She told me to sit down in a meadow, measure out with my eyes a patch of ground one yard square and do nothing but gaze at it for an hour. I got to know every blade of grass, noted the different textures of fallen leaves, followed every movement of ants and ladybugs, and the time went before I knew it. I was never so exhilarated. I have done it many times since."

### 6. Extracurricular duties

No parent would want to overload a child with an impossible number of tasks and responsibilities. The ADD adult's workaholism and dread of the word "no" leads her to overextend herself. A large proportion of the ADD clients I have seen are juggling too many projects, commitments that leave them with nary a moment to finish a thought. We engulf ourselves in hubbub, chase our minds in ten directions at once and then wonder why we cannot stand still long enough to notice anything. This "symptom" of ADD, too, is self-perpetuating. It creates itself. If a mind in a different relationship to itself is a goal, we need to clear some ground for its development. We may need to let some activities go.

### 7. Recreation

There is a difference between entertaining diversions and recreation. Watching television may be entertaining but it is not a process that re-creates. One does not flick off the set feeling refreshed. Re-creation needs activities that nourish the mind or liberate the body. What these may be will vary from person to person, but universally ADD adults deny themselves regularly scheduled times for mental and physical regeneration.

### 8. Creative expression

It is unusual for me to meet an ADD adult who does not have some secret longing for artistic expression, and almost as unusual to find one actively doing something about it. Essential to finding meaning and purpose in life is the liberation of one's creative instincts.

On Internet chat rooms about attention deficit disorder, one can find lists of success stories: individuals who, despite their ADD, became great artists, writers, geniuses. It is even argued—dubiously, in my opinion—that ADD confers advantages such as creativity and a good sense of humor. Mozart, Einstein and Edison are some of the illustrious examples.

The tendency to creativity of the ADD mind cannot be denied. Even those without an artistic interest will show a creative streak, being able to apply their fertile minds to difficult situations and to come up with solutions others would never dream of.

I would myself love to believe that the neurophysiological impairments and psychological dysfunctions I have been writing about in this book also have their positive side, granting me, like others, some powers of creative expression. Unfortunately, though, what gifts I may have been blessed with have not been helped in their development by my disorganization, drivenness, distractibility, lack of persistence, forgetfulness and periods of psychic lethargy. But for such ADD traits, they would, I believe, have found their way to whatever sunlight they merit much earlier in my life.

I do not believe ADD leads to creativity any more than creativity causes ADD. Rather, they both originate in the same inborn trait: sensitivity. For creativity, a temperamental sensitivity is indispensable. The sensitive individual, as we have seen, draws into herself the unseen emotional and psychic communications of her environment. On some levels of the unconscious, she will, therefore, have a deeper awareness of the world. She may also be more attuned to particular sensory input, such as sound, color or musical tone. Thus the sensitivity provides her with the raw materials her mind will rework and reshape. Thus sensitivity contributes to the emergence of attention deficit disorder, as well as to creativity.

Colin, a forty-year-old I diagnosed two years ago with ADD, had been working as a bartender for the past twenty years, making good money, drinking more than he should and berating himself for not having a university degree like his siblings. His real interest was in filmmaking. Part of my treatment approach is to explore with people their creative natures, to urge them to do some self-inquiry why this side of the personality may have been disregarded. If self-esteem means esteeming the self, the individual's deepest creative urges must be honored. The self-parenting part of healing ADD must, I am convinced, involve paying attention to one's need to create.

Colin came to see me recently. He has begun to work in Vancouver's thriving film industry. He is loving it and will soon take a courageous plunge into economic insecurity by quitting his hotel job. "There is only one thing I feel bad about," he says. "I am working with all these people who knew what they wanted. They are twenty years ahead of me. I have a lot of catching up to do."

"It's a loss," I agreed. "But first you had to catch up to yourself."

Not everyone would be able to earn a living in his chosen field of creative expression, but I always urge people to identify the direction in which their creative energies would naturally flow, and to allow them expression. Many ADD adults don't have to search for anything new in following this advice; they just have to reconnect with something they had lost contact with long ago.

### 9. Meditation and mindfulness

The problem of ADD, like any other problem facing people individually or collectively, can only be resolved if we take a balanced view of our needs as human beings. We have seen how it is important to be attentive to the body and also to seek help in untying the psychological knots binding us. The third pillar of a balanced human existence is spiritual work. This could take place in a religious context, but not necessarily. Spiritual work is the cultivation of a mindful solitude. All traditional meditative and contemplative practices, including many types of prayer, have as their purpose helping us to disengage for a time from our concerns with people, objects, desires, thoughts and fears, to actively strive for connection between ourselves and the rest of creation. Enormously beneficial to everyone, spiritual work is essential in the self-treatment of ADD.

The age-old wisdom of traditions from all continents and cultures tells us that reality has aspects more profound and more universal than we tend to imagine in our harried and isolated workaday lives. The person who feels that he is not being "himself" recognizes this implicitly. Without being able to explain why, he senses there is a truer self he does not experience directly but which exists nonetheless—otherwise how would he know that he is not being that self? Intimations of the true self, a vague awareness, seeps into our consciousness, if only in the form of the dissatisfaction we feel at not being able to contact it. We sense somehow that in many of our pursuits we are chasing shadows, but the very existence of shadows implies the existence also of the real objects, beings, or entities represented by them. When a human being says that she does not know who she is, she is communicating her conviction that what she does know of herself is only a partial reflection of the completeness which is her true self.

The quintessential achievement of Western civilization, the scientific method, has come to be interpreted so narrowly that it has been used to exclude essential knowledge human beings have worked and studied and struggled over hundreds of generations to gain: the knowedge that we are not just the molecules that accidentally have come together to form our bodies, the thoughts that temporarily engage our minds, the feelings that agitate or soothe us from one moment to the next. So "scientific" have we become, that our science has come to ignore or deny the work and experience of the greatest teachers of humankind.

Lest I present myself as a proselytizer or as one who has any right to claim authority about such things, I must confess that I have never had the spiritual experiences that would allow me to speak of these matters from direct knowledge. For one thing, only recently have I begun to pay some deeper attention to my own spiritual needs—and so far only in a typically inconsistent

ADD fashion. Yet it seems to me somehow that I *remember* these spiritual realities, which to me means that somehow I am not completely cut off from them, although I used to think that I was.

People who have examined the question of "the real self" in some depth, for example the psychiatrist and Buddhist practitioner Mark Epstein and the spiritual master and psychologist A.H. Almaas, say that for the full realization of the self one must employ the understandings and insights of modern Western psychology, and also the spiritual explorations of the Eastern and Middle Eastern traditions, or, no doubt, of the native spiritual teachings of other continents. They do not suggest a *synthesis* of Eastern spirituality and Western psychology—they show that both these pathways explore the same ground. You do not need to synthesize that which is already a unity. I am convinced they are right.

The search of the fragmented ADD mind for oneness must, therefore, involve also the spiritual quest, however an individual may wish to define that for him or herself. Meditation is the method I have chosen for myself. The ADD mind is most uncomfortable with meditation, is intensely bored with it. It's all the more amazing to me that recently I have actually come to enjoy and look forward to it. It becomes fun, after a while, to watch the fretful and anxious mind do its backwards flips, somersaults, and disappearing tricks—to observe it all, and work at not being identified with it, not mistaking it for *me*.

Of all spiritual traditions, Buddhism has cultivated meditation most deeply. Nietzsche called Buddha "that profoundest physiologist." He may well have said neurophysiologist. We have seen that part of the neurophysiological basis of ADD is the tenacious survival of neurological pathways first activated in early childhood, resulting from the tendency of a group of nerves to fire off together repeatedly if they have fired off together once. Meditation aiming at mindfulness, at strengthening the observing "third eye" in the mind, is a direct way of weakening the hold of ingrained neurological responses. "Pay precise attention," writes Mark Epstein, "moment by moment, to exactly what you are experiencing, right now, separating your reactions from the raw sensory events."[2]

Meditation is one way of acting on the neurophysiology of ADD. It is an important way, but not the only one. Any activity, from gardening to martial arts, that promotes mindful concentration will bring benefits. Adults with ADD should at least consider giving themselves some daily opportunity for contemplative solitude. Contemplative solitude is different from being alone in a room, reading, listening to music or being lost in reverie. It means putting some attention on one's life, one's thoughts and feelings. Like nature, it has an integrating and harmonizing effect.

Without some sort of practice, we can no more develop the skill of concentration than we can learn to play the piano. Nothing is more difficult for the ADD mind than to meditate, or to contemplate anything with determined attention. A brain used to decades of inattention and disorganization will not overnight reorganize itself. If attention and presence of mind are the long-term goal, time and effort need to be devoted to their cultivation each and every day. In the beginning, a person does well if out of the, say, twenty or thirty minutes he devoted to such a practice each day, he succeeded in focusing for even 10 percent of the time. It really is a matter of developing sinews long weak from disuse.

With all these self-parenting tasks, the catch-22 for the ADD adult is that the very state he is wanting to grow out of hinders his capacity to create the conditions required for growth. In order to settle the chaos inside, we have to clear up the chaos outside, which was generated in the first place by the chaos inside. After a lifetime of discouraging experiences, people naturally hope that the help they need will be found in a pill or in the wisdom of some expert. "Many people want to remake their lives," the physician and writer Andrew Weil points out, "but cannot imagine doing so without outside help. If only some skilled hands could apply the necessary force to get them going, they could do it, but on their own they remain in habitual ruts."

As we have already seen, no one can instill motivation in anyone else. No one can forcibly induce motivation in oneself either. The best attitude to adopt is one of compassionate patience, which has to include a tolerance for failure. When it comes to changing unhealthy habits or instituting healthy ones, writes Weil, "whether you succeed or fail is less important than making the attempt."[3]

When to begin? No better moment than the present. Or, in the memorable and eternally inspiring words of a former British Columbia cabinet minister: "It's time to grab the bull by the tail and look him firmly in the eye."

# 30

# In Place of Tears

# and Sorrow:

# Addictions and

# the ADD Brain

It is not true that when the heart is full the eyes necessarily overflow; some people can never manage it, especially in our century, which in spite of all the suffering and sorrow will surely be known as the tearless century.

— GÜNTER GRASS, *The Tin Drum*

ALL ADDICTIONS ARE anesthetics. They separate us from the distress in our consciousness. We throw off our familiar and tired consciousness to assume another mind state we find more comfortable, at least temporarily. Desperate to be out of our mind and unaware, we surrender to the addiction, to be lulled into a walking sleep.

Whether they know it or not, a large number of people addicted to behaviors and substances of various sorts have attention deficit disorder, no matter what their proclivity may be: for gambling, compulsive sexual roving, chronic impulse buying, workaholism, excessive physical training, danger-seeking pursuits like drag racing or for nicotine or cocaine, alcohol or marijuana. As an example, according to some surveys, the rate of smoking among the ADD population is three times that among the non-ADD population.

It is easy to understand the appeal addictive substances would have for the ADD brain. Nicotine, for one, makes people more alert and improves mental efficiency. It also elevates mood, by stimulating the release in the brain of the neurochemicals dopamine, important in feelings of reward and motivation, and endorphins, the brain's natural opioids, which induce feelings of pleasure. The endorphins, being related in chemical structure to morphine, also serve as analgesics, soothing both physical and emotional pain. (One reason for the amazing resilience of the tod-dler, cheerfully bumping his head and bruising his knees on sundry objects as he explores the world, is thought to be the abundant presence in the brain of endorphins at this stage of life.) This com-bination of arousal and soothing enables the nicotine addict, like the caffeine addict, to be an alert sleepwalker. By contrast, the alcoholic lurches about in a state of stupor, his nerve endings dead-ened. He, as they say, is feeling no pain.

Less obvious but no less physiological are the effects on the brain of self-stimulating behaviors. The gambler and the sexaholic, the compulsive shopper and the man or woman who insists on ski-ing uncharted glaciers are all looking for the same hit of dopamine and endorphins that the ingestion of substances gives the drug addict. Whatever gets you through the night. Those of us with attention deficit disorder love dopamine and endorphins.

There have been times when my workaholism did not satisfy my need for oblivion. I needed more and found it in pursuits that vicariously fed my creative and spiritual needs—vicariously, because the driven ADD personality has no idea what his true needs are and must find for them some displaced, symbolic expression. My route was the compulsive buying of classical records and compact disks, alternating with—or conjointly with—the frenzied purchase of books. On the surface these may seem like innocent and even admirable pastimes—as they would be if undertaken consciously and in moderation. The addict has no such control. The compulsion beckons; the addict runs to serve it. Gradually, in each orgy of buying, I felt myself shrinking into a ghost of myself, full of self-contempt and apologetic for my existence. I have treated heroin addicts, and I recognized in myself the same vacant and driven look I saw in their eyes. The behavior addict knows, or ought to know, that what separates him from the drug addict's fate is little more than good fortune.

Over the years, I spent thousands of dollars on compact disks. Dropping a few hundred dollars in an hour or two was easy. My all-time record for expenditure, I believe, approached $8,000 in one week. (I have kept the receipts from that week, as a memento of my driven days.) I was cushioned from economic disaster by the income earned through my work as one of the self-sacrificing—read workaholic—physicians much admired by the world. It was easy for me to justify all the spending as compensation for all my hard work: one addiction provided an alibi for the other. My confusion—and I see this in the ADD addict repeatedly—was that both behavior dependencies represented genuine parts of me, though exaggerated. The addiction to music or books could masquerade in my own eyes as an aesthetic passion, and my addiction to work as a service to humanity—and I do have aesthetic passion, and I do wish to serve humanity.

In itself there would be nothing wrong, by this society's standards at least, with buying massive numbers of recordings and books.* It's possible, I suppose, that a man could love music and reading so fervently that he decides, with due consideration, to devote much of his income and life energy to these activities. The truth was that for me, as for all addicts, the excitement was not in the ostensible goal—listening to the music—but in the process of acquiring. Now years down the road, I still have not heard many of the operas and symphonies I bought, let alone the many disks I sold unheard for pennies because some other version that caught my fancy needed space on the shelf.

There is a fine but clearly discernible line between addiction and passion. Any passion can become an addiction. It's simply a question of who is in charge: the individual or the behavior. The addiction is the repeated behavior engaged in despite the certainty that it harms oneself or others. Passion loves the goal or process that is its object (the painting one buys or the painting one does), but the real object of addiction is the *thrill* of plunging into the behavior, not the love of it. (The objective of the gambler is not winning, but the thrill of gambling.)

The effects on my family life were devastating, not because of financial privation or even primarily because of the time I spent away from home while haunting the stores. The major effect was that I could not be present—in both senses of being at home or attentive to my family—whenever I was in the grip of the fever. For an addict, morality, truth, devotion to a partner and children can pale into abstraction. I would keep my children waiting or hurry them along to suit my purposes. I lied to my wife, daily, for weeks and months at a time. When the reckoning came, as it always did, I made guilty confessions and soon-to-be-broken promises. I would rush into the house, stashing my newest purchases on the porch temporarily, and pretend to be present.

---

* Except for the glaring contradiction of how people with supposed humanitarian principles can justify such a degree of self-indulgence while only a few streets away others are hungry. This is not an issue I have even come near to resolving. Clearly, I am not ready to deal with it.

Inwardly, I could think of nothing but the music. Naturally, I hated myself, and the more I did, the harsher, more controlling and more critical I became with my sons and my daughter. We cannot endure seeing the needs of other people, least of all those of our children, when we are preoccupied with serving our own false needs. Perhaps the nadir, but not the end, of my addictive years was when I left a woman in labor in hospital to run downtown to pick up whatever music was then my latest obsession. I would even then have had time to return for the delivery had I not begun to cast about for other recordings to buy. I murmured apologies when I got back, but no explanations. Everyone was most understanding, even my disappointed patient.* After all, I am a busy doctor. I cannot be everywhere at once.

I could not have been more focused when engaged in my addiction. I remembered titles, conductors, record labels, music reviews. My brain was fully alert. I would make appointments to have lunch with two different people at two different restaurants at the same time, but I never forgot to call the store when I wanted to order a recording. My prefrontal lobes were awash with endorphins and dopamine, released by the thrill of the hunt and acquisition. The addiction, in a strange way, makes the addict feel more connected to life. The downside is that it separates him further and further from himself. He is feeding only his appetite, not his hunger.

In biochemical terms, any addictive substance or behavior is self-medication, self-administered emotional pain relief. But the ADD person is also treating herself for a condition she is not even aware of having.

Whatever behavior or substance one is addicted to, the treatment of attention deficit disorder cannot make headway until one accepts the fact of the addiction and takes steps to end it. It is not possible to lull feelings to sleep and hope to be truly awake. When the addiction dominates, the true self—how one really is in the

---

* Her name is Joyce, and she has long known this story.

world—slumbers. To own the addiction is to begin to take ownership of the pain. Until that happens, the pain owns the addict and
the addiction rules him. "The task of integrating thought and feeling is called *striving for ownership*," writes the psychologist and
addiction expert Robert J. Kearney:

> When people are response-able and not in denial, they are
> *aware*...of what they feel and they *know*...what has gone on in-
> side them to generate those feelings. It is a three-part chain
> connected by awareness: awareness of events, awareness of in-
> terpretation of those events, and awareness of the emotional re-
> action following those interpretations. If the chain is broken,
> ownership of the feeling is lost. When the task of ownership is
> being performed, the chain is solid.[1]

I read everywhere, I once said to my therapist, that I am supposed to heal myself by "feeling my pain and my grief." Try as I
might, I could not force myself to conjure up emotions according
to some formula in a book. Feelings either come or they don't. So
where was my pain, my grief?

"Quite right," he agreed. "How could you know?" I was
spending all my waking hours, as he pointed out, stimulating myself with ceaseless activity, working overtime to keep my brain
spinning, gorging it with mind candy—what exactly was I expect-
ing to feel? Where did I leave even a small crack for feeling to seep
through?

It has become evident that the brains of people who are prone
to addiction are biologically predisposed by some imbalance of
brain chemicals. Narcotic addicts, for example, are thought to suffer from a relative undersupply of endorphins, the brain's endog-
enous narcotics. People with ADD seem to be short on dopamine,
the reward chemical. There probably exist, too, combinations of
imbalances. What causes the abnormal brain chemistry? The scien-
tifically simplistic answer would again put the onus on genetic inheritance, although there are also compulsive moralizers who insist

on seeing everything in terms of ethically flawed and weak-willed culpability. The moralizers are chewing on a kernel of truth when they reject genetic determinism; the genetic-minded are right to insist on the importance of biology and physiology. And they both miss the point.

The deficient neurochemistry of addiction, like the deficient neurochemistry of ADD, can be traced to events in the first year or two of life, as we know, the brain's most crucial formative period.[2] We saw in chapter 12 that emotional stresses can affect the supply of brain chemicals—recall, for example, that infant monkeys suffer a drop in dopamine levels in their frontal lobes after only a few days' separation from their mothers. "Social isolation, the early deprivation of empathic care, causes a permanent reduction of brain opiate receptors," writes the researcher and theorist Allan Schore.[3] The catastrophic incidence of substance abuse that afflicts oppressed minority populations in North America can, in this light, be accounted for by the unbearable stresses society has imposed on family life among the poor and powerless. Yet the media leap with alacrity anytime someone reports the latest rhubarb about the so-called alcoholism gene, for instance.

We see, then, that the *pain* the substance abuser does not want to feel has as its original source the same experiences that deprived her of the *chemical* she is trying to replenish by means of her habit. The emotions the behavioral addict is running to escape were imprinted in his implicit memory circuits at the same time as the dopamine circuits were stunted, which now, by his thrill-seeking behaviors, he is trying to stimulate. The harder these people work to compensate for their deficient biochemistry through their respective addictions, the more they perpetuate the emotional emptiness that only the ownership of their problem and the recognition of its causes in past and present will begin to fill.

A significant proportion of the adults I see with ADD admit to substance addictions at some time in their lives, and not a few continue to engage in them into the present. When I find that parents who seek treatment for their child's ADD have a substance addiction, say, alcoholism, I tell them as gently as I can that little meaningful help can be given their son or daughter unless they, the parents, confront their addiction. A number of times such parents have declined to return. Adults who hope to outgrow their ADD problems need to make a similar choice. While they stick with their addiction, they are being no kinder to themselves than the parents who are unable to give up theirs even to help their child.

There are many potential sources of help for the addict wishing to heal, although too many put the emphasis purely on the addiction rather than the underlying causes. "We so often become so preoccupied with the problem the drug use creates," write Drs. Hallowell and Ratey in *Driven to Distraction*, "that we fail to consider what purpose the drug must be serving for the user."[4] While attention deficit disorder cannot be successfully treated as long as the addiction continues to dominate, neither can the addiction be given the appropriate attention if the ADD is ignored and if the common origins of both remain unexplored.

In his novel *The Tin Drum*, the German author Günter Grass depicts a nightclub where the jaded clientele come to sniff pungent onions to the sound of a frenzied drumbeat. Their tears flow and they feel their sorrow, which otherwise is too deeply repressed in their psyches. What they are addicted to is the artificially induced intensity of deep emotion. As Grass writes, we are far away from our griefs, which are the truest parts of ourselves. There is no path toward oneself that leads away from the pain.

# PART SEVEN

Conclusion

# 31

# I Never Saw the

# Trees:

# What Medications

# Can and Cannot Do

I believe that one of the main efforts of neurobiology
and medicine should be directed at alleviating suffering.
... But how to deal with the suffering that arises from
personal and social conflicts outside the medical realm is
a different and entirely unresolved matter. The current
trend is to make no distinction at all and utilize the
medical approach to eliminate any discomfort.

— ANTONIO DAMASIO, M.D., PH.D., *Descartes' Error*

A S A PRACTICAL MATTER, the use of medications in treating attention deficit disorder is straightforward. It's how they are currently employed and their status as first-line treatment that are complicated.

There is a legitimate perception that too often drugs have been prescribed with the intention of making a child more manageable from the adult point of view. I have seen a child put on Ritalin because the parents have been told that unless the child is medicated, he cannot come to school. It is not unusual to hear such stories. It has been estimated that in Quebec the number of children using Ritalin has almost quadrupled from 1990 to the present. According to a *Globe and Mail* report, Pierre Paradis, a professor of education at the University of Quebec, has said that this is in large part because schools ask parents to have their children use the drug.[1] Professor Paradis points out that the increased use of Ritalin has paralleled reductions in the number of special education teachers, psychologists and social workers in the educational system—results of the cutbacks in funding that throughout North America are considered to be among the duties of "responsible" governments.

It is also true, however, that some of the opposition to the use of medications comes from people without the least knowledge of the subject. I was once sharply challenged by a radio host who demanded to know how I could justify prescribing to children a new and untried medication such as Ritalin—the reality being, of course, that this drug has been known and used for at least four decades. I find, too, that the people most closed-minded on the question of medications are also the ones least aware of what attention deficit disorder is. Not appreciating its complex physiological dimensions, they tend to imagine ADD to be a simple matter of authoritarian schools trying to control the spoiled or troubled children of negligent parents.

Only people who have not witnessed or personally experienced how helpful medications can be could maintain a categorical opposition to their use. The positive effects are often dramatic and immediate. One patient of mine, a fifty-four-year-old woman, came back excitedly after taking a low dose of the psychostimulant Dexedrine. "I never saw the trees," she said. "We live across from a park and have a beautiful view, but I never noticed before how green it was." Almost three years later, she continues on the same low dose and reports the same effects, which to her still seem miraculous. One gets similar testimonials from other adults. "You know what I'm doing for the first time in my life?" asked a forty-year-old man, after three weeks on Ritalin. "I am asserting myself." People report that they can get through the workday without losing track of what they're doing every three minutes, or that they can complete pages of writing at a time. A university student found that her migraines had abated. I had worried about giving her Ritalin because of its potential to cause headaches; it turned out her migraines resulted from anxiety over her difficulties studying, which the medications resolved so well that she attained higher marks than she ever could before.

A teenager for whom I recently prescribed Ritalin, a fifteen-year-old with a cunning sense of humor, approached her parents a half hour after taking her first dose. "I feel like listening to a boring lecture from a geography teacher," she said. What she did, in fact, was watch the educational channel, a first. That evening she also had the first calm and intimate talk with her mother in years. One could relate similar positive outcomes with elementary-grade children.

In many other cases, the results are not so impressive. The medications will not work or will cause unpleasant side effects, such as headaches, loss of appetite, listlessness, insomnia or anxiety,* or, simply, the positive changes will not be so dramatic.

---

* Who develops side effects and who doesn't is unpredictable. Fear of side effects is no reason not to try medication, if otherwise doing so is advisable.

There is no way to predict how a given individual will react to a particular medication. I explain to everyone who chooses to try a psychostimulant that each human brain has its own chemistry; one cannot know just how it will be affected. Although as a class, stimulants have been used clinically since 1937 and are about as safe and well understood as any drugs used anywhere in medicine, each person taking them for the first time is being, in a sense, his own guinea pig. There is no reason to be afraid of them, however. More exactly, if we are to be reluctant to use them, it should be for the right reasons, not because of misinformation, such as that these drugs are addictive if used for ADD. While they are subject to abuse, as are other legitimate medications, their administration in medically prescribed doses does not induce addiction. A better case can be made that they may *prevent* addictions, by correcting some of the biochemistry that predisposes a person to substance abuse, as described in the previous chapter.

The main drugs in ADD treatment are the psychostimulants, the most familiar being methylphenidate, known by its trade name Ritalin, and dextroamphetamine sulfate, commonly referred to as Dexedrine. Although they have different modes of action, they both stimulate the activity of the cerebral cortex by balancing the levels of the neurotransmitters (chemical messengers) in the frontal lobe of the brain and in other centers concerned with arousal and attention. As we saw with the "sleeping cop" analogy in chapter 5, with the inhibiting power of the cortex enhanced, there is less chaos in the mind and a greater capacity to resist distraction. The person feels calmer, more focused and purposeful.

Neither methylphenidate nor dextroamphetamine can be said to be better than the other; individual predisposition determines what works best. Alternative medications are available, including other psychostimulants, antidepressants in low doses and some

---

They go away within hours of stopping the drug and cause no long-term damage. On the whole, the psychostimulants are tolerated quite well by the majority who try them.

different classes of drugs as well. I will not conduct here a technical discussion of which drug and in what doses; the subject is well outlined in a number of other books on ADD. Far more important are the principles that should guide drug treatment, and not least, the very question of whether medications should even be used in the case of any particular child or adult.

### Only one person has the right to decide whether a medication is taken: the one about to be treated

For adults, this is self-evident, but in the treatment of children, this principle is often not recognized. It is essential that the child not perceive that she is sick, that something is wrong with her. She does not have a disease and does not have to be cured. The medication may improve functioning, if that is her own chosen goal, but no one should impose on her the demands of the adult world. When you take a chemical substance, it alters how you feel internally and how you relate to the world. Even if these changes are positive, it is a major boundary violation for parents or schools to insist that an unwilling child subject herself to fluctuations in her internal chemical states.

One can understand the frustrations of the teacher facing a classroom full of children, of whom perhaps two to four may have ADD. Unless he ignores those children completely or coerces them into passivity, a good half of his energies will be taken up interacting with these few, to the detriment of the others. In most cases, he is not trained or equipped to teach such children. The awareness of what attention deficit means is as unpredictably variable from teacher to teacher as it is from doctor to doctor. What is outrageous is that cash-deprived educational systems should have to think in terms of chemical straitjackets. Children are being altered to fit the schools, rather than schools being organized to meet the needs of the children who, due to their life experience in this society, have needs and personality traits that call for greater flexibility and creativity than most institutions of learning are currently able to offer them.

The desperation of parents for some relief from what often seems like the impossible task of dealing with their ADD child is also understandable, as is their worry that without medication the child will do poorly in school. One couple I have seen have gone so far as to mix Ritalin into their son's breakfast drink. He refuses to take it knowingly, and without it he is constantly in trouble in school. I urged them to stop this practice immediately.

Parents are sometimes upset that I insist so heavily on the child's autonomy. "He will fail if I don't make him take the medicine," they argue. Apart from the principle involved, my reasons are quite practical, if we have in mind long-term rather than short-term objectives. It may well be that one can push a young child through the early grades by the enforced use of medication. But then what? Well before adolescence, all but the most intimidated children are capable of putting up a strong resistance. All their counterwill-driven oppositionality, hitherto suppressed, will erupt. They will have been driven into a position of obstinate refusal of medication, no matter how useful it could be to them. Along with that, pressuring the child and violating his boundaries will sabotage the long-term developmental goals that should really be the main aim of treatment. Far better for the parents to work on the attachment relationship with their child and on their own parenting approaches than to worry about his passing a grade. Children who feel good about themselves and secure in their bonding with their parents are unlikely to refuse the help of medications, if such help is truly needed.

### The prescriber should be knowledgeable

The medications employed in attention deficit disorder cannot be prescribed according to the fixed recipes appropriate for most medical drugs. Doctors are familiar with the cookbook approach, which is how most medications are prescribed. The dosage of penicillin given for a bacterial throat infection, for example, does not vary between an eight-year-old and an eighty-year-old. Some other medications are dosed according to body weight. With the psychostimulants, neither is there a fixed dose nor can one judge by body size. A small child may need more than a large adult, or vice versa. The principle is to begin with a very small amount of the drug and to build it up gradually. If a child experiences unpleasant effects from psychostimulants taken over a long period of time, the problem is due to prescriber error, not to the medications. It is very simple to reduce the dose or to stop the medication altogether if problems are encountered.

### *The aim of medication is not to control behavior but to help children focus*

The vast majority of preadolescents receiving Ritalin are boys, and even for the boy with attention deficit disorder there are reasons for rambunctious behavior other than his ADD. If a physician increases the dosage of the drug until classroom perfect behavior is achieved she may end up tranquilizing the child into an overly subdued state, with loss of the special vivacity and spark that characterize many ADD children. The end point should be the child's experience of himself, not only observed behaviors. No child should have to take medications that give him side effects, any more than an adult would want to do so.

### *Adults should have clear and limited expectations for what medication can do for them*

At an adult ADD conference I attended, the buzz of conversation between sessions was largely about which person was prescribed what medication, and about what other drugs they could be using instead, or along with it. There was a general sense of disappointment that despite the pharmacological treatment, people continued to experience significant difficulties in their lives. Drugs, of course, do not alter the major issues a person needs to struggle with. In some cases they can be of tremendous help, and in others their benefits are more limited. In no case do they resolve the basic problems of low self-esteem, fear of intimacy, driven lifestyles and lack of self-knowledge. The medications, if taken, should be used with the specific purpose of reducing distractibility and improving concentration and focusing, not of changing people's lives.

### *The adult should be aware of her emotional state when setting out to take medications for ADD*

Not infrequently, the ADD adult may be suffering from chronic low-grade depression or anxiety. If this is the case, the psychostimulants may not help, or in some cases may make matters worse. If depression or anxiety is present, it needs to be addressed first, or at least at the same time.

### *Medications should never be the only treatment, or even the first treatment*

The most serious problem with the widespread use of medications in the treatment of attention deficit disorder is that very often—probably in the vast majority of cases—they are the only form of intervention consistently pursued. Yet in themselves they do not promote long-term positive changes. When children or adults stop taking them, they find that none of their problems have gone away.

Attention deficit disorder is not primarily a medical problem. Neither its causes nor its manifestations are due to illness. The factors that maintain the ADD-related mental turmoil and behaviors are only in part biochemically internal to the individual, and have more to do with the circumstances in which an adult or child lives her life. The easy route of relying on a pill is tempting but leads in the wrong direction. Much more difficult, and much more essential, is to address the issues of psychological security, family relationships, lifestyle and self-esteem.

One of the many astute recommendations made by the psychologist Thomas Armstrong in his book *The Myth of the ADD Child* is that medications have no place as the first-line treatment for ADD. "Most importantly," he writes, "medication can be used *as a last resort*, after a sincere attempt to employ a number of appropriate non-drug interventions has failed to produce significant results."[2] I might not put it as categorically as that, but despite my initial enthusiasm for medications when I first learned about ADD, and despite the clear benefits they can have, I do now tend toward that view.* There are some cases where early pharmacological intervention is sensible—if the child voluntarily accepts it—for example, the relentlessly hyperactive child whose family and school life are in crisis. The exclusive use of medications can never be endorsed and the development goals outlined throughout this book must always be foremost.

### Consider the long-term implications of medication use, not just its short-term benefits

The fifteen-year-old who felt like "listening to a boring lecture by a geography teacher" after taking her first dose of Ritalin had, nevertheless, some mixed feelings about the medication. "It's not the me that I'm used to," she told me. "It's kind of weird to see my mind working differently." Before and all throughout their teenage years, children have the task of consolidating a sense of themselves, of who they are. Medications impose an artificial state, affecting the child's moods and thoughts. Even if such changes are positive, they still may introduce further confusion into a process already teeming with changes and internal conflicts. They may, as Stanley Greenspan points out, "undermine the adolescent's long-term goal of forming a united sense of self."[3]

One of the main reasons not to pressure children into taking medications is that this integrated sense of self is far less likely to be disrupted if they themselves choose pharmacological treatment. When they are making a free choice, they are not simply electing to take a medication, but indicating that their sense of self is ready to accommodate an awareness that they may have problems in some areas of functioning, and that they will accept help. In

---

*Unfortunately, in all but rejecting the very existence of ADD, Dr. Armstrong throws out the baby with the bathwater. For all that, his book is a most useful read for the parents of ADD children.

supporting the young person's freedom of choice, parents express their faith in his own processes and do not convey a belief that there is something wrong with him. They also do not reinforce the child's anxiety that he is not accepted by his parents just the way he is.

### Do not read more into the effects of medication than they merit

It would be easy to come to the wrong conclusions from experiences like that of the same teenage girl who, having taken Ritalin, had a meaningful talk with her mother for the first time in years. The story may be seen as proof that the only thing wrong between mother and daughter had been the teenager's ADD, now "cured." Not so. Many problems remain in that family, which the parents are only now beginning to work on. The girl herself, despite the contact with her mother while on Ritalin, still spoke despondently of her relationship with her parents. "Why can't they just accept me for who I am?" she said. "I don't understand why they even want me at home." That the medication worked to calm and focus her certainly indicates that she does have a neurophysiological problem, but the episode also highlights the mother's problem: something in the mother tenses up when her daughter is tense. Her own anxieties are triggered so that she can not remain calm, loving and attentive. Unless her daughter is well controlled, she cannot be accepting toward her. There has not been enough individuation, or differentiation between them. In his own way, the father, too, has been involved in the triangle. It is the parents' responsibility to recognize such dynamics and to move to change them, which this couple are keen to do.

Given the importance of nonpharmacological approaches, how to explain the huge imbalance in favor of medication use in the treatment of attention deficit disorder? There is, of course, the North American propensity for the quick fix and the hope of fast relief from a nagging and difficult problem. But it is not as spontaneous as all that.

"While until very recently the bedside usually determined

what was done in the medical research laboratory," the physician and author Sherwin Nuland has written, "the findings coming out of the laboratory nowadays are just as likely to tell the clinician what he can do at the bedside. The tail often wags the dog. In fact, the tail is becoming the dog."[4] The fact is, researchers and doctors find it much easier to raise funds for drug evaluation studies than for treatments that do not hold out the promise of huge profits for anyone. Pharmaceutical companies, the major source of research dollars, have no incentive to support alternative approaches that will do nothing for the size of their coffers. If, as Dr. Nuland suggests, the laboratory tail is wagging the clinical dog, it is largely because the poor dog is starving even as the tail becomes bigger and bigger.

# 32

# What It Means

# to Attend

People have, with the help of so many conventions,
resolved everything the easy way, on the easiest side of
the easy. But it is clear we must embrace struggle. Every
living thing conforms to it. Everything in nature grows
and establishes itself in its own way, establishing its own
identity, insisting on it at all cost, against all resistance.
We can be sure of very little, but the need to court struggle is a surety that will not leave us.

    — RAINER MARIA RILKE, *Letters to a Young Poet*

**"I** HAVE SPENT MY WHOLE LIFE pretending to be
normal," said fifty-year-old Elizabeth, an inte-
rior designer. The pretense of normality is famil-
iar to any adult with attention deficit disorder. She works at fitting
in by toning down the strength of her feelings about matters that
others seem to think unimportant, by struggling to suppress her
intensity and by feigning an interest in what bores her to tears. The
game is precarious. No matter how clever the alien becomes at

attempting to pass as an earthling, some telling awkwardness in his manner, some fatal expression of his true nature will, in unguarded moments, betray him for what he is: *different.*

Although the soul-destroying fear of being different is shared by many in North American culture, conformism is less a painful struggle for those who really do fall in with social norms. Those who do not consciously experience themselves as different may also shrink from any temptation to be themselves, but they are not compelled to live every day aware of the mask they are wearing, tense for fear it will slip.

The irony is that the energy ADD adults expend on their attempts at sameness is wasted, as is the anxiety parents generate over their child's differentness. The world is much more ready to accept someone who is different and comfortable with it than someone desperately seeking to conform by denying himself. It's the self-rejection others react against, much more than the differentness. So the solution for the adult is not to "fit in," but to accept his inability to conform. The child's uniqueness has to first find a welcome in the heart of the parent.

None of this is achieved by an act of will, and it is possible one will not succeed completely. That is not important. What is important is to engage in the process, difficult as that is. Healing is not an event, not a single act. It occurs by a process; it is in the process itself.

By no means is it an easy process. A person with ADD does start off with a sense of isolation. It is good to realize that many other people have had the same experience, are having the same experience. There are millions in North America whose lives are affected by attention deficit disorder in one way or another. It is certainly helpful for adults with ADD, or parents with ADD children, to join for mutual support with others who must confront the same problems they themselves face every day. There is strength in numbers.

This strength in numbers is essential for another purpose, too. Beyond the question of individual psychological support is the issue of effecting changes in the way society in general views attention deficit disorder, and in particular how the helping professions view it. Current attitudes toward attention deficit disorder are characterized by foggy awareness, confusion and/or hostile skepticism.

The state of medical knowledge about ADD today reminds me of the way doctors used to conduct deliveries about twenty years ago, when I first began to practice medicine. It was routine to perform an episiotomy on every woman giving birth. "Time to make a little cut now," I would announce as the infant's head was ready to exit the birth canal. Having injected local anesthetic near the vaginal opening, I would then make an incision a few inches long, catch the baby and hand it to the nurse. Then I set to repairing the wound I myself had caused. This is what I had been taught to do in medical school; I knew no other way. I happened to learn from some midwives—in those dark ages still working illicitly in British Columbia—that an episiotomy is not necessary in most labors. Other surprises followed: women could deliver babies without their feet in stirrups or even without lying down. When there were no complications, the baby could be handed to the mother without being poked and prodded under bright lights and having plastic suction tubes shoved in her mouth. These heretical doctrines have since been validated by solid medical research, so doctors can now practice with peace in their hearts what midwives have been doing safely for hundreds of years. Years of pressure from pregnant women and laypeople have now established natural birth procedures in many hospitals—although far from everywhere.

Three conclusions may be drawn from that experience. First, the medical view of the world tends not to trust nature very much. Second, there are things in the world that are true, even if they're not taught in medical school. Third, sometimes doctors have to be educated by the public—under duress, if necessary. Since I have become interested in attention deficit disorder, I have seen that the same lessons apply. They apply also in the educational system, and equally in the fields of psychology and therapy. People will have to demand the help they require, and they will have to educate the professionals from whom they seek help about the realities of their lives. Parents as well as adults with attention deficit disorder must insist that the world pay more attention to their needs, even as they learn how to pay attention to themselves and to their children.

I have learned through my own process that a goal in life cannot be the avoidance of painful feelings. For people like me with ADD, and for everyone else, emotional pain is a reality. It does not have to exclude joy and a capacity to experience the beauty of life. We each for ourselves have to discover the age-old wisdom that the thing is not to struggle against pain, but to be able to endure it when it is unavoidable. "Many parents have an especially hard time when their children are feeling sad and disappointed," writes Stanley Greenspan. "It's an especially hard situation for parents of sensitive children, because these children feel emotions so strongly. But parents can help their children come to grips with these difficult feelings, learn to tolerate a sense of loss and disappointment, and move on."[1] We don't do our children any favors when we try to protect them from experiencing sadness or failure. What we really want for them when they feel sad is to be able to endure disappointment and hurt feelings, not to hide behind defenses, angry acting-out and driven behavior in order to avoid emotional distress. Not, in other words, for them to become ADD adults. It takes a lot of loving to help a child accept sadness, to know that it can be endured, that sadness, like all other mind states, is evanescent. It will pass.

Throughout this book, I have insisted on the connection between human relationship and attention. Love, it turns out, is intimately related to attention. In *The Road Less Traveled* Scott Peck brilliantly defines love as action, as the willingness to extend oneself in order to nurture another person's spiritual and psychological growth, or one's own. Extending oneself means to do precisely what we find difficult to do. Most parents do not need to be taught how to love their children in the feeling sense, but we can all use practice in how to be actively loving toward them in day-to-day experience. I hope people will find this book of some help.

Adults with ADD face the most difficult task of all: learning how to be loving toward themselves. This is the greatest struggle because it requires that we gradually shed the defenses we have come to identify as the self and venture into new territory.

To love is to extend oneself toward another or toward oneself, says Dr. Peck. It so happens that this is also the precise meaning of giving *attention* to another person or to oneself. The origin of the word *attend* is the Latin *tendere*, "to stretch." *Attend* means to extend, to stretch toward.

If we can actively love, there will be no attention deficit and no disorder.

# Notes

INTRODUCTION

1. In the professional literature Stephen P. Hinshaw, associate professor of psychology at the University of California, Berkeley, has been a distinctive voice, suggesting the possiblity of complex biological, social, and psychological interactions together forming the roots of ADD: "Notions of complex causal pathways in which psychobiologic risk factors, problematic family functioning, and wider system influences might combine to shape problems in attention regulation, activity level modulation, and response inhibition have been slow to gain acceptance." (Hinshaw, *Attention Deficits and Hyperactivity in Children*, ix.)

CHAPTER 3: WE COULD ALL GO CRAZY

1. Canadian statistics regarding Ritalin use: *The Vancouver Province*, April 3, 1998.
2. Regarding our still rudimentary knowledge about the microfunctioning of the brain, "We are still far away from explaining even one aspect or piece of an integrated act by a neural circuit, neural assembly, or neural code," writes the brain researcher Patricia S. Goldman-Rakic. (Dawson and Fischer, *Human Behaviour and the Developing Brain*, xi.)

CHAPTER 5: FORGETTING TO REMEMBER THE FUTURE

1. Singer and Revenson, *A Piaget Primer*, 95.
2. Goleman, *Emotional Intelligence*, 34.
3. University of Alberta study: Janzen, Troy *et al.*, "Differences in Baseline Measures for ADD and Normally Achieving Preadolescent Males," in *Biofeedback and Self-Regulation*, Vol. 20, No. 1 (1995): 65.

4. "The cortex's job is to prevent the inappropriate response rather than to produce the appropriate one," writes neuroscientist Joseph LeDoux. (LeDoux, *The Emotional Brains*, 165.)

5. Greenspan, *The Growth of the Mind*, 143.

CHAPTER 6: DIFFERENT WORLDS: HEREDITY AND THE ENVIRONMENTS OF CHILDHOOD

1. The paucity of evidence for the genetic basis of personality traits is not limited to ADD. Robert Plomin, an internationally known behavioral geneticist at the University of Colorado, Boulder, touched on this issue in his book *Development, Genetics and Psychology*. The study of hereditary effects on the development of personality, he pointed out, would require the identification of single genes that code for specific characteristics. "Unfortunately," he concluded, "there is no example of a single gene that accounts for a detectable amount of variance in any psychological characteristic such as cognitive ability, personality, or psychopathology." (Plomin, *Development, Genetics, and Psychology*, 4.)

2. "Because parents share family environment as well as heredity with their offspring, parent-offspring resemblance does not prove the existence of genetic influence." (Plomin, 9.)

3. There is one more argument regarding identical twins made on behalf of the genetic view: that since identical twins adopted out have a higher concordance rate than fraternal twins, the difference again must be due to genetics. To some degree this is true, of course. Whatever genetic susceptibility one identical twin inherits will also affect his/her sibling. However, there is an important environmental factor at play here, too. The world is much more likely to respond in similar ways to identical twins—same sex, same inherited tendencies, identical physical features—than to fraternal twins who may be of different sex and have very different looks and reactivity patterns. In other words, for identical twins the environmental factors are still more likely to be similar, even after adoption into different families.

4. Wender, *Attention-Deficit Hyperactivity Disorder in Adults*, 98.

5. Greenspan, *The Growth of the Mind*, 143.

6. "The influence of birth order, like that of gender, can be traced throughout history with clear and dramatic consequences... The psychological consequences of birth order provide compelling evidence for the role of

the family environment," says Frank J. Sulloway of the Department of Brain and Cognitive Science at the Massachusetts Institute of Technology, in his recent book, *Born to Rebel: Birth Order, Family Dynamics, and Creative Lives*, xiv.

7. Mahler, *The Psychological Birth of the Human Infant*, 3

## CHAPTER 7: EMOTIONAL ALLERGIES: ADD AND SENSITIVITY

1. Vagal stimulation study: Dawson and Fischer, 349.

## CHAPTER 8: A SURREALISTIC CHOREOGRAPHY

1. "The number of synaptic contacts in human cerebral cortex is staggeringly high," writes Peter Huttenlocher, a neuroscientist at the University of Chicago. "It is clear that this large number cannot be determined by a genetic program, in which each synapse has an exact assigned location. More likely, only the general outlines of basic connectivity are genetically determined." (Dawson and Fischer, 138.)

2. Damasio, *Descartes' Error*, 260.

3. Regarding the vulnerability of the infant brain to environmental influences: "At any point in this process you have all these potentials for either good or bad stimulation to get in there and set the microstructure of the brain," Dr. Robert Post, chief of the U.S. National Institute of Mental Health's biological psychiatry branch said in an interview with *Chicago Tribune* science writer Ronald Kotulak. (Kotulak, *Inside the Brain*, 8.)

4. Neural Darwinism: "Both neurons and neural connections compete to survive and grow," write two researchers, Kurt W. Fischer and Samuel P. Rose: "Neurons that receive little input and so are not active are pruned away; those that are active are sustained. Similarly, synapses connecting neurons compete with each other, and those that receive ample input thrive, while those that receive minimal input become weaker or are pruned away. This competition is an important part of development and apparently accounts for many of the effects of specific experience. Experience causes some neurons and synapses (and not others) to survive and grow." (Dawson and Fischer, 9.)

5. "All the evidence indicates," writes the anthropologist Ashley Montagu, "that while the duration of the gestation period in man differs by only a week or two from that of the great apes, a large number of factors, all combining to

lead to the much more prolonged development of the human infant, causes him to be born before his gestation has been completed." (Montagu, *The Human Revolution*, 86.)

CHAPTER 9: ATTUNEMENT AND ATTACHMENT

1. *Scientific American* article quoted in Schore, *Affect Regulation and the Origin of the Self*, 73.

2. Seattle EEG infant study: Dawson and Fischer, 367.

3. British studies on postpartum depression: Murray and Cooper, *Postpartum Depression and Child Development*, 97.

4. Daniel J. Siegel, *Cognitive Neuroscience Encounters Psychotherapy*, notes for a plenary address to the 1996 Annual Meeting of the American Association of Directors of Psychiatric Residency Training.

5. The intricate processes of attunement are described in the following manner by Daniel Stern, professor of Psychiatry and chief, Laboratory of Developmental Processes, Cornell University Medical Center: "First, the parent must be able to read the infant's feeling state from the infant's overt behavior. Second, the parent must perform some behavior that is not a strict imitation but nonetheless corresponds in some way to the infant's overt behavior. Third, the infant must be able to read this corresponding parental response as having to do with the infant's original feeling experience and not just imitating the infant's behaviour." (Stern, *The Interpersonal World of the Infant*, 139.)

In other words, the mother (or mothering figure) has to be exquisitely aware of the minute and rapidly changeable gradations of the infant's emotions. She (or he) then has to be able to communicate to the infant by means of facial expression, tone of voice and body language, that she understands those emotions and is with the child in experiencing them. These messages are processed and encoded in the front part of the infant's right hemisphere, the right prefrontal cortex.

6. Bowlby, *A Secure Base*, 7.

7. Attachment was explained by John Bowlby, the pioneer of attachment theory: "To say of a child that he is attached to, or has an attachment to, someone means that he is strongly disposed to seek proximity to and contact with a specific figure and to do so in certain situations, notably when he is frightened, tired or ill..." (*Attachment*, 371.)

8. Greenspan, *The Growth of the Mind*, 53.

CHAPTER 10: THE FOOTPRINTS OF INFANCY

1. The research data and the psychological observations pointing to the central role of the OFC in self-regulation, motivation, emotional processing and attention are detailed masterfully in *Affect Regulation and the Origin of the Self* by Allan N. Schore, destined to become a classic in the literature of brain development.

2. Schore, 195.

3. "There are many subtle ways in which disruptions in electrical and chemical functions can adversely affect a brain region, with lesions being just an extreme example of this," the psychologist and neuroscientist Joseph LeDoux points out. (LeDoux, 250.)

4. Damasio, 78.

5. Dubovsky, *Mind ↔ Body Deceptions*, 193.

6. Study on anxiety and natural benzodiazepines in rats: Christian Caldji, Beth Tannenbaum *et al.*, "Maternal care during infancy regulates the development of neural systems mediating the expression of fearfulness in the rat," in *Neurobiology*, Vol. 95, No. 9 (April 28, 1998): 5335–40.

CHAPTER 12: STORIES WITHIN STORIES: ADD AND THE FAMILY (III)

1. The quotations on pages 98-99 are from Barkley, *Attention Deficit Hyperactivity Disorder*, 147–48 and 157.

2. 1994 study: van der Kolk, *Traumatic Stress*, 31.

3. Barkley, *Attention Deficit Hyperactivity Disorder*, 149.

4. Barkley, *Attention Deficit Hyperactivity Disorder*, 148

5. Bowlby, *Separation*, 266.

CHAPTER 13: THIS MOST FRENETIC OF CULTURES: THE SOCIAL ROOTS OF ADD

1. Hallowell and Ratey, *Driven to Distraction*, 191.

2. Bowlby, *Attachment*, 46.

3. Hollowell and Ratey, *Driven to Distraction*, 191.

CHAPTER 14: SEVERED THOUGHTS AND FLIBBERTIGIBBETS: DISTRACTIBILITY AND TUNING OUT

1. "In its broadest terms," writes the psychologist Etzel Cardena, "dissociation simply means that two or more mental processes or contents are not associated or integrated." (Lynn and Rhue, *Dissociation*, 15.)

The value of dissociation is explained in the following manner by Dr. Bessel van der Kolk, associate professor of psychiatry at Harvard Medical School and director of the Trauma Centre at Human Resources Institute Hospital, in Brookline, Massachusetts: "During a traumatic experience, dissociation allows a person to observe the event as a spectator, to experience no, or only limited pain or distress; and to be protected from awareness of the full impact of what has happened. (van der Kolk, 192.)

2. Freyd, *Betrayal Trauma*, 68.

3. Fischer and Rose, writing in Dawson and Fischer, 33.

4. LeDoux, 287.

5. Greenspan, *The Growth of the Mind*, 45.

6. When the maternal face expresses positive internal emotional states, infants are more likely to seek the mother's gaze. Toward the end of the first year, as babies begin walking, checking the mother's face becomes an important guide to exploring the world. A happy, supportive look from mother encourages interest in the environment. It takes but a moment—on the average 1.33 seconds—for the infant to read in mother's facial expression the signals allowing continued exploration and interest, or the signs of discouragement. (Data from Schore.)

7. Schacter, *Searching for Memory*, 154.

## CHAPTER 15: THE PENDULUM SWINGS: HYPERACTIVITY, LETHARGY AND SHAME

1. The scanning behavior described on this page, as well as other automatic behaviors observable in ADD children and adults, strikingly resembles the descriptions given in John Bowlby's work on the demeanor of infants after a period of separation from their mothers: "For hours on end sometimes the infant would crane his neck, scanning his surroundings without apparently focusing on any particular feature and letting his eyes sweep over all objects without attending to any particular one." (Bowlby, *Separation*, 54.)

Older children who are able to move around exhibit a form of mobile hyperactivity that may alternate with dejected inactivity. These are also the pendulum swings that characterize ADD behavior. Another study quoted by Bowlby observed: "This increased activity frequently took the form of anxious searching or agitated movement. There was occasionally a quite opposite kind of reaction to the stress of being alone: a kind of frozen immobility ... Also, it occasionally happened that a child who was upset over separation would alternate between unfocused running activity and immobility." (*Separation*, 50.)

Data from animal experiments is revealing. At Pennsylvania State University, it was found that rats deliberately lesioned—damaged—in the orbitofrontal area of the cortex became hyperactive. Similar observations were made at the University of Colorado Medical Center when young monkeys were separated from their mothers. Together, these findings suggest that interference with the mother-infant attachment has consequences similar to those resulting from physical damage to the orbitofrontal cortex. The difference is that the manmade lesion cannot be reversed, but the attachment disruption can be.

2. Kaufman, *Shame*, 13.

3. All research observations in this chapter, unless otherwise specified, are quoted from Schore's *Affect Regulation and the Origin of the Self*, 199–230.

CHAPTER 16: IT AIN'T OVER TILL IT'S OVER: UNCONDITIONAL POSITIVE REGARD

1. All three quotations on this page are from Diamond, *Enriching Heredity*, 150, 157 and 164 respectively.

2. Plasticity of the brain in infancy: Dawson and Fischer, 147.

3. Benes, writing in Dawson and Fischer, 198.

4. Damasio, 112.

5. Greenspan, *The Growth of the Mind*, 151.

6. Rogers, *On Becoming a Person*, 283.

7. Diamond, 163.

8. Rogers, 283. Rogers was summing up the qualities of a good therapist in relation to her/his clients. Substitute parent for therapist and child for client, and we see an eloquent description of what is needed in a parent-child relationship.

CHAPTER 18: LIKE FISH IN THE SEA

1. Kerr and Bowen, *Family Evaluation*, 203.

2. Freeman, *Family Therapy with Couples*, 8.

CHAPTER 19: JUST LOOKING FOR ATTENTION

1. Deci, *Why We Do What We Do*, 28.

CHAPTER 20: THE DEFIANT ONES: OPPOSITIONALITY

1. Greenspan, *The Growth of the Mind*, 68.

2. Magic marker study: M. R. Lepper, et al, "Undermining Children's Intrinsic Interest With Extrinsic Rewards," *Journal of Personality and Social Psychology*, 28, 1973, 129–37: *237*: Deci, 18 and 25.


CHAPTER 22: MY MARSHMALLOW CAUGHT FIRE: MOTIVATION AND AUTONOMY

1. Rathvon, *The Unmotivated Child*, 25.

2. Deci, 30, 42.

3. Greenspan, *The Challenging Child*, 50.

4. Greenspan, *The Challenging Child*, 44.

5. Rathvon, 119.


CHAPTER 23: TRUSTING THE CHILD, TRUSTING ONESELF: ADD IN THE CLASSROOM

1. Allyson Golding's article, "The Incoherent Brain," appeared in *Harper's Magazine*, May 1998.

2. *The New York Times*, April 7, 1998.


CHAPTER 25: JUSTIFYING ONE'S EXISTENCE: SELF-ESTEEM

1. Miller, *The Drama of the Gifted Child*, 33.

2. Damasio, 240.


CHAPTER 26: MEMORIES ARE MADE OF THIS

1. Herman, *Trauma and Recovery*, 235.

2. Schacter, 161.

3. LeDoux, 198.

4. Schacter, 233

5. LeDoux, 204.

6. Greenspan, *The Growth of the Mind*, 56.


CHAPTER 27: REMEMBERING WHAT DIDN'T HAPPEN: THE ADD RELATIONSHIP

1. Epstein, *Thoughts without a Thinker*, 165.

2. LeDoux, 203.

3. On the interaction of the orbitofrontal cortex and the amygdala: "The orbital cortex provides a link through which emotional processing by the amygdala might be related in working memory to information being processed in sensory and other regions of the neocortex," writes Dr. LeDoux (*The Emotional Brain*, 278). In short, the OFC collects data about incoming information, especially the emotional content of stimuli, interprets them in the light of the implicit memory imprinted in its circuits from our earliest months and years and connects all this input with the emotional messages flooding toward it from the lower regions of the brain.

4. Bowlby, *Separation*, 12.

5. Kerr and Bowen, 165.

6. Greenspan, *The Growth of the Mind*, 248.

7. Hendrix, *Getting the Love You Want*, 35.

## CHAPTER 28: MOSES SAVED BY THE ANGEL: SELF-PARENTING (I)

1. Ginzberg, *The Legends of the Jews*, 294.

2. Storr, *Solitude*, 22.

3. Damasio, 255.

## CHAPTER 29: THE PHYSICAL AND SPIRITUAL ENVIRONMENT: SELF-PARENTING (II)

1. Storr, 25.

2. Epstein, 110.

3. Weil, 7.

## CHAPTER 30: IN PLACE OF TEARS AND SORROW: ADDICTIONS AND THE ADD BRAIN

1. Kearney, *Within the Wall of Denial*, 62.

2. The role of natural opiates in infant attachment: "Opiates play a unique role in socioemotional, imprinting, and attachment developmental processes. In face-to-face affective interactions, the emotionally expressive face of the imprinting object, the mother, induces alterations in opioid peptides in the child's developing brain." (Schore, 145.)

3. Schore, 438.

4. Hallowell and Ratey, *Driven to Distraction*, 368.

CHAPTER 31: I NEVER SAW THE TREES: WHAT MEDICATIONS CAN AND
CANNOT DO

1. *The Globe and Mail,* May 27, 1998.

2. Armstrong, *The Myth of the A.D.D.* Child, 48.

3. Greenspan, *The Growth of the Mind*, 204.

4. Sherwin Nuland in an article in *The New York Times*, May 10, 1998.


CHAPTER 32: WHAT IT MEANS TO ATTEND

1. Greenspan, *The Challenging Child*, 46.

# Bibliography

I have not attempted to list all the works consulted for this book, nor all the works the general or professional reader may find useful. Cited only are those publications used as references in the text, or which were found to be of special importance in the preparation of it. — G.M.

GENERAL WORKS ON ADD

Armstrong, Thomas, Ph.D. *The Myth of the A.D.D. Child: 50 Ways to Improve your Child's Behavior and Attention Span, without Drugs, Labels or Coercion.* New York: Dutton, 1995.

Hallowell, Edward M., M.D., and John J. Ratey, M.D. *Driven to Distraction: Recognizing and Coping with Attention Deficit Disorder from Childhood through Adulthood.* New York: Touchstone, 1994.

———. *Answers to Distraction.* New York: Pantheon Books, 1994.

ACADEMIC AND PROFESSIONAL WORKS ON ADD

Barkley, Russell A. *Attention Deficit Hyperactivity Disorder: A Handbook for Diagnosis and Treatment.* New York: The Guilford Press, 1990.

———. "Impaired Delayed Responding," in Routh, Donald K., ed. *Disruptive Behavior Disorders in Childhood.* New York: Plenum Press, 1994.

———. *ADHD and the Nature of Self-Control,* New York: The Guilford Press, 1997.

Hinshaw, Stephen P. *Attention Deficits and Hyperactivity in Children.* Thousand Oaks, CA: Sage Publications, 1994.

Nadeau, Kathleen G., Ph.D. *A Comprehensive Guide to Attention Deficit Disorder in Adults: Research, Diagnosis, Treatment*. New York: Brunner/Mazel, 1995.

Wender, Paul H., *Attention-Deficit Hyperactivity Disorder in Adults*. New York: Oxford University Press, 1995.


WORKS ON PSYCHOLOGY, PSYCHIATRY AND CHILD DEVELOPMENT

Bowlby, John. *Attachment*. New York: BasicBooks, 1969.

————. *Separation: Anxiety and Anger*. New York: Basic Books, 1973.

————. *Loss: Sadness and Depression*. New York: Basic Books, 1980.

————. *A Secure Base: Parent-Child Attachment and Healthy Human Development*. New York: Basic Books, 1988.

Chess, Stella, and Alexander Thomas. *Origins and Evolution of Behavior Disorders: From Infancy to Early Adult Life*. Cambridge, MA.: Harvard University Press, 1984.

Deci, Edward. L. *Why We Do What We Do: Understanding Self-Motivation*. New York: Penguin Books, 1995.

Dinnerstein, Dorothy. *The Mermaid and the Minotaur: Sexual Arrangements and Human Malaise*. New York: Harper Perennial, 1977.

Dreikurs, Rudolf. *Children: THE Challenge*. New York: Hawthorn/Dutton, 1964.

Dubovsky, Steven L. *Mind ↔ Body Deceptions: The Psychosomatics of Everyday Life*. New York: W.W. Norton & Company, 1997.

Epstein, Mark, M.D. *Thoughts without a Thinker: Psychotherapy from a Buddhist Perspective*. New York: Basic Books, 1995.

Erikson, Erik. H. *Childhood and Society*. New York: W.W. Norton and Company, 1985.

Firestone, Robert W., Ph.D. *The Fantasy Bond: Effects of Psychological Defenses on Interpersonal Relations*. New York: Human Sciences Press, Inc., 1985.

Freeman, David, S. *Family Therapy with Couples: The Family-of-Origin Approach*. New York: Jason Aronson Inc., 1992.

Goleman, Daniel. *Emotional Intelligence: Why It Can Matter More Than IQ*. New York: Bantam Books, 1995.

Greenspan, Stanley I. *The Challenging Child: Understanding, Raising and Enjoying the Five "Difficult" Types of Children*. Reading, MA: Addison-Wesley Publishing, 1995.

Greenspan, Stanley I. *The Growth of the Mind*. Reading, MA: Addison-Wesley, 1997.

Herman, Judith Lewis, M.D. *Trauma and Recovery: The Aftermath of Violence—From Domestic Abuse to Political Terror*. New York: Basic Books, 1992.

Kagan, Jerome. *The Nature of the Child*. New York: Basic Books, 1994.

Kaufman, Gershen. *Shame: The Power of Caring*. Rochester, VT: Schenkman Books, 1980.

Kearney, Robert J. *Within the Wall of Denial: Conquering Addictive Behaviors*. New York: W.W. Norton and Company, 1996.

Kerr, Michael E., and Murray Bowen. *Family Evaluation: The Role of the Family as an Emotional Unit that Governs Individual Behavior and Development*. New York: W.W. Norton and Company, 1988.

van der Kolk, Bessel A. *et al*, ed. *Traumatic Stress: The Effects of Overwhelming Expereince on Mind, Body and Society*. New York: The Guilford Press, 1996.

Lynn, Steven Jay, and Judith W. Rhue, ed. *Dissociation: Clinical and Theoretical Perspectives*. New York: The Guilford Press, 1994.

Mahler, Margaret S., *et. al., The Psychological Birth of the Human Infant: Symbiosis and Individuation*. New York: HarperCollins, 1975.

Miller, Alice. *The Untouched Key: Tracing Childhood Trauma in Creativity and Destructiveness*. New York: Anchor Books, 1988.

———. *The Drama of the Gifted Child: The Search for the True Self*. New York: Basic Books, 1994.

Montagu, Ashley. *The Human Revolution*. New York: Bantam Books, 1965.

Murray, Lynne and Peter J. Cooper. *Pospartum Depression and Child Development*. New York: The Guilford Press, 1997.

Plomin, Robert. *Development, Genetics, and Psychology*. Hillsdale, NJ: Lawrence Erlbaum Associates, 1986.

Ratey, John J., and Catherine Johnson. *Shadow Syndromes: Recognizing and Coping with the Hidden Psychological Disorders that Can Influence Your Behavior and Silently Determine the Course of Your Life*. New York: Pantheon Books, 1997.

Rathvon, Natalie. *The Unmotivated Child: Helping Your Underacheiver Become a Successful Student*. New York: Fireside, 1996.

Rogers, Carl R. *On Becoming a Person: A Therapist's View of Psychotherapy*. New York: Houghton Mifflin Company, 1995.

Singer, Dorothy G., and Tracey A. Revenson. *A Piaget Primer: How a Child Thinks*. New York: Penguin Books, 1978.

Stern, Daniel N. *The Interpersonal World of the Infant*. New York: Basic Books, 1985.

Sulloway, Frank J. *Born to Rebel: Birth Order, Family Dynamics and Creative Lives*. New York: Pantheon Books, 1996.

Winnicott, D.W. *The Child, the Family, and the Outside World*. New York: Penguin Books, 1964.

————. *The Maturational Process and the Facilitating Environment: Studies in the Theory of Emotional Development*. Madison, CT: International Universities Press, 1985.


BRAIN, MIND AND BRAIN DEVELOPMENT

Damasio, Antonio R. *Descartes' Error: Emotion, Reason, and the Human Brain*. New York: G. P. Putnam and Sons, 1994.

Dawson, Geraldine, and Kurt W. Fischer, *Human Behavior and the Developing Brain*. New York: The Guilford Press, 1994.

Diamond, Marian Cleeves. *Enriching Heredity: The Impact of the Environment on the Anatomy of the Brain*. New York: The Free Press, 1988.

Edelman, Gerald M. *Bright Air, Brilliant Fire: On the Matter of the Mind*. New York: Basic Books, 1992.

Freyd, Jennifer F. *Betrayal Trauma: The Logic of Forgetting Childhood Abuse*. Cambridge, MA: Harvard University Press, 1996.

Greenspan, Stanley I. *The Growth of the Mind and the Endangered Origins of Intelligence*. Reading, MA: Addison-Wesley Publishing Company, 1997.

Kotulak, Ronald. *Inside the Brain: Revolutionary Discoveries of How the Mind Works*. Kansas City, MO: Andrews and McMeel, 1996.

LeDoux, Joseph. *The Emotional Brain: The Mysterious Underpinnings of Emotional Life*. New York: Simon and Schuster, 1996.

Restak, Richard M. *The Modular Brain: How New Discoveries in Neuroscience are Answering Age-Old Questions About Memory, Free Will, Consciousness, and Personal Identity*. New York: Simon and Schuster Inc., 1994.

Restak, Richard M. *Receptors*. New York: Bantam Books, 1994.

Schacter, Daniel L. *Searching for Memory: The Brain, the Mind and the Past*. New York: Basic Books, 1996.

Schore, Allan N. *Affect Regulation and the Origin of the Self: The Neurobiology of Emotional Development*. Hillsdale, NJ: Lawrence Erlbaum Associates, 1994.

Siegel, Daniel J. "Cognitive Neuroscience Encounters Psychotherapy: Lessons from Research on Attachment and the Development of Emoton, Memory and Narrative," presented in a plenary address to the 1996

Annual Meeting of the American Association of Directors of Psychiatric Residency Training (to be published in Siegel, Daniel J., *Memory Matters*, Guilford).

Storr, Anthony. *Solitude*. London: Flamington, 1989.

OTHER WORKS CITED

Bly, Robert. *The Sibling Society*. New York: Vintage Books, 1996.

Dostoevsky, Fyodor. Trans. Constance Garnett. "Notes from Underground," in *Three Short Stories of Dostoevsky*. New York: Doubleday, 1960.

Frank, Anne. Trans. Susan Massotty. *The Diary of a Young Girl*. New York: Doubleday, 1995.

Ginzberg, Louis. *The Legends of the Jews*. New York: Simon and Schuster, 1909; 1961.

Hendrix, Harville. *Getting the Love You Want: A Guide for Couples*. New York: HarperCollins, 1990.

Illich, Ivan. *Limits to Medicine*. London: Marion Boyards, 1976.

Krishnamurti, J. *On Relationship*. New York: Harper San Francisco, 1992.

Miller, Henry. *Sexus*. New York: Grove Weidenfeld, 1965.

Morrow, Lance. *Heart: A Memoir*. New York: Warner Books, 1995.

Nietzsche, Friedrich. Trans. Walter Kaufman. "Ecce Homo," in *The Basic Writings of Nietzsche*. New York: Random House, 1992.

Peck, Scott F. *The Road Less Traveled*. New York: Touchstone, 1978.

Proust, Marcel. Trans. C.K. Scott-Montcrieff and Terence Kilmartin. *Swann's Way*. London: Vintage, 1996.

Ricci, Nino. *In a Glass House*. Toronto: McClelland & Stewart, 1983.

Suzuki, Shunryu. *Zen Mind, Beginner's Mind*. Tokyo: Weatherhill, 1970; 1984

Sacks, Oliver. *An Anthropologist on Mars*. Toronto: Alfred A. Knopf Canada, 1995.

Salinger, J.D. *The Catcher In the Rye*. New York: Bantam, 1964.

Weil, Andrew. *8 Weeks to Optimum Health*. New York: Fawcett Columbine, 1997.

Winnicott, D.W. *Home Is Where We Start From*. New York: W. W. Norton, 1986.

# Index